Plunging into Haiti

Plunging into Haiti

into

CLINTON, ARISTIDE, AND
THE DEFEAT OF DIPLOMACY

BY RALPH PEZZULLO

University Press of Mississippi /*Jackson*

An ADST-DACOR Diplomats and Diplomacy Book

www.upress.state.ms.us

The views and opinions in this book are solely those of the author
and the author's sources and not necessarily those of the Association
for Diplomatic Studies and Training and Diplomatic and Consular
Officers, Retired, Inc.

The University Press of Mississippi is a member of the
Association of American University Presses.

First edition 2006

∞

Library of Congress Cataloging-in-Publication Data

Pezzullo, Ralph.
  Plunging into Haiti : Clinton, Aristide, and the defeat of diplomacy /
by Ralph Pezzullo.— 1st ed.
    p. cm.
  "An ADST-DACOR diplomats and diplomacy book"
  Includes bibliographical references and index.
  ISBN 1-57806-860-6 (cloth : alk. paper) 1. Aristide, Jean-Bertrand.
2. United Nations Mission in Haiti. 3. Multinational Force and
Observers. 4. Haiti—Politics and government—1986–
5. United States—Foreign relations—Haiti. 6. Haiti—Foreign
relations—United States. I. Title.
  F1928.2.P49 2006
  327.7294073'09049—dc22   2005029232

British Library Cataloging-in-Publication Data available

"The reasonable man adapts himself to the world. The unreasonable man persists in trying to adapt the world to himself. Therefore all progress depends on the unreasonable man."
—GEORGE BERNARD SHAW

Dedicated to the people of Haiti.

CONTENTS

FOREWORD

Since 1776, roughly 230 years ago, extraordinary men and women have represented the United States abroad under all kinds of circumstances. What they did and how and why they did it remain little known to their compatriots.

In 1995 the Association for Diplomatic Studies and Training (ADST) and Diplomatic and Consular Officers, Retired (DACOR) created the Diplomats and Diplomacy book series to increase public knowledge and appreciation of the involvement of American diplomats in world history. The series seeks to demystify diplomacy by telling the story of those who have conducted our foreign relations, as they lived, influenced, and reported them.

We are pleased to add *Plunging into Haiti* by Ralph Pezzullo to the series. This timely study of America's 1994 intervention provides a richly detailed inside account of senior-level policymaking during the Haiti crisis of the early to mid-1990s.

Based on thorough research and interviews with central participants from the Haitian, international, and American sides, the book emphasizes the candid perspectives of Lawrence Pezzullo, a key player in the story as President Clinton's special advisor for Haiti, and of three others deeply involved in the events: Michael Kozak of the State Department and Dante Caputo and Leandro Despouy, both of the United Nations. A fifth personality, Robert Malval, an interim Haitian prime minister, also provides a key insider's account.

The story, told largely from interviews with these five men, is interspersed with chapters that outline Haiti's history and evolution. The book concludes with useful "lessons learned."

The author offers important insights into subjects not covered extensively elsewhere, such as the Governors Island Agreement, negotiations with Haitian military leaders, and the evolution of U.S. policy on Haiti. He also recounts how some Defense Department and CIA participants undercut official U.S. policy, sending mixed messages to the Haitian authorities. That some of the episode's players and issues remain current lends further importance to the book's insights.

Ralph Pezzullo is a screenwriter and former journalist and an award-winning playwright. He is the author of *Eve Missing*, of *Jawbreaker* (coauthored with Gary Berntsen), and of *At the Fall of Somoza*, coauthored with his father, Lawrence Pezzullo, who served as ambassador to Nicaragua and to Uruguay.

A serious and well-sourced account of the post-Duvalier period, *Plunging into Haiti* makes a major contribution to the historical record on Haiti and provides an authoritative analysis of a major foreign policy effort in the early years of the Clinton administration. Students, diplomats, area specialists, and journalists, as well as Haitian readers, will find this a valuable addition to the literature.

—KENNETH L. BROWN
President, Association for Diplomatic Studies and Training

—MICHAEL E. C. ELY
President, Diplomatic and Consular Officers, Retired

Plunging into Haiti

CHAPTER 1

Clinton's Pledge

"I can't believe I left Little Rock for this bullshit."

—VINCENT FOSTER in his suicide note

It was a Saturday in March of 1993—March 13, 1993, to be exact—and the snow outside fell in a steady hiss. A solidly built gray-haired man in a cream-gold Acura cursed his bad luck. He could barely see five feet in front of him as he skidded from one side of I-95 to the other. Time seemed to be suspended in the magical white world beyond his windshield. He thanked God there was no one else on the road.

But Lawrence Pezzullo had to get to Washington. After all, the sixty-seven-year-old career diplomat was on his way to his first meeting with President Clinton at the White House. It was a moment he had been waiting for, a culmination of his forty-year involvement in international affairs.

Only two weeks earlier Pezzullo had been called by Peter Tarnoff at his office at Catholic Relief Services headquarters in downtown Baltimore. He had known Peter in the Carter administration when Tarnoff was head of the State Department secretariat and Pezzullo was serving as ambassador to Uruguay and, then, to Nicaragua. After that, Tarnoff had directed the prestigious Council on Foreign Relations, located on Park Avenue in

New York City. Now he was the deputy under secretary of state for political affairs.

"Larry, we would like you to help us on the Haiti issue," Tarnoff said. "I'm sure you've been following it in the newspapers."[1] Pezzullo knew from news reports that a Catholic priest, Jean-Bertrand Aristide, had been elected president of Haiti in December 1990 by 67 percent of the voters. A military coup had deposed him nine months later after charges that he had violated the constitution and incited mobs to "necklace" his opponents. Since then international efforts to restore Father Aristide to power had failed.

"Peter, I'm flattered," Pezzullo answered. "But I'm running Catholic Relief Services and I can't just bug out." Actually, Pezzullo had been the head of the Catholic Relief Services for ten years and was intrigued by the offer to get back into the foreign policy work he loved.[2]

Two days later Tony Lake called. Pezzullo and Lake, a fair-haired, preppy-looking man with an affable manner, went back to the early sixties when they were both junior Foreign Service officers and played together on a championship softball team. They had also served together in the U.S. embassy in Saigon during the days of Madame Nhu and the Tonkin Gulf Incident. But fortunes turn. In the early days Pezzullo had played shortstop, while Tony was a late-inning sub. Now Lake was President Clinton's new national security advisor. Depending on one's perspective he was either the most influential man in the making of U.S. foreign policy or the second most important after Secretary of State Warren Christopher.

"Larry, we have a high regard for you and your performance in Nicaragua in dealing with Somoza," Lake said.[3]

Pezzullo didn't need much convincing. After nearly ten years of the Machiavellian machinations of the Catholic Church as it dealt with poverty and development, he was ready to move on. The next day he was at the State Department being briefed on Haiti.

At this first briefing, Peter Tarnoff introduced him to Bernard Aronson, the departing assistant secretary of state for American Republic Affairs, and the man who had been nominated to replace him, Alexander Watson. In the more-muddled-than-usual transition from one administration to another, neither Tarnoff nor Watson had been confirmed by Congress.

Tarnoff instructed Pezzullo to get organized and put together a staff. His official title would be Special Advisor to the Secretary of State on Haiti.

Bernie Aronson, an intensely focused man who spoke and wrote with great precision, had been overseeing the day-to-day situation in Haiti since President Aristide was ousted in a military coup d'état on September 2, 1991. "I've dealt with the Haitian military and General Raul Cédras," Aronson told Pezzullo, "and they're experts at rope-a-dope. That's exactly what they'll do. Procrastinate, procrastinate, and procrastinate some more."[4] He characterized deposed president Aristide as a narrow, rigid man, who though friendly in person was difficult to deal with. Aronson described two agreements negotiated and signed by President Aristide since his overthrow—one in Washington and one in Cartegena, Colombia—in which Aristide had agreed to things that he later backed away from. "It seems to be a pattern," Aronson concluded.[5]

He also seemed to have doubts that a multinational approach—either through the United Nations or the Organization of American States—would resolve the crisis. Nevertheless, he was gracious enough to arrange a lunch between Pezzullo and Dante Caputo, the former foreign minister of Argentina, who had been appointed the new United Nations/Organization of American States Special Envoy to Haiti in December.

While Aronson was talking, a call came from Richard Feinberg inviting Pezzullo to the White House the next day for a major meeting on the Haiti crisis. Feinberg, whom Pezzullo knew from the Carter administration, was now heading the Latin American office of the National Security Council (NSC). Feinberg informed Pezzullo that he was preparing an NSC policy paper, which Aronson characterized as a "mish-mash."[6] He went on to describe Feinberg's draft as a long, disjointed prescription of what the Clinton administration should do that ended up raising more questions than it resolved.

Back in Baltimore that night, as Pezzullo sat down to a plate of his wife's penne with vodka sauce, the snow began to fall. It was falling sideways when he got up early Saturday morning. He called the White House immediately.

"The meeting is on for twelve noon," he was informed.

In no time, he was digging out his car. Minutes later he was sliding from one side of I-95 to the other. Little did he know that his skidding car would become a fitting metaphor for the Haitian policy of the Clinton administration.

His career in the State Department had conditioned him to expect a new challenge every two or three years. He had gone from visa and protection work on the Mexican border to two years at the operations center of the State Department during the Berlin blockade and the Cuban Missile Crisis; to Saigon, Vietnam (1962–64), during the fall of the Diem regime, numerous terrorist attacks by the Viet Cong, and the escalating involvement of U.S. troops; to La Paz, Bolivia (1965–67), where Che Guevara was trying to build a guerrilla base among skeptical Bolivian campesinos; to Bogotá, Colombia (1967–69); to Guatemala (1969–71); to deputy assistant secretary for congressional affairs in Washington; to ambassador to Uruguay (1977–79).

In the spring of 1979, Pezzullo was asked by his superiors to jump from Uruguay into war-torn Nicaragua. He landed there on June 26, in the midst of a civil war. The last scion of the Somoza dynasty was holed up in his bunker, and it was Pezzullo's job to tell him that the United States was not going to bail him out. This is not what the dictator wanted to hear. Or, as Anastasio Somoza put it in his colloquial English: "Let's not bullshit ourselves, Mr. Ambassador. You have your dirty work to do and I have mine."[7] Three weeks after Somoza resigned and fled the country, Pezzullo returned as the first U.S. ambassador to the victorious Sandinista regime.

When the Reagan administration came into office with a radically different agenda for Central America from the patient political and economic pressure that the Carter administration had been using, Pezzullo figured it was time to retire. In 1983 he was hired to head Catholic Relief Services. In ten years he had helped it grow into one of the preeminent relief organizations in the world with over three hundred programs in seventy-six countries.

So there he was: sixty-seven years old, raised in the Bronx, the seventh son of Italian immigrants. He had reason to think he was prepared for the next challenge. But no one who conforms to our Western way of doing things—based primarily on reason and logic—can be prepared for the Hieronoymus Bosch world of Haiti.

On that snowy Saturday in March, Pezzullo was optimistic. Even as his car slid around the beltway and skidded off at Connecticut Avenue, he had reason to be hopeful. The last years of Republican rule in Washington had been difficult for a man of his intelligence and experience to sit through, what with the Reagan nonsense of Nicaragua being eight hundred miles away from Harlingen, Texas, and the United States funding contras to invade Nicaragua and supporting an all-out war in El Salvador. It seemed to him that now was an opportunity for a thoughtful, rational approach to foreign policy.

Pezzullo parked across the street from the west rear gate of the White House. Norman Rockwell would have wept. Fir and holly trees had been swept with snow; smoke rose from the many chimneys. Huddled in the West Wing foyer were Bernie Aronson and Richard Feinberg. The three of them waited for another presidential meeting to end and were then summoned into the Roosevelt Room.

In FDR's day, this room across from the oval office was used as a waiting area for presidential visitors. So many callers spent so many hours staring at mounted fish, that it had been dubbed "the morgue." In the spirit of bipartisanship, President Nixon had the room decorated with mementos to both Roosevelts. A dramatic equestrian portrait of Teddy Roosevelt hung on one wall and a wise-looking head of FDR looked on from another.

President Clinton was seated halfway down the grand mahogany table in a brown sweater, nursing a mug of coffee. Vice President Gore, like Clinton a big man, sat across from him in blue jeans and a blue sweater. Sitting next to the president was Tony Lake. Lake's anxious deputy, Sandy Berger, was at the head of the table.

Lake walked over and extended a hand to his former shortstop. "Larry, it's good to see you. Thanks for doing this."[8]

Warren Christopher followed Lake in an expensively tailored sports jacket with a silk handkerchief. The last words Pezzullo and Christopher had exchanged dated back to the summer of 1979 when Pezzullo was calling from Nicaragua trying to convince his superiors at the State Department to recall him after Somoza had pulled a fast one on the United States. "What is wrong with you people?"[9] Pezzullo had screamed into the phone. He didn't know that then deputy secretary of state Christopher was listening in on the other end.

Pezzullo sat next to Sandy Berger, who had been a friend of the Clintons since 1972 when they worked together to organize a rally at the Alamo for George McGovern's presidential campaign. Feinberg and Bernie Aronson took their places next to Christopher. The president was in a bad mood. "Let's get on with this," he said, gruffly.[10]

The burly, rumpled Berger started in a burst of nervous energy: "Mr. President, I'll give a recap, then I'm going to ask Bernie Aronson to give you a sense of what's going on in Haiti. Then Feinberg will talk about your meeting with Aristide on Tuesday."[11]

Berger tried to weave together bits and pieces of everything—recent history, past history, personalities, goals—but it all came apart, setting a tone of disarray and confusion. President Clinton sipped his coffee and looked on. At some point, the Senior Advisor on Policy and Strategy, George Stephanopoulos, slipped in, sat behind them, and started scribbling notes on a legal pad.

Next came Aronson, who spoke with great precision about conditions in Haiti. Gradually the issue started to come into some kind of focus. At one point the president broke in and said something to the effect: "This is our hemisphere, and this is something we should be able to do."[12]

"What, exactly?" Pezzullo wondered as Richard Feinberg took the floor. Feinberg's amateurish presentation quickly wrecked the cohesive framework that Aronson had started to put together. He ended by reading a quote from Aristide's autobiography: "You cannot eat okra with only one finger."

President Clinton pounded the table. According to Pezzullo, he said: "You've given me nothing here that I haven't heard already during the transition. We don't have a policy here. This is not the kind of work I want to see."[13]

Christopher, who had said nothing up to this point, assured the president that he would oversee the development of a coherent policy.

Then Tony Lake spoke: "Mr. President, I want you to meet Larry Pezzullo, whom we've brought in to help us with Haiti. He's the one who got Somoza to leave Nicaragua. I think he's the kind of man who can deal with the Haitian military."

The president looked at Pezzullo as if to say: "Who is this guy?"[14]

Clearing his throat, the veteran diplomat spoke briefly: "I just came into this, but I think we have to make it very clear to the Haitian military what we intend to do. We have to be resolute and disciplined. I think the argument we've got to make is similar to the one I made to Somoza, namely: 'Change is inevitable and you should play a historic role that speaks to the greater good of your country.'"[15] Pezzullo said he would be traveling to Haiti to meet with the Haitian military right after the meeting with Aristide.

"Thank you for joining us," said President Clinton.[16]

The president and vice president were running late. Secretary of Commerce Ron Brown was waiting. Pezzullo, trying to process his impressions of the new administration, followed the others minus George Stephanopoulos through the narrow West Wing hallways to Tony Lake's office. It was generous by White House standards, but would never do for even a junior vice president in an investment house. Reflecting his recent past as a professor of foreign affairs at Mount Holyoke College, Lake's office was lined with books. The wall opposite his desk was dominated by a painting of a large cow lolling on a field of grass. Lake pointed out proudly that it was on loan from the National Gallery.

From a chair beside his desk, Tony Lake opened the meeting. According to Pezzullo, he said: "We have to get the briefing material together for the president's meeting with President Aristide on Tuesday and we need to put Feinberg's paper to bed so that we have something outlining our basic policy." Secretary Christopher sat next to Pezzullo and never uttered a word.

Lake was thinking out loud. He said something like: "Given Aristide's difficult personality, at some point in time we might have to walk away from him."

Pezzullo was astonished that no one objected. So he broke in: "Tony, if you walk away from Aristide, you lose your moral position."[17]

Lake told Pezzullo that he wasn't saying they should do it, but that should be an option.

Then Lake thought out loud some more. He said that at some point they might have to consider using military force. Again, no one said anything.

"Military force?" Pezzullo broke in. "That's ridiculous, Tony. The use of U.S. military force in a country like Haiti with its political history would be a prescription for disaster."[18]

Lake told Pezzullo he wasn't suggesting it; he was just raising it as a contingency.

What followed, according to Aronson, was a completely disjointed discussion, with people adding fragments of thoughts and ideas that were practically non sequiturs. Secretary of State Warren Christopher said nothing.

After thirty-five or forty minutes Tony Lake turned to Aronson and asked him to "take out the gems" from the discussion and incorporate them into a policy paper.

Bernie Aronson asked incredulously: "What gems? This has been a completely disjointed conversation. What do you want me to say?"[19]

Lake asked Aronson to write a summary highlighting the areas of consensus.

"I don't know what to write," responded Aronson.

After the meeting ended, Pezzullo joined Aronson in the lobby just as he exploded.

"You people are setting up the president," Aronson said to Feinberg. "You're giving him the impression that this can be done easily and that's not true. That's not going to happen in Haiti. I'm telling you, you're not serving the president. I hope you understand that."[20]

As Pezzullo drove away, Aronson's words resonated in his mind. He understood the temptation to want to please the president and make him look like an international hero. Having spent most of his professional career in Latin America, Pezzullo also knew something about the wildly complicated love-hate relationship that those countries have with the United States. And Haiti was even more complex because of the issue of race.

As he left the White House that Saturday, Pezzullo realized that no one had mentioned the refugee crisis, which had put Haiti on the political front burner. He knew that President Clinton and his advisors wanted to avoid a repeat of the period of late 1991 through early 1992 when over 35,000 Haitians had fled in boats to the shores of Florida.

On May 24, 1992, in an attempt to stem the tide of refugees, President George Bush had signed an executive order requiring all interdicted Haitians to be returned to Haiti without being given the chance to apply for political asylum. It smacked of discrimination since people escaping Cuban were readily admitted as political refugees.

Then-Democratic-candidate Bill Clinton had criticized President Bush for playing "racial politics" with Haitian refugees. "I wouldn't be shipping those people back," he said during the heat of the presidential campaign.

But in a January 14, 1993, radio address as thousands of Haitians prepared to flee by boat to Florida, President-elect Bill Clinton reversed himself. He justified continuing the Bush administration's policy on the grounds that it would save lives. "Many hundreds of Haitians, including women and children, have already lost their lives in dangerous sea voyages," he explained. "For this reason, the practice of returning those who flee Haiti by boat will continue for the time being after I become President. Progress toward a political settlement will improve the human rights situation for all Haitians and create a brighter future for your country. That is why, as we work to restore democracy in Haiti, I urge all Haitians not to leave by boat."[21]

Newspaper columnists and members of the Black Caucus on Capitol Hill, who had been taunting the president for not living up to his campaign promises on Haiti, applauded the news of Pezzullo's appointment. "The administration has finally engaged the issue," said columnist Earl Caldwell in the *Daily News*.[22] One of the first calls to Pezzullo's new office came from Congressman Charles Rangel, who represented Harlem. He complained that the State Department, rather than getting tough with the Haitian generals, had been "playing footsie."[23] Pezzullo told him in no uncertain terms, "that's over."

On Monday, after a weekend spent digesting all he could about Haiti, Pezzullo met President Aristide's ambassador to Washington, Jean Casimir. Casimir traveled to the State Department accompanied by a charming Haitian-American lawyer named Mildred Trouillot (who later became President Aristide's wife). A big bear of a man, Casimir had been described to Special Advisor Pezzullo as a professor who had spent most of his professional life outside of Haiti. Divorced and living with his ninety-year-old mother, he could, as one Haitian put it, "dedicate himself twenty-four hours a day to the logic of power."[24] He was also a newcomer to President Aristide's Lavalas movement.

But Ambassador Casimir was not an equivocator, as Pezzullo found out. They had barely finished shaking hands when Casimir launched into a lengthy diatribe against the Bush administration and the United States. Pezzullo had heard that since the fall of the Duvaliers, Haitian leftist intellectuals and political activists had referred to U.S. policy as the "American plan." According to their paranoid logic, the intention of the

United States was to prevent Haiti's political and economic development and, thereby, preserve Haiti as a source of cheap labor.

Casimir was from this camp. In 1992, he wrote: "The international elite, to satisfy its own vested interests, has to solve an embarrassing equation: the distinctiveness of the Haitian people, the pertinence of their project of society in light of a new international order, and inadequacy of the international power structure to accommodate this pertinent project."[25] A political ally of Aristide later characterized Casimir as an anti-American leftist, who believed that the CIA, the U.S. military, and American imperialism were to blame for all the problems in Haiti. Needless to say, Casimir did not leave Pezzullo and other U.S. officials feeling warm and fuzzy.

It was not an auspicious introduction to President Aristide himself, who was next on Pezzullo's list of calls. Pezzullo already knew that the former Catholic priest was a highly controversial figure. His supporters in Haiti and the United States regularly referred to him as a prophet, while his detractors called him "the Devil." The former spoke reverently about his commitment to the poor as a parish priest in Port-au-Prince and his continued outspoken opposition to Duvalierist thugs in spite of having barely escaped at least three attempts on his life. They saw a beatific visionary who spoke eight languages, wrote poetry, composed songs on his guitar, and fought uncompromisingly for truth and justice. But his political opponents considered him an unbalanced demagogue with messianic visions. They cited the fact that he had repeatedly incited mobs to "necklace" his political opponents with burning tires and had brazenly violated the very constitution that he had sworn to defend.

The special advisor suspected that the truth lay somewhere in between. One of Aristide's American advisors had described him as "a cross between the Singing Nun and Idi Amin."[26]

The frail president greeted the six-foot Pezzullo warmly. Aristide spoke in a whisper and was impeccably dressed. Pezzullo couldn't help noticing the large gold watch around his wrist. Aristide's face was soft and boyish, but his eyes were strange. The right one looked straight ahead, hard and calculating. But the left eye was opened wide and seemed to stare into space. They sat and exchanged homilies.

President Aristide was living on Government of Haiti assets seized under an executive order issued by President George Bush soon after the September 1991 coup. They amounted to between $30 million and $50 million and consisted mainly of fees for international phone calls and airplane landing, but also included some private funds. Although his rented rooms were nicely furnished, they were relatively small. One modest room down the hall was reserved for his Secret Service detail and another was being used as his apartment. The room they were in, his office, featured a big photograph of Martin Luther King leaning against one wall.

"Two lovers cannot stay apart without reaching out to the other one," President Aristide said, referring to himself and his country. "It is a natural feeling. It is a natural way to be. You love your country, and so it is natural to do everything to save it. That's the Haitian life. And I am glad to be the son of a country where the roots of love are filled with sap."[27] As he spoke excitedly about his impending visit to the White House, a fax machine spewed out a stream of documents that fell to the floor.

But the next morning a very different President Aristide spoke from the Op-Ed page of the *New York Times*. In blunt terms he called for the United States to oust the coup leaders in Haiti, threaten an embargo of oil and weapons, and set a deadline for his return to Haiti. It struck Pezzullo as a strange way to appeal for help. It also showed that Aristide knew how to use the press and was not above trying to publicly pressure the U.S. government.

As Secretary of State Warren Christopher and Special Advisor Pezzullo approached the White House on Tuesday, March 16, they saw hundreds of enthusiastic Aristide supporters gathered across the street in Lafayette Park. Christopher and Pezzullo waited in the Roosevelt Room. After several minutes a jaunty President Aristide entered with ex-prime minister René Préval, Ambassador Casimir, and Mildred Trouillot. Nancy Soderberg of the NSC was by his side, making no effort to hide her unabashed admiration of the Haitian president.

An aide ushered them through a narrow hall where they ran into Coretta Scott King coming out of the Oval Office. Aristide and Mrs. King exchanged effusive hugs and kisses. Then they entered the Oval Office where President Clinton was the picture of graciousness.

The visitors were shown their places, then a signal was given and the press photographers descended on them like locusts. What seemed like fifty thousand clicks later the photographers were sent out into the cold Rose Garden.

"To those who block the restoration of democracy, I want to make clear in the strongest terms that we will not now or ever support the continuation of an illegal government in Haiti," President Clinton began. "We will step up dramatically the pace of negotiations to restore you under conditions of national reconciliation and mutual respect for human rights, with a genuine program of genuine economic progress."[28] It was a mouthful, but the president said it well, displaying the empathy and openness that had served him famously during the presidential campaign.

President Aristide beamed as President Clinton offered to commit one billion dollars to resuscitating Haiti once political reconciliation was achieved. Referring to Aristide's editorial in the *New York Times*, President Clinton said he didn't think it was a good idea to set a deadline for President Aristide's return and urged him to be flexible.

"I agree with you completely," responded Aristide. "I feel good." As the meeting ended, Aristide smiled and said that he would work with Ambassador Pezzullo.[29]

Then the press was invited in. They came this time with a phalanx of microphones. One of their first questions, directed at President Aristide, had to do with his previous insistence that the leaders of the coup that ousted him be jailed. "I'm saying—asking—to all Haitians to not go to vengeance," the Haitian president answered, "to wait for justice instead of doing it for themselves. We can work peacefully to remove the coup leaders from the army, and that way to free the army and let justice be done, not then to feel happy because we've put them in jail."[30]

"That sort of attitude on the part of President Aristide is the very thing that should enable us to resolve this in a peaceful way," added President Clinton.[31]

After the one-hour meeting broke, George Stephanopoulos was asked when Pezzullo would be traveling to Haiti. He announced that the special advisor would be leaving later in the week and "he will send a tough message that we expect progress now, and he will also send a message that our patience is running thin."[32]

In this hurried whirl of political posturing, Pezzullo was trying to get his bearings. "Okay," he thought to himself, "President Clinton has made his goals clear to everyone. Now it's up to me to carry them out." But he had the uneasy feeling that Bernie Aronson was right and the president's advisors saw Haiti as an easy foreign policy victory. From his limited knowledge of Haiti, he was sure that the problems would be more complex. A Haitian scholar had once told him: "When you think you know Haiti, throw out everything you know and consider the exact opposite."[33]

He might have added some words written by British poet and scholar D'Arcy Wentwood Thompson at the end of the eighteenth century: "Against a foe I can defend myself, but Heaven protect me from a blundering friend."

CHAPTER 2

Welcome to Haiti

"Haiti is a land of unlimited improbabilities."

—a Haitian proverb

The sky outside was a calm, reassuring blue. Special Advisor Lawrence Pezzullo returned to the article in his lap and the words of a prominent Haitian psychiatrist: "You might find us resigned or unrealistic, but that may be because, as people of all social categories will tell you, this is not the real world."

"Not the real world?" he repeated to himself and sat up. He felt uneasy, being a man who prided himself on being rooted in reality. "Not the real world?"

It was two days after the meeting between President Clinton and President Aristide at the White House and a week after he had taken on the job. Seated beside him was Charles Redman, a former ambassador to Sweden, who had just been appointed chargé d'affaires in Port-au-Prince. They were on their way to Haiti, a place called "the best nightmare on Earth." The U.S. embassy there had been without an ambassador since Alvin Adams Jr. was recalled in June 1992, nine months after the coup that had deposed President Aristide.

Their plane passed over the azure waters of the Straits of Florida, where hundreds, maybe thousands of Haitians, had lost their lives since 1990 in rickety, overcrowded boats. Pezzullo had heard that for two thousand dollars one could hitch a ride on a freighter that would leave you off in the Bahamas. From there it was just a hop in a small boat to Miami. For three thousand dollars you could purchase a false passport, visa, and papers. Most Haitians couldn't afford that kind of money. For some, land, a girlfriend, or the use of a car could be bartered for a trip on a boat crowded with one hundred to two hundred people.

"It's infested with sharks," said Chuck Redman nodding down at the Windward Passage. According to a fatalistic Haitian proverb: "Every creature in the sea eats people; it is the shark which bears the bad name."

As the American Airlines jet cut through the white, cumulus clouds, Pezzullo once again saw the isle of Hispaniola. This is where Columbus first landed in October 1492. In 1986, after the fall of Jean-Claude Duvalier, a two-ton statue of Christopher Columbus, which presided over the Port-au-Prince harbor, was toppled into the sea. On its empty pedestal was scrawled the message: "*Pa de blancs en Hayti!*" (No more whites in Haiti!) But the United States was back, once more propelled into this country's murky history. This time they were invited by Haiti's democratically elected president to try to deliver it from its own tragic fate.

The jet was approaching from the east, passing over a harsh chaos of mountains slashed by deep, white gulches and parched savannas without a scrub in sight. It's been said that when Queen Isabella of Spain asked Admiral Columbus to describe the newly discovered isle of Hispaniola (Little Spain), he took a sheet of her writing paper, crumpled it, and dropped it on a table. "It looks like that." Once one of the world's most productive agricultural regions, Haiti today relies on imports for much of its food.

The blue water around the island was clouded with silt, the result of tons of precious topsoil spilling monthly to the bottom of the ocean. Pezzullo had traveled to Haiti before as executive director of the Catholic Relief Services, and he had seen the ecological devastation close up: Miles and miles of arid countryside covered with cactus and parched bushes; deeply eroded gorges sometimes fifty feet deep; and winds blowing dust constantly. "If you want to see an environmental disaster," wrote Dwight

Worker in August 1994, "go to Haiti. It's our local worst-possible-case of eco-catastrophe."[1] Experts say that up to 97 percent of the country is deforested and over half of the original ecoplane is eroded. And wood exports ended in 1900.

How did it happen? One only has to look at the streets of Port-au-Prince where two-wheeled wooden carts (brouetes) distribute charcoal to all parts of the city. You see them sometimes piled with as many as two dozen bags. This is the stuff that fuels tens of thousands of cooking fires and covers the slums in brown smoke.

In the countryside, completely barren hills are dotted with smoke, too. But this smoke comes from the pits used for making charcoal. Dwight Worker found a man named Jean Baptiste at one of them who said it hadn't rained in his region for five years. "He used to grow produce," Worker wrote, "now he cuts down trees for charcoal."[2]

Travelers to Haiti in the early nineteenth century praised it for its never-ending verdure and romantic landscapes—marshes of wild ginger, plantations of bananas and Indian corn, and forests of redwood, mahogany, and pine. In his monumental biography, *The Life and Voyages of Christopher Columbus*, Washington Irving describes Hispaniola as "one of the most beautiful islands in the world, doomed to be one of the most unfortunate." It was Admiral Columbus's ambition to gather enough gold in Hispaniola so that King Ferdinand and Queen Isabella could realize their dream of wresting the Holy Land from the infidels.

Soon the island's "beehive of people," whom Father Bartolomé de las Casas described as "the most guileless," were forced to work in gold mines under the cruelest of conditions. Within fifty years over half a million Taino-Arawak Indians perished and pre-Columbian civilization started to vanish from the island. In his *Brevisima Relacion de la Destruccion de las India Occidentales*, written in 1552, Las Casas (who accompanied Columbus on his third voyage) described how the Spanish fell upon the Indians "like ravening wild beasts, ... killing, terrorizing, afflicting, torturing, and destroying the native peoples" with "the strangest and most varied new methods of cruelty."

Father de las Casas so vehemently condemned the "impossible and intolerable" practice of Indian slavery that it was abolished in 1542. As a practical alternative he suggested the importation of Christianized blacks from the Spanish colonies. Thus began the first shipment of blacks to the New World and the beginning of a tragic legacy that we're still wrestling with today. To this odd twist of philanthropy we owe, according to the Argentine poet and novelist Jorge Luis Borges: "the mythological dimensions of Abraham Lincoln; the five hundred thousand dead of the Civil War; and the entrance of the verb lynch into the thirteenth edition of the dictionary of the Spanish Academy...."

The two U.S. envoys were descending through the blue sky into the sprawling capital of Haiti. Port-au-Prince hugs the contours of a deep and marshy horseshoe bay encircled by mountains. "Beyond the mountains lie more mountains," says the Creole proverb. The mountains give the illusion of space. But once on the ground this illusion disappears. There are people everywhere. Haiti is a land of over six and a half million people in an area that's about the size of Maryland (about fifteen thousand square miles). A third of them live huddled together in Port-au-Prince.

Thick air greeted them outside the plane, smelling of fuel, charcoal, rotting garbage, and flowers. Pushing through throngs of beggars, taxi drivers, and money-changers, the diplomats were struck by the vibrancy of the colors. Psychedelic buses called tap-taps careened through the streets. They had names like "Peace and Love," "Michael Jackson Machine," and "Baby Love All Night." A Haitian woman with a pyramid of purple eggplants on her head weaved nonchalantly through the pulsing, dusty downtown chaos.

The U.S. envoys were climbing up a hill from the squalor of the city to the suburb of Pétionville, where the wealthy people lived. The so-called MREs, or "morally repugnant elites," had survived wars, coups, and invasions and always managed to cling to their privileges. As their driver swerved to avoid the many potholes, they passed gingerbread houses, which seemed to be spun out of sugar. There were signs for local Prestige beer and Panther condoms, known in Creole as *kapotes pante*, or Dante Caputos as they would soon be called. Higher up they passed spotless houses surrounded by high security walls softened with tropical foliage and bougainvillea. Most seemed to feature satellite dishes.

This was a world away from the fetid slums of Cité Soleil, built on landfill near the harbor's edge. There some 150,000 Haitians lived in a rat's warren of *bidons*—primitive shelters patched together with adobe, abandoned sheet metal, and cardboard. Swollen-bellied children picked through great mounds of garbage and played in open sewage. "I have just seen children fighting with dogs for bones," reported one shocked Dutch journalist.[3]

By U.S. standards, the MREs lived very well. By Haitian standards they lived like royalty. But even in this rich suburb one could sense that something was wrong. UN special envoy Dante Caputo put his finger on it: "When you go to some countries in Latin America, although poverty is everywhere, you find rich ghettos. You have nice trees, nice streets, of course, nice houses. There's a tremendous duality in those societies, but at least the rich people are able to build rich neighborhoods with some nice things that they share. In Haiti they were not able to build common things in that society, even for the rich."[4]

The diplomats turned into the driveway of chargé Leslie Alexander, who would be leaving in a few days to become ambassador to Mauritius. Gathered on a verandah overlooking the city were senior members of the embassy staff. Pezzullo wasted no time: "I want you to understand that President Clinton is committed to the return of President Aristide and constitutional government and I've been brought in to implement that policy."[5]

After a few awkward minutes the CIA station chief, his officers, the military attaché, the head of the United States Information Agency (USIA), and others started to speak. All of them, in one way or another, tried to describe the mood of the country. They agreed on two things: The policy of returning Aristide was a mistake. They also felt they had been ignored by the Inter-American Affairs (ARA) bureau of the State Department. State Department officials had been talking to Haitian military leaders directly without keeping the embassy informed.

Redman assured them that was going to stop.

But they kept coming back to the first point, repeating the charges against Aristide—that he violated the constitution, that he incited his followers to riot and "necklace" people, that he had threatened the business community and members of Parliament, that he had covered up the human rights abuses of military officers loyal to him. Both Redman and Pezzullo had read all these charges in voluminous reports filed by Ambassador Alvin Adams. Adams, who had been enthusiastic about

Aristide's potential when he assumed the presidency on February 7, 1991, had grown increasingly pessimistic as the weeks went by. By the time President Aristide was overthrown on September 29, 1991, Adams had come to view him as a dissembler who had either deliberately or unwittingly created a politically explosive climate.

One younger officer spoke up. "The disaffection was more than just a political disagreement," he explained. "Aristide just wasn't getting anything done."[6]

"Look," Pezzullo said, "Aristide is coming back and the Clinton administration will be doing everything it can to bring that about. Chuck Redman is staying behind to make sure the policy gets implemented. Aristide might not be your choice for president, but he was elected by 67 percent of Haitian voters."[7]

After stopping at the flower-festooned Montana Hotel, Pezzullo and Redman went back down the hill to military headquarters. The old colonial building faced both the gleaming, white National Palace and the tattered, ochre-colored police headquarters. These three buildings stood on the edge of the Place des Héros de l'Indépendence, a palm-lined plaza, popularly known as the Place des Zéros. The least conspicuous of the three, the headquarters of the Armed Forces of Haiti (FADH), was a rectangular white colonial mansion with a colonnaded balcony running the length of the second floor.

The two U.S. diplomats passed a public waiting room on the first floor filled with what seemed like brightly dressed wives and girlfriends. They mounted rickety steps to the balcony, where sleepy soldiers rested their rifles on their knees. An officer directed the two Americans to General Cedras's office on the far left. He greeted them in a low voice. His manner seemed more that of a shy history professor than that of the leader of a renegade army. At forty-four, his body appeared as slim as his lantern-jawed face. He wore a starched khaki uniform that matched his complexion.

They both knew that Cédras had graduated first in his class from Military Academy in 1973. According to a former FADH commander, that class had been handpicked by Baby Doc Duvalier from families most loyal to his regime. In July of 1990, Cédras was in charge of the military library when he was appointed to head a five-man Security Coordinating

Committee to oversee the fairness of upcoming elections. On the day of his inauguration in February 1991, President Aristide had passed over many senior officers to appoint Colonel Cédras deputy commander of the FADH. Five months later, he elevated Cédras to commander. The appointment violated military procedures and never received parliamentary approval as required by the constitution. Cédras's betrayal of his patron only two months later had left Aristide understandably angry and bitter.

Pezzullo had also heard that General Cédras loved to scuba dive and that his favorite book was *The Stranger* by Camus. "At a certain point in our lives, we ask what is the sense of this life?" he confided to a journalist. "Just what Camus had asked with his theory of absurdity. There is another essay by Camus on the myth of Sisyphus. It is about a man pushing a rock up a mountain. Whenever he gets to the top . . ."[8]

They took their places at a long conference table that ran the length of the thirty-foot room. The general lit a Benson & Hedges and sat at the head of the table surrounded by his general staff. There were three other generals: Duperval, an amiable man who spoke perfect English; Mayard, a very tall, good-looking man, who seemed "out to lunch"; and Phillipe Biamby, Cédras's chief of staff, whose benign, soft face belied his true nature. Of the three, Biamby would prove to be the most important. All Pezzullo and Redman knew at the time was that this friendly-looking guy was supposed to be a health nut and was rumored to be sleeping with Cédras's wife. The others were all colonels representing the country's nine military departments.

To call the 7,300-man FADH an army was something of a misnomer. Not only did it lack equipment and organization, but also its recruits had little training and its officers were chosen almost exclusively on the basis of family ties and political orientation. It hadn't fought in a real war since 1855 and that was against the neighboring Dominican Republic. Traditionally, the FADH had been a breeding ground for political chicanery and corruption. Full colonels were paid a meager five thousand gourdes a month, or the equivalent of U.S. $147. Enlisted men made about $38. This left a lot of room for corruption. According to one former general: "When officers reach the rank of captain or major they are routinely approached by politicians or businessmen who seek alliances. And most recruits are quickly corrupted. It might be a house for their parents, a new car, . . . but it starts there. And the pattern is established."[9]

Still, the FADH was the only government institution in Haiti that operated with some regularity. In its present incarnation it controlled the police force, the country's prisons, and all state corporations, from the telephone system to flour imports.

A servant served coffee in little demitasse cups covered with flowers. Pezzullo took a quick glimpse around the simple room adorned with flags and coats of arms. High up on the wall, running the length of the table, was a series of photographs of the previous commanders of the FADH. The faces in the top row were white! These where the U.S. Marines who had commanded the FADH during the U.S. occupation of Haiti from 1919 to 1935. "What the hell are they doing there?" Pezzullo asked himself.

Clearly, this was more than just a surrealistic joke. It said volumes about how the Haitian military saw their relationship to the United States. "I don't think there's an army in the world that would put pictures of the occupying army in the headquarters of their general staff," Dante Caputo said later.[10]

Pezzullo told the general staff that Chuck Redman would be staying on to work closely with them. Then he outlined the position of President Clinton. "I've been brought aboard to implement that policy," he explained. "I will be working closely with the new UN special envoy Dante Caputo. So when you speak to one of us, you will be speaking to the other. There will be no difference in view. We want to see this transition occur in a dignified manner. But we are resolute and you should understand that President Aristide will return. It will serve you as senior members of the FADH to play a helpful role."[11]

There was a painfully long pause after Pezzullo finished. General Cédras stared at the ceiling. He looked down, made a little note to himself, and looked up again. Finally, the general began to speak in very formal French. He thanked the envoys for coming to see him. He said he appreciated their candor. He said he understood what they had said, but wanted them to hear some of his concerns.

Pezzullo and Redman had been told to expect masters in circular conversation. Cédras was obviously of this school. Eventually, he started to speak with some passion.

According to Pezzullo's notes, Cédras said: "First, you make a mistake when you think that I'm the person who can make these decisions. I am only a soldier sworn to uphold my responsibility as commander-in-chief, which I will do. The army had to restore order after the crisis created by Aristide. We never developed a junta. There is now a civilian government headed by Marc Bazin. It's his government that will have to make the decision. I ask you to speak to them."[12]

The United States had never recognized the government of Marc Bazin, who became prime minister in June 1992, and Cédras knew that. "I understand your position, General," Pezzullo countered. "But as far as I'm concerned, you're the man who holds power here, not Marc Bazin. I'll talk to Marc Bazin. I have no problem talking to anybody. But let's not live behind this fiction, because I don't accept it."

Cédras didn't bat an eye. Instead he launched into a long speech about Aristide. According to Redman, it went something like this: "Aristide continually violated the constitution and left the country because of his own failures. Now he's sitting in Washington trying to hurt this country. You can talk to a lot of people and they'll tell you the same thing."[13]

Pezzullo didn't challenge him. "You know our policy, General," he reiterated. "We intend to carry it out."

The general thanked the special advisor. He said that Ambassador Redman was free to call on him any time.

The next two days were filled with more talk on flowering verandahs, including a meeting with President Aristide's Presidential Commission. After a breakfast hosted by General Cédras and his wife, Yannick, Chuck Redman and Pezzullo drove back to the chargé's house.

Since the Pétionville suburb was divided by deep gorges, they had to descend down to the city and take another road up. They drove past dilapidated wooden structures that looked like they had been gnawed on for years by termites. Newer concrete structures often featured storefronts. Their brightly colored façades were baked with grime. Battered signs read "Sacred Heart Art and Snack," "College Decartes," and "Super Marriage Numbers Bank." On one wall was scrawled the graffiti "FUCK US."

Waiting at the chargé's house sat a group of private businessmen representing all the major families—the Mevs, the Brandts, the Accras, the

Bigios, the Berhmans. Among them they controlled Haiti's commerce in sugar, poultry, cooking oil, textile, steel, construction materials, automobile and truck imports, and, probably, illicit drugs. According to one estimate, 2 percent of Haitians controlled 45 percent of the country's wealth. For the most part, their forefathers had come to Haiti from Europe, the Middle East, and Jamaica during the past hundred years. "They attend the University of Miami and l'Université de Paris," reported Peter Katel in *Newsweek*. "They play the commodities market and learn to distinguish a Bordeaux from a merlot. These people make weight-loss remedies popular in a country plagued by hunger."[14]

During the thirty-year reign of Papa Doc Duvalier and his son, the Haitian elite had been ordered to make money and stay out of politics. But it was no secret that some of them had financed the coup that overthrew President Aristide.

Special Advisor Pezzullo now told them that the return of President Aristide was inevitable. "It would be in your best interest to put pressure on the military," he said. He warned them that the OAS embargo, which was already hurting the country, would be stepped up. "We're going to get tougher, you can count on that."

The burly, light-skinned Mev brothers, Fritz and Greg, told Pezzullo the United States could count on them for help. Some of the others got very emotional.

"You don't understand what Aristide did!" one man shouted. "I had a brother-in-law killed by a mob; they attacked one of my factories!"[15] Others stopped him. The anger and fear in their voices was real. The conversation seesawed back and forth for two more hours. Pezzullo and Redman were blunt. According to one report, "the mouths of the Haitians were hanging open" when the diplomats left.

The next morning found the envoys sitting on the colonial verandah of Marc Bazin's house, which was crammed with Haitian art. Marc Bazin couldn't have been a more gracious host. A distinguished-looking gray-haired man, Bazin was a Western-trained economist. For years he had been an official in the World Bank. In the early eighties he led a highly publicized crusade against corruption as Jean-Claude Duvalier's finance minister. He was quickly fired. Given his background, it was easy to understand why ex-president Jimmy Carter had once seen him as the solution to Haiti. In the 1990 presidential elections Bazin had come in second to Aristide, receiving 14.2 percent of the vote.

Although the FADH had forced President Aristide out of the country, they had allowed the elected legislature to continue. Under Haiti's constitution, the legislature elects the prime minister and approves the cabinet. In 1992, after some complicated coalition building, Bazin was elected prime minister. But Bazin's regime was viewed in Washington and capitals around the world for exactly what it was—a façade covering a military regime. When asked why he had forsaken his reputation as "Mister Clean" to head the de facto government Bazin responded: "If you get a chance to jump over the volcano, you do it."[16]

Bazin was joined by François Benoit, who was serving as his foreign minister in the de facto regime. Back in April of 1963, Benoit was a young lieutenant in the FADH when the limousine carrying Papa Doc's children to school was attacked with machine-gun fire. Although the president-for-life's eleven-year-old son, Jean-Claude, and fourteen-year-old daughter, Simone, escaped injury, their chauffeur and three bodyguards were killed. Evidence pointed to Duvalier's friend and former leader of the Ton Ton Macoutes, Clement Barbot, as the perpetrator of the attack. But Papa Doc decided that Lieutenant François Benoit must have been the assassin. Why? Because Benoit was a champion sharpshooter.

Papa Doc Duvalier would later announce from the balcony of the National Palace that "I am neither red nor white, but the indivisible bicolor of the Haitian People. I am already an immaterial being."[17] On the night of April 26, however, the very real and terrifying dictator sent Macoutes to storm Benoit's house. They machine-gunned his parents, infant son, visitors, servants, even the family dog.

Pezzullo told the two men the purpose of their visit. Bazin, who had been called "the Haitian Kennedy," said he felt the United States should reconsider its support of President Aristide. "I don't want to say that he's unbalanced," said Bazin, "but he's a very difficult man. He created this situation for himself."[18]

Pezzullo then turned to another issue. "The leadership of the FADH must change," he said. "But the FADH as an institution can survive. The United States is willing to invest in its reorganization and training. The FADH requires a new mission commensurate with the needs of the country. We are also prepared to help create an independent police force as stipulated in your constitution."[19]

When François Benoit spoke, he emphasized the importance of retraining and restructuring the FADH as part of a solution to the current crisis. "The military is both the abuser and the abused," he explained. "They're abusers because they have no constraints on them. They've been badly trained and pushed by events to take on a role that they're not trained for. Haitians are not difficult people, but the confidence level is zero."[20]

Both Pezzullo and Redman understood. Building the confidence of Haitians—whether military officers, business persons, politicians, or Aristide supporters—would be necessary for any political solution that would return President Aristide to power in a stable environment. But how could the international community build confidence in a country that had never really become a nation? And how could they restore civility to a country formed in the crucible of French colonialism and slavery?

CHAPTER 3

From Slavery to Independence

"Beyond the mountains are more mountains."

—popular Haitian proverb

"Things have got to change here," said Pope John Paul II in his *Address to the Haitian Nation* in March 1983. He was referring to the fact that the western third of the isle of Hispaniola was (and continues to be) the poorest country in the Western Hemisphere. Indeed, few countries in the world can point to a present and future as alarmingly bleak as Haiti's. Not only is the per capita GNP a mere $380 a year and the per capita annual government expenditure for health care $2, but its 6.5 million people live in frightening ecological desolation. According to UN estimates, only 39 percent of the population has access to safe water and 27 percent to sanitation.

It's hard to imagine that in the closing decades of the eighteenth century, Haiti—then the French colony of Saint Domingue—was the envy of all of Europe. Back then thirty-six thousand whites and an equal number of free mulattos dominated half a million African slaves. The colony generated two-thirds of France's overseas trade—a productivity that easily surpassed that of the newly formed United States. In the year of 1789 alone, exports of coffee, indigo, cacao, tobacco, hides, and sugar filled the holds of over four thousand ships.

In 1697, as a result of the Treaty of Rijswijk, which concluded the Nine Years War in Europe, the western third of Hispaniola was ceded to the French by Spain. A French presence on the island had been established decades earlier by pirates and men banned from France because "they had forgotten the God of their fathers." Travelers to Hispaniola at the time described these men as a strange assembly of political dissenters and soldiers of fortune who lived without women, often in couples.

Operating out of speedy little fly boats that they built for themselves on the Ile de Tortue, these pirates harassed lumbering Spanish galleons, heavy with the wealth of the Aztecs and Incas as they ploughed across the Caribbean—known as the Spanish Main—on their voyage home.

The Arawak Indians, the original natives of Hispaniola, taught these pirates how to cure meat by smoking it on frameworks of green wood *boucans*. Known as *boucaniers* (or buccaneers), these men gradually took to subsistence farming on the mainland of Hispaniola. When they started to cultivate indigo in 1685, the transition to a plantation-oriented economy began. Because of the dearth of ready labor on the island, plantations required that laborers be imported. The first were indentured servants, or *engagés*, from western France, who served under three-year contracts. French King Louis XIII encouraged the importation of Negro slaves, arguing that it was "for the good of their souls" and would advance the cause of Christianity.

By the first decade of the eighteenth century there were eight hundred plantations in Saint Domingue and twelve thousand slaves. By 1789, the number of plantations had soared to over seven thousand—over three thousand in indigo, twenty-five hundred in coffee, eight hundred in cotton, and some fifty-odd in cacao. But the cornerstone of the colony's economy was sugar. If prior to 1690 Saint Domingue had only one sugar plantation, by the mid-1700s there were six hundred, making it the most important sugar colony in the New World.

It was the cultivation of cane and the multistage process of producing sugar that necessitated dramatic increases in the importation of slaves. From 1764 to 1793 roughly 26,400 Africans per year were imported into

Haiti. From 1783 to 1792 that average rose dramatically to 37,000 per year. The constant need for new slaves was fueled in part by their stagger-ing death rate, caused by disease, overwork, and brutal treatment.

To supply Saint Domingue with sufficient labor, French merchants known as *armateurs* mounted vast shipping operations, sending out no fewer than 374 slaving ships in seven years, with as many as 69 ships in 1740 alone. This complex enterprise involved operations on three conti-nents. Since the western colonies produced virtually nothing besides trop-ical produce and its byproducts, only Europe and Asia could provide the exotic wares of interest—things like cotton cloth, beads, guns, gunpowder, alcohol, iron bars, brass bars, brass bowls, and knives—to barter with African buyers. Thus, the starting point of the so-called slaving triangle was a half dozen ports in France, especially Nantes and Bordeaux. Here *arma-teurs* organized expeditions by fitting out ships and finding investors.

Once docked on the west coast of Africa, a slaving captain had to pay a price specified by the local chief before trading could begin. In most cases, a captain had to buy his slaves one at a time from an African mid-dleman. An average cargo of 350 slaves could take anywhere from three weeks to three months to assemble. In February 1768 one French cap-tain recorded his purchase of 78 African slaves—40 men, 15 women, and 23 teenagers. According to his journal, he traded two rifles, four barrels of powder, and a dozen pieces of cloth for each man.[1]

Where did the slaves come from? A study of 179 liberated slave informants supplied by S. W. Koelle in his *Polyglotta Africa* shows that 34 percent were war captives, 30 percent were kidnapped, 7 percent sold by relatives or superiors, 7 percent sold because of debts, 11 percent con-demned to slavery through the judicial process, and the other 11 percent for unspecified reasons.[2]

Olaudah Equiano was only eleven years old when he and his sister were kidnapped by neighboring tribesmen and sold into slavery. In his memoirs written in 1791, he described the terrifying experience of being put under the deck:

There I received such a salutation in my nostrils as I had never
experienced in my life: So that with the loathsomeness of the stench and
crying together, I became so sick and low that I was not able to eat.[3]

Once disembarked in the Saint Domingue ports of Cap François, Port Daupin, Mole Saint-Nicolas, or Port-au-Prince, they were separated from their kinsmen, their names were changed, and the Africans were branded with red-hot irons to designate their new owners. Less than 5 percent of the Africans were sold as house personnel. The remaining 95 percent were dispatched to plantations, where after a period of tutoring and acclimatization, they were organized into work groups or *ateliers*.

From the age of fourteen to sixty, men and women worked from sunrise to sundown under the absolute domination of their owners. At five in the morning, the *commandeur*, or slave driver, would sound the bell and after a brief prayer, work would begin. At eight they would be allowed to stop and consume a meager breakfast. The crack of a whip signaled that work would resume until noon. The midday break lasted till one or two, then it was back to the fields until sundown. After the evening meal, slaves often had to work sorting and husking coffee beans, or grinding sugar until midnight. The only day they had to themselves, Sunday, was usually spent cultivating their own little garden on a small plot of land allotted to each slave by the owner.

This harsh life took its toll. The French observer Hilliard d'Auberteuil estimated that between 1680 and 1776 over 800,000 African slaves had been imported to Saint Domingue. By the end of that period, he estimated, only 290,000 survived.[4] Through his research of colonial records, French historian Gabriel Debien has calculated that 50 percent of all slaves died within the first three to eight years of their captivity.[5]

The documented excesses of some plantation owners defy belief. Branding, indiscriminate flogging, rape, and killing were a matter of course. Field hands caught eating cane were forced to wear tin muzzles while they worked. Common tortures included spraying the flesh with boiling corn syrup, sewing the lips together with brass wire, castration, sexual mutilation, live burial, and stuffing the anus with gunpowder which was then ignited, a practice known as "blasting a black's ass."

Confronted with this unrelenting intimidation and torture, the options of slaves were few. Some took their own lives. Others escaped the plantations under cover of night. These runaways, known to their French masters as *maroons*, were hunted by professional bounty hunters and their dogs. The practice of *maroonage* was apparently widespread. Between the years of 1764 and 1793, colonial records report some forty-eight thousand cases.[6]

Some fugitive slaves tried to slip into anonymity in the cities, while others made for the Spanish frontier of Santo Domingo. Others, seeking revenge for the injustice imposed on them and their people, joined organized bands in remote sanctuaries in the mountains.

The most famous of these *maroons*, François Mackandal, lost his arm in the iron rollers of a sugar cane press. Allowed to herd cattle in the northern district of Limbé, he organized a band of some fifty or more *maroons* with the aim of terrorizing and eventually overthrowing the white masters. Mackandal was captured on January 26, 1758, and burned at the stake, but his legend lived on. Slaves believed that his soul flew away and returned years later as a mosquito to spread yellow fever through the French troops.

White masters, known as the *grande blancs*, stood at the top of a strict caste system that divided Saint Domingue and grew more varied as time went by. Chroniclers of the time have pointed out that in most cases the *grandes blancs* wanted to make their fortunes as soon as possible and then enjoy it in the cultured ease of Parisian society. French colonialists who remained in Haiti were said to have "fallen in with the Negress." In the words of one eighteenth-century historian: "Whenever their sex drives stirred, they took whatever slave servants that pleased them ... living a life tormented by the thoughts of possible infidelity to their spouses." The erotic attraction that black women exerted over white planters resulted in a growing population of mulattos in the colony, so that by the end of the eighteenth century they equaled the number of whites.

"These exotic beings," wrote one Haitian historian, "conceived of in lust and by chance, coupled the beauty of dark Africa with pale Europe, and so often did they conquer paternal hearts with their familiar features etched into darker skin and framed by curlier hair, that new rules were made for them and they were considered to constitute a new breed of humanity."[7]

The mulattos formed a growing class, known as *gens de couleur*, who were officially declared free citizens on their twenty-first birthdays. But their citizenship came with restrictions. They were forced to serve in the police force to hunt *maroons*, forbidden to wear European fashions, excluded from most professions and public offices, and deprived of civil liberties, including the right to defend their women against sexual attacks by white men. They responded by quietly acquiring property, slaves, and education. By 1789, the *gens de couleur* owned one-third of the plantation property, one-quarter of the slaves, and one-quarter of the real estate in Saint Domingue.[8]

To some degree laws limiting the rights of the *gens de couleur* grew out of the jealousy of white colonial women and another class of whites, known as *petits blancs*. This group of middle-class plantation overseers, artisans, grocers, and city rabble despised the white planters as their social superiors, but had an even stronger antipathy toward the mulattos, who were often their superiors in every respect except skin color.

Given this volatile mix of social hatreds, it is no surprise that in 1783, the Marquise du Rouvray observed: "This colony of slaves is like a city under the imminence of attack; we are treading on loaded barrels of gunpowder."[9] It was the French Revolution six years later that ignited them. Exploiting the chaos in France, the *grands blancs* tried to establish an independent government in Saint Domingue that would exclude their economic competitors, the *gens de couleur*—which they called a "bastard and degenerate race"—and set property qualifications to exclude the *petits blancs*. Reacting in fury, the mulattos, led by forty-year-old Jacques Vincent Ogé, staged a revolt. The violent clashes that resulted were only a preview of the cataclysmic violence that would rock Saint Domingue.

Because on the night of Sunday, August 14, 1791, a huge black plantation foreman and voodoo priest (or *houngan*) named Boukman held a rally at Lenormand deep in Alligator Woods, about seven miles from Cap Haitien. It was near the spot where the *maroon* leader Makandal had been burned at the stake. Under the cover of a tropical storm, several hundred slaves assembled to hear Boukman issue his instructions.

According to eyewitnesses, an old prophetess named Roumaine drove a knife into a pig's throat just as a thunderclap from the tropical storm lit up the mountains. When the thunder died away, Boukman plunged the knife once more into the pig's entrails and pronounced that a pact of blood had been sealed between the initiated and the great gods (loas) of Africa. Then he gave the call to action:

Time of vengeance has come; . . . all whites should die. . . . No more delay, no more fear! We must not leave any refuge, or any hope of salvation.

Eight nights later, at the appointed hour, drums beat out the signal and fires were set throughout the north end of the colony. The huge conflagration could be seen from as far as the Bahamas as it raged over cotton-filled sheds, sugar cane fields, coffee plantations, and sugar mills and into the gigantic warehouses of the masters of the island.

The light of day revealed its gruesome aftermath: smoldering, toppled houses and buildings, groaning and screaming people. "Human blood poured forth in torrents; the earth blackened with ashes, and the air tinted with pestilence," wrote the English eyewitness Byron Edwards.[10]

Fifty thousand slaves under the leadership of Boukman continued their savage campaign of revenge. Within days, two thousand whites were killed and 180 sugar plantations and 900 coffee plantations destroyed. Among the victims was the mother of John James Audubon, to whom she had given birth near Las Cayes on April 25, 1785.

Then the whites struck back. Believing that had they been harsher and crueler with the slaves the rebellion would never have happened, any black suspected of supporting the revolt was slaughtered. During the three-week counterterror as many as twenty thousand blacks and mulattos were murdered. Boukman himself was captured and beheaded.

Tens of thousands of slaves deserted their plantations. Crudeiy organized, they retreated into the hills, armed with knives, sticks with sharp points, and swords stolen from the houses of planters.

A forty-eight-year-old freed slave named François-Domingue Toussaint became their leader. Toussaint, the barely literate grandson of an African chieftain, had studied the Commentaries of Caesar. He was, in the words of one contemporary, "possessed of an iron constitution. Soldiers regarded him as a superior being, and the cultivators prostrated themselves before him as being a divinity."[11]

Toussaint drilled his forces in the tactics of guerrilla war, which proved highly effective against the regimented grands blanc army. The black army prevailed, and by 1793 surviving white colonists hastily abandoned the island.

Hoping to restore prosperity to the war-ravaged island, Toussaint invited white planters to return. But few accepted. Ironically, his economic and political plans did not include changing the plantation basis of production. Instead Toussaint replaced slavery with a system of contract labor enforced by a *gendarmerie*. And foreshadowing the practices of future political leaders, Toussaint alone managed the treasury and was unaccountable to any institution. This led one ex-slave to remark: "We are free, but in worse shape than during the time of slavery. Toussaint replaced our old bonds with new ones."[12]

The uneasy truce between France and Saint Domingue lasted only until December 1801, when Napoleon dispatched seventy warships and twenty-five thousand soldiers under the command of his brother-in-law General Charles LeClerc to take control of the island. General LeClerc was accompanied by his wife and Napoleon's sister, the infamous beauty Pauline. Famed for her promiscuity and audacity, she once remarked: "I am on excellent terms with my brother; I have slept with him twice."

As the French fleet sailed within sight of Saint Domingue, Toussaint is reported to have wept: "Friends, we are doomed. All of France has come. Let us at least show ourselves worthy of our freedom."[13]

In the first days after they landed, the better-armed French troops captured most of the important coastal towns. Still, in his first report to Napoleon, LeClerc wrote:

These people here are beside themselves with fury. They never withdraw or give up. They sing as they are facing death and they still encourage each other while they are dying. They seem to know not pain. Send reinforcements![14]

Moving stealthily at night, Toussaint managed to elude the larger French army. Soon the French started to suffer from a scarcity of food and supplies. Even more lethal was the yellow fever that grew more virulent with the onset of the rainy season in November. Transmitted by mosquitoes, the disease cut a devastating swath through the Europeans. Death was horrible, relatively quick, and certain. One convoy of fifteen hundred reinforcements was completely felled by the disease within fourteen days.

Given the suffering of his troops, LeClerc invited Toussaint to a reconciliatory meeting on May 6, 1802. Pauline Bonaparte greeted the black general in a snow-white dress that almost completely exposed her breasts. The two men agreed to stop fighting, if the French would guarantee the freedom of all blacks.

A month later when Toussaint met with the French again to outline the terms of the reconciliation, he was captured. Taken aboard the French frigate *Héro* in chains, he uttered defiantly: "In overthrowing me, you have cut down only the trunk of the Tree of Liberty in Saint Domingue."

Although he was to die in a cold French prison on April 7, 1803, Toussaint's words proved to be prophetic. On November 2, 1802, his rival, General LeClerc, himself fell victim to yellow fever. The "blond Napoleon's" wife, Pauline, cut off all her hair and set it beside her husband in the cedar coffin.

LeClerc's successor Marshal Donatien de Rochambeau reinstated slavery and fought the blacks with a depravity that was extreme even for Saint Domingue. Despite his spectacular cruelty, Rochambeau's war of extermination failed. In the summer of 1803, Napoleon sent 2,570 Polish reinforcements. Like their French predecessors they met with disaster.[15] Those Polish soldiers not cut down by yellow fever soon realized that the blacks were fighting for the same freedom and liberty that they yearned for in Europe. At the end of November 1803, having lost over sixty thousand veteran troops, the French finally evacuated Saint Domingue.

On January 1, 1804, Toussaint's successor, Jean-Jacques Dessalines proclaimed the entire island an independent republic under the Arawak name Haiti. An aide reportedly marked the occasion by saying: "We will write this act of independence using a white man's skull for an inkwell, his skin for parchment, blood for ink and a bayonet for a pen." After an estimated 350,000 deaths between 1791 and 1804, Haiti became the first and only nation created by a slave revolt.

CHAPTER 4

Working with the UN

"In vodoun one and one make three."

—MAYA DEREN

On the afternoon of March 30, 1993, Special Advisor Lawrence Pezzullo entered the Situation Room of the White House. He had been back in Washington one week. Since his return from Port-au-Prince, Pezzullo had crisscrossed the capitol talking to congressmen, senators, and fellow diplomats from the Organization of American States (OAS). All had expressed optimism that the focused intent of the Clinton administration would yield a resolution to the crisis in Haiti.

Gathered around the table in the oak-paneled Situation Room were Tony Lake, Sandy Berger, and Richard Feinberg of the NSC; Peter Tarnoff and Warren Christopher from the State Department; CIA director James Woolsey; Secretary of Defense Les Aspin; and Chairman of the Joint Chiefs of Staff General Colin Powell. Behind President Clinton's foreign policy advisors, young men and women on assignment from the Pentagon monitored developments around the world on sophisticated computers.

NSC advisor Tony Lake opened the meeting by asking CIA director Woolsey for an intelligence update.

Woolsey read from the assessment that the CIA would use throughout the entire crisis. It concluded that the Haitian military wouldn't deal and Aristide was unstable. Pezzullo had already been briefed by the CIA and read its profile of Aristide. What he didn't know was that the profile was based in part on personal papers, diaries, paintings, clothes, and drugs pilfered from Aristide's bedroom. These had been turned over in late 1991 by the Haitian military through a Canadian named Lynn Garrison, who described himself as a diving buddy and friend of Lieutenant-General Raoul Cédras. A former fighter pilot for the Canadian Air Force who later flew stunts in the movie *Those Magnificent Men and Their Flying Machines*, Garrison had provided eight-headed doodlings of voodoo figures, appliquéd pajamas said to be the uniform of a voodoo secret society, a medicine chest full of drugs, and a statement from a professor who had taught Aristide at the Port-au-Prince Institute of Neuropsychology. The professor claimed that in 1977 he had prescribed lithium carbonate for his brilliant young student, whom he concluded was a "psychotic manic depressive."[1]

Pezzullo had learned to take the CIA's intelligence with a grain of salt. His skepticism was the product of extensive experience overseas dealing with contacts in local government, political parties, labor organizations, journalists, students leaders, campesino groups, and other diplomats. He had come to prefer the views of people with insight over CIA reports. But he also knew there was a tendency among newcomers in Washington to take the assessments in intelligence reports as gospel truth.

When Woolsey finished, Tony Lake turned to the special advisor. He asked Pezzullo, who had just returned from Haiti, to give his reading of the situation.

Pezzullo tried to keep his comments to the point. "It's clear to me," he said, "that we have a problem that stems from Aristide's performance in Haiti while he was president. He left behind a tremendous amount of resentment. Also, Haitians seem to have a genius for making things worse than they are. It's not going to be easy to get the military to move. The military leaders have their rationale, they're comfortable, they're making money. We have to put pressure on them. Aristide, on the other hand, is a wild card. Nobody trusts him. We've got to convince him that he must be the principal reconciliator. Unfortunately, his tendencies, and those of people close to him, run in the other direction."[2]

Tony Lake then spoke about the need for a major peacekeeping force in Haiti. He said it was his belief that there was so much internal political division that without peacekeepers, the crisis would never be resolved.

Pezzullo cut in. "Wait a minute, Tony," he said. "We're talking about a society that is deeply polarized. How are peacekeepers going to resolve political differences? It seems to me that we've got to put together a policy that forces Haitians to try to resolve some of their differences so that they can live together."[3]

Dismissing Pezzullo's comments, Lake turned to General Powell, who was sitting across from Pezzullo, and asked him how many soldiers it would take to do the job.

Powell grimaced. He said he couldn't answer the question, because he didn't understand Lake's reasoning. In his opinion, troops wouldn't help in a situation like the one described in Haiti. They would get trapped between contending forces and were not trained for that kind of mission.

Lake kept pushing. He felt strongly that U.S. soldiers were needed to prevent a bloodbath.

An alarm went off in Pezzullo's head. "Tony, if we're working in the direction of trying to prevent a bloodbath, I think we should back away from this whole thing. Because the key ingredient here is getting the Haitians to reconcile. If we try to get in the middle, we'll be attacked from both sides."

But Lake kept pressing General Powell. He wanted to know how many troops were needed. Fifteen thousand? Twenty thousand?

Colin Powell was getting annoyed. He said it was irresponsible to send in U.S. troops if they didn't have a clear mission. "What's the mission?" he asked.

According to Pezzullo, Lake rattled on sounding more and more like a college professor, which he had been until recently at Mount Holyoke College. Finally, Defense Secretary Les Aspin said that what Lake had been describing sounded to him more like a police function.

Pezzullo agreed: "If we need anything, we're talking about a police function, a gendarmerie. Our military got involved in Haiti before and it turned out to be a big mistake."

But Lake wasn't through. "Can we stand idly by while Haitians are killing Haitians?"

"Why are we talking about a bloodbath, Tony, if we create the political reconciliation that is essential?" Pezzullo asked.[4] Colin Powell was the only one who seemed to understand.

The meeting in the Situation Room broke up, or rather dissolved. And Pezzullo left in a haze of unanswered questions and confusion. "What exactly had been accomplished?" he wondered. No one had taken notes. The bloodbath scare had been posited and left hanging. Add to that the assumption that Aristide was unstable and that Cédras and company would never budge. It seemed to him that the administration was trapping itself in a maze of misunderstandings before they had even begun.

Fortunately, Pezzullo found a highly intelligent and capable partner in UN/OAS special envoy Dante Caputo. But they had some rough ground to get over first. Dante Caputo was an intensely rational man with a mop of gray hair and a drooping gray mustache. Picture, if you can, a cross between Emiliano Zapata and Confucius. Even in mid-March, barely three months into his job, he was exasperated with General Cédras and de facto prime minister Marc Bazin. Lately, he had been trying to get them to accept a contingent of OAS and UN observers to monitor the human rights situation in Haiti.

He admitted that Haiti and Haitians were hard for him, later confiding: "One of my major mistakes was trying to present my arguments in a rational way. If there is a phrase that I repeated most in Haiti when I was dealing with Cédras and the others, it was 2 + 2 = 4. It comes from the end of the play *Don Juan* by Racine when his aide asks: 'Sir, what do you believe in?' And Don Juan says: 'I just know that two plus two equals four.'"

According to the anthropologist and experimental filmmaker Maya Deren, the Haitian worldview was decidedly unEuropean. "In voudoun," she wrote, "one *and* one make three; two *and* two make five; for the *and* of the equation is the third and fifth part respectively, the relationship which makes all the parts meaningful."[5]

In another sense, however, Caputo's experience made him acutely sensitive to the human stakes in the Haiti crisis. "I was not just coming from a personal history where I believed in the principle of human rights," he explained. "I had lived that principle and risked my life for it."[6] An academic and a politician, he had studied in France and the United States before returning to Argentina in 1972, just as his country was entering a state of siege. Right-wing militants backed by elements of the Argentine armed forces had declared war on groups of leftist guerrillas, most notably the Montaneros. The victims of this so-called dirty war eventually grew to include some twenty-five to thirty thousand leftist politicians, student leaders, journalists, and anyone else who spoke out against the military dictatorship. Dante Caputo, as a member of the Radical Party, spent ten painful years watching friends and colleagues disappear and wondering when he might he next.[7]

When the Radical Party candidate Raúl Alfonsín won the presidential election in 1983, Caputo was named foreign minister. He was elected to the Chamber of Deputies in 1989.

Although Caputo had never been to Haiti, he had worked closely with the United Nations, serving as president of the General Assembly in 1988. He was convinced that with the end of the cold war the UN, a forum for the world community, had a unique opportunity to build a rational model for international relations. "Because now there is not this balance of power, the threat of nuclear holocaust," he explained, "so we can use our rationality, our principles, our values to build a different world." He understood that in order to achieve this the United States would have to find a new way to define its leadership, one that emphasized the impor-tance of a multilateral approach through the mechanism of the United Nations.

At the end of 1992, Haiti seemed like a perfect place to start. When Dante Caputo met with President-elect Bill Clinton, in mid-January 1993, the newly elected president seemed to understand. Clinton asked: "What is it that we need to achieve a political solution in Haiti?"

Caputo answered: "Mr. President, it's important that we don't have a double discourse with the Haitians, where the United States is telling them one thing and the international community is saying something else."[8]

In early January 1993, Caputo initiated a series of trips to Haiti to acquaint himself with the country and its political and military lead-ers. "Haiti was even worse than I expected," he said later. "One of the things that shocked me the most, besides the incredible poverty, was the absence of anything in common in Haiti. You don't have state institutions, you don't have a state apparatus, but even worse, they have not been able to build something in common during two centuries." There seemed to be no social contract.

Haitian society reminded him of the prisoner's dilemma in the political science game theory. Caputo sensed that the most irrational possibility applied to the political actors in Haiti. They would rather accuse one another and destroy themselves, than lie or remain silent in order to help one another.

In his initial contacts with Haitians, Caputo was also impressed by their capacity to use words. "I would say that their reality is so unacceptable, so unbearable," he explained, "that they need to deny that reality, building the reality of words. If you're Haitian, how do you explain your country? It's not a colonial country. It's not a country that got its independence in the 1960s. They have two hundred years of independence."

General Cédras and Caputo did not get off on the right foot. The coup had not been a "coup d'état," Cédras argued, but a "coup de force" since the FADH was not interested in taking power, only in removing a president who had continually violated the constitution.

And Cédras had a particular way of reasoning. He would answer Caputo's questions with more questions. "What do you mean by this? What do you mean by that?" Or: "What do you mean by general staff, Mr. Caputo?"

"General, staff," Caputo answered. "You know, you people sitting here."

"Well, well, well . . . It's not so easy . . ."[9]

They would go around and around in circles for hours. One character, a Colonel Carl Dorelien, would play the role of the bad cop. "He'd be shouting all the time," remembered Caputo, "saying that they were going to defend Haiti from the international community. They called the international community the international, which made it sound like some kind of communist conspiracy."

Dante Caputo also couldn't fathom Cédras's strange attachment to the constitution. "He would argue: 'Because of this article we can't do that,'" remembered Caputo. "At a certain moment I just exploded. I said: 'What are you talking about? You are saying we cannot do this because of your interpretation of the constitution, but you made a coup!'

"And you know what his answer was? 'There is no single article of the constitution which prohibits a coup.' It was unbelievable!"

In addition to the general staff, Caputo also had to deal with the de facto prime minister Marc Bazin. "This was another experience," said Caputo. "Here was Bazin, who had a good background as an international economist, but you put him back in Haiti and he starts behaving strangely."[10]

Bazin and Cédras were playing a double game. Bazin would say: I understand what you want to do and that's correct, but I can't do it because Cédras and the military have all the power.

Caputo remembered that when he took the same proposal to the general staff of the FADH, General Cédras responded: "We are not in power here. Mr. Caputo, you have to understand that we're not the government. I'm not allowed to discuss these matters."

On this first visit Caputo brought with him Leandro Despouy, a fellow Argentine, great raconteur and charmer, and a politician down to his fingernails. Despouy was made for Haiti, not only for his ability to insinuate himself into very delicate situations, but also because of his great talent for seeing the absurdity and humor in life.

Caputo and Despouy were so fundamentally different that it was hard to imagine that they could work together at all. But each had a deep, abiding respect for the other. While Caputo was impatient, Despouy seemed to thrive on the endless talk that characterized political discourse in Haiti. While Caputo focused on defining realistic goals and how they could be achieved, Despouy was getting to know the players—how they saw the world, how they felt about themselves.

Despouy, the son of a congressman from the western department of San Luis, Argentina, had been forced into exile during the "dirty war." Arriving in Paris in 1974 without money, friends, or a knowledge of French, he spent eight years before he could even write or call or see his family for fear of putting them in danger. He did manage to hone his political skills as a legislative aide to the French Socialist Party.

It didn't take long for Caputo and Despouy to understand that the political situation in Haiti was deeply fractured. "The challenge was to convince the forces in Haiti, to persuade them," said Despouy, "to find common ground that would allow Aristide to return under conditions positive to the survival of democracy."[11]

When the two Argentines concluded their first visit to Port-au-Prince in early January 1993 they left convinced that General Raoul Cédras and the de facto prime minister Marc Bazin had agreed to accept the deployment of several hundred international human rights monitors as a first step. The Inter-American Commission on Human Rights estimated that fifteen hundred Haitians had died in political violence since the September 1991 overthrow of President Aristide. When Caputo and Despouy returned to Port-au-Prince on the first of February, with an agreement to sign, they were met at the airport by hundreds of angry demonstrators calling them "international devils" and vowing to resist any foreign intervention with force.

It was only after Caputo left and the United States threatened to tighten the OAS embargo that Bazin relented and signed the agreement without conditions. Within a week the first of 240 OAS/UN human rights observers were deployed in Haiti. Armed with little more than knowledge of the law and a crash course in Haitian history and culture, the observers started patrolling the country in white four-wheel-drive vehicles. Slowly, Haitians started to come forward. In the southern town of Jacmel, for example, they told the story of Gottfriend Krause, a Swiss school director who had lived in Haiti for twenty years.

In May 1992, after a neighboring school was surrounded by police officers because they were holding a pro-Aristide rally, Mr. Krause intervened. For daring to speak up, he was dragged from his house the next day, taken to Port-au-Prince, and thrown into prison. "The soldiers told me I was arrested because I had books about Aristide, but none about Cédras," said Krause.[12] After protest by the Swiss consulate, Krause was released.

In early March, UN special envoy Dante Caputo decided that, given the high level of antipathy to the UN effort, it was a good idea for his colleague, Leandro Despouy, to stay behind in Port-au-Prince to initiate a dialogue with the diverse political actors. "In Haiti, you must remember that everything is so polarized," Despouy explained, "there is so much bad blood. Even in the Catholic Church. Some priests loved Aristide, some priests loathed him. Never have I seen priests with so much hate inside them."[13]

One Protestant sect was run by a man named Richard Vladimir Jeanty from the PARADIS party. Jeanty was one of the many candidates who ran against Aristide in the 1990 presidential elections. According to the Provisional Electoral Council, he received 12,296 votes (or three-quarters of 1 percent). "He was completely crazy," said Despouy. "Always on the radio, saying rabid things about the international community."

One day at the end of a political discussion, Jeanty came up to him and said: "Despouy, you are going to bring the devil. And when the devil comes there's going to be blood. And when the blood flows everyone gets stained. And you'll get stained, too."[14]

It turned out that the most moderate groups were the voudouns. Despouy's first interview with voudoun priests (or *houngans*) was arranged by Max Beauvoir, the chief of the voudoun federation. A very modern, urbane man who spoke fluent English, Spanish, and French, Beauvoir explained that most Haitians were poor and believed in voudoun. He said that people were worried about the effects of the embargo, but "we *houngans* are not taking sides."

The next time Despouy met with the *houngans*, they set the agenda: "This time we're going to hear from you."

But no sooner had he started than they interrupted him. Two beautiful voudoun princesses were led in. "Their faces were gorgeous and their bodies were perfectly sculpted," remembered Despouy with many oohs and aahs. "They were all dressed in white."

"These are our assistants," announced the *houngans*.

One sat on Despouy's left and the other sat on his right. They didn't move. But when Despouy spoke, they listened intently and their noses seemed to quiver like they were smelling him.

Unnerved, Despouy asked: "Why do they have to be here?"

"We're not interested in what you have to say," answered one of the *houngans*. "We're interested in your intent. It's the intent behind your words that our assistants are interpreting for us." After a while the princesses left.

"The talks served to humanize us with these people," Despouy concluded. "No longer were we just symbols of the international community, we were men who were trying to achieve a political neutrality."

Despouy was also learning something else that would serve him in the future. "There are a few rare Haitians who don't believe in voudoun," he explained. "So if you assume everyone believes, you're better off."

While Despouy was getting to know the political actors in Haiti, Special Envoy Dante Caputo was ready to put pressure on the de facto regime.

When he met Lawrence Pezzullo on April 7, 1993, Caputo explained that he was traveling to Port-au-Prince the next week to propose a settlement that called for Aristide's quick return, the removal of the military leaders who overthrew him, and a vast one-billion-dollar package of grants and loans designed to jump-start Haiti's ravaged economy. The sticking point was the passage of some kind of amnesty for the leaders of the coup.

To no one's surprise, Caputo's proposal was rejected by Cédras. Prime Minister Marc Bazin, in a defiant speech to the nation, said the UN plan was "doomed to failure."[15] Part of the problem was that Haitian military leaders didn't trust President Aristide and vice versa. At Caputo's urging, President Aristide broadcast a speech that was heard in Haiti on Sunday, April 11, on the eve of the UN special envoy's visit. President Aristide claimed that he was offering political amnesty to army leaders. But his speech contained the following passage: "Our ancestors wish for us to safeguard each other, according to the country's Constitution. Toussaint l'Ouverture accorded an amnesty to General Rigaud and his supporters."[16]

The threat implied in the exiled president's words was not lost on General Cédras and the de factos. They knew that within months of the amnesty of General Rigaud referred to by President Aristide, Toussaint l'Ouverture supervised the slaughter of thousands of his rivals' supporters in one of the most violent betrayals in Haitian history.

Caputo returned from Haiti exasperated with Cédras and Bazin. And, his impression of President Aristide had changed. "I started to realize that Aristide isn't a hero," said Caputo. "He's quite a complicated guy. Part madman, part political genius. I started to realize that he wasn't committed to finding a political solution for his country. It was clear that he wanted us to apply pressure to the military, but he didn't want to make any commitments himself. He also wanted to destroy the army to take revenge."[17]

When Pezzullo met with Caputo after his return, the Argentine declared: "We have to put more pressure on the military."

And Pezzullo said: "Dante, we've got to move this thing slowly."[18] Before adding to the misery of Haiti, the Clinton administration wanted to make sure that the messages to its de facto government and ousted president were clear.

Since October 8, 1991, Haiti's weak economy had been choked even further by an OAS trade embargo. A month later, the United States suspended about $85 million in aid and froze Haiti's assets in U.S. banks.

The effects of the embargo were visible on the streets of Port-au-Prince. Factories and light industries had been forced to shut down, resulting in the loss of tens of thousands of jobs. According to Howard French of the *New York Times*: "Port-au-Prince, a bustling city in normal times, now often seems a dusty ghost town. A quarter or more of the population of more than one million have left for the countryside, hoping to live off the land. The salaried workers who remain are reduced to half-day shifts of three-day weeks. By the afternoon, streets are empty except for the cars that park overnight in long lines, thirsty for some of the dwindling supply of gasoline. Most services in the city have been interrupted for lack of gasoline and mounds of garbage are piled high on many streets."[19]

After Dante Caputo's ill-fated visit to Haiti in mid-April, the U.S. chargé d'affaires, Chuck Redman, began holding talks with General Cédras at FADH headquarters. In Redman's view, Cédras was amenable to some kind of agreement, but it had to be handled carefully.

Pezzullo asked: "Do you think you can get a letter from him agreeing to step down?"[20]

And by the end of April, Redman had a letter from General Cédras promising to resign as commander in chief under an agreement that would guarantee the survival of the FADH. Pezzullo immediately called Caputo in New York and told him. "Now what?" the UN/OAS special envoy asked.

In his talks with Cédras, Chuck Redman had raised the possibility of offering military training as part of the transfer of power. A plan to restructure the FADH had already been drawn up at the Pentagon by Lieutenant General Jack Sheehan, who had served in Haiti earlier in his career. The plan called for the establishment of an independent police force and the reorganization and reduction of the FADH from its current seven thousand down to three thousand. Combat forces would be replaced by engineering units, which would concentrate on civic action projects, road repairs, and disaster relief. To discourage the army from playing a political role, the plan envisioned moving military units away from Port-au-Prince.

Chargé Redman said that the United States was willing to offer training and advisory services to help bring about the transformation, which was estimated to take three to four years.

Cédras liked the idea. He felt that if he were seen as a man who began to transform the military, he could retire with honor. A new commander could be appointed and, then, President Aristide could return.

After Pezzullo discussed the idea with Caputo, the two men decided to try it out on President Aristide's U.S. advisors, Michael Barnes and Robert White.

Pezzullo had gotten to know Mike Barnes when Pezzullo was the U.S. ambassador to Nicaragua from 1979 to 1981 and Barnes was chairman of the Western Hemisphere subcommittee of the House Foreign Affairs Committee. Since losing his suburban Maryland seat, Barnes had been practicing law in Washington, first at Arents Fox and, more recently, at Hogan & Hartson. His relationship with Aristide went back to early 1991 when the newly installed president of Haiti asked him to help recover assets stolen by the Duvalier regime. Barnes's value to the ousted president soared after he ran candidate Bill Clinton's presidential campaign in Maryland and helped him win.

The deputy NSC director Sandy Berger and Barnes were close friends. In fact, when Berger left his partnership at Hogan & Hartson to take up his post in the Clinton administration, Barnes pulled up stakes at the rival firm of Arents Fox and moved the Aristide account to Hogan & Hartson. It was reported to be worth at least fifty-five thousand dollars a month and was paid by President Aristide out of frozen Government of Haiti funds.

Bob White was another story. The big-boned Irishman, who bore a slight resemblance to the actor Lee Marvin, had been a highly visible and outspoken U.S. ambassador to El Salvador during the Carter administration. Since resigning from the State Department in 1981, Bob White had become president of the Center for International Policy (CIP), a nonprofit education and research organization that followed U.S. policy toward the Third World, especially as it related to human rights. As president of CIP, White had developed close ties to the Congressional Black Caucus, Representative Joseph Kennedy, and others on Capitol

Hill with a strong interest in Haiti. Among his friends in the Clinton administration he counted Sandy Berger, Richard Feinberg, and Nancy Soderberg of the NSC.

White claimed that his relationship with Aristide was different from Mike Barnes's for one important reason: He wasn't on Aristide's payroll. "Sometimes," White said, "President Aristide would like to say: 'Do this.' And he could say that with Mike Barnes and with others, but he couldn't do that with me."[21]

Dante Caputo and Pezzullo had lunch with Mike Barnes and Bob White at Barnes's law offices on April 22, 1993, and presented the idea of restructuring the FADH and introducing military trainers.

Both Barnes and White objected. Aristide would never accept foreign troops in Haiti before he returned, they said. Trainers would have to be brought into Haiti *after* President Aristide was reinstalled.

"But that's going to be awkward," Pezzullo explained.

While Pezzullo was in the men's room, Caputo told the two Aristide advisors that he didn't think the diplomatic effort to return Aristide would work, because the United States wasn't putting enough pressure on the Haitian military. When the U.S. diplomat returned, Mike Barnes repeated what Caputo had just said.

"That's nonsense," Pezzullo answered, annoyed. "The Haitian military leaders don't want to talk to Dante. They'll talk to us because we're the United States."

Mike Barnes said that he thought Caputo had a point. The United States should be putting more pressure on the Haitian military.

"Look, Mike," Pezzullo countered, "there comes a point at which, if you push this, you're talking about using military force."

According to Pezzullo, Mike Barnes smiled and said: "I think it's going to come to that."

"Well, I disagree," Pezzullo said. "That would be a sad day for Haiti and President Aristide, too."[22]

As the two diplomats left, Pezzullo turned to Caputo and asked: "What's the purpose of going around talking about putting more pressure on the military? Maybe I should bow out and let you do this yourself."

Caputo shook his head: "No, I'm going to quit."

Pezzullo responded: "Well, that's up to you. Quit if you want."

When he returned to the State Department, Pezzullo was summoned to Secretary Christopher's office. The special advisor was taking his seat, when the secretary asked: "How are things going?"

Pezzullo was still stewing. "As a matter of fact, I just had a very abrasive meeting with Dante Caputo. I don't think he trusts us. He goes around saying that we've got to apply more pressure. There might come a point where we have to make a break."

Christopher told Pezzullo that the president wanted to resolve the Haiti crisis with or without the cooperation of the UN and the OAS.

The next Tuesday, April 27, Special Advisor Lawrence Pezzullo traveled up to New York to meet with Marrack (Mig) Goulding, the UN under-secretary-general for political affairs, at Dante Caputo's request. Dante Caputo started by saying: "I don't know if I can continue on because there are different signals by the U.S."

Pezzullo jumped in immediately. "What the hell are you talking about? If we're going to work at cross-purposes I don't see how we can go on."

"I can't depend on the relationship," said Caputo, raising his voice. "I'm getting sick and tired of you people doing things by back channels."

"What back channels?" asked Pezzullo.

"The second channels that are operating behind my back!" shouted Caputo.

"There are no back channels or second channels," Pezzullo replied. "President Clinton has made his position public and that's what I'm trying to implement."

Caputo wasn't convinced.

"Well, maybe we need to reconsider this whole thing," Pezzullo said. "Because I'm not going to put up with this crap and I don't think my country is either."

At that point Mig Goulding cut them off. "Can't you two cool down? You're both first-class guys and you're arguing over things that you shouldn't be arguing about."[23]

The meeting ended and Pezzullo returned to Washington. About a week later Dante Caputo called him to invite him to a meeting at the OAS.

It was a beautiful spring day. As they walked, Caputo spoke: "I have to apologize to you about what happened. I've come to realize a couple of things. First, you and your staff are the best friends I've got. I can trust your people more than I can trust my own staff at the UN."[24]

Caputo went on to explain that several members of his staff, including Frencesc Vendrell and Nicole Lannegrace, had been trying to convince him that the United States was negotiating secretly with Cédras through a "second channel." These aides told him that while President Clinton publicly supported the return of President Aristide, other agents of his government were working secretly with General Cédras to bolster the military regime.

After his confrontation with Pezzullo in Mig Goulding's office, Caputo had done some checking of his own and found out that his aides had been speaking darkly of a "second channel" without telling Caputo that they were referring to Chuck Redman's talks with General Cédras in Port-au-Prince, on which Caputo had been thoroughly briefed.

Caputo had more to get off his chest. "You also have to understand," he continued, "I grew up with the political history of the Radicales Party in Argentina. We looked upon the United States as the great imperialist. I was always critical of the United States. I lived through the Reagan years. I was foreign minister when the U.S. was involved in those idiocies with the contras in Nicaragua. When I came up to the UN, I encountered anti-Americanism of a quality that I have never found in my life, anywhere. They detest the United States."[25]

"That was the break," remembered Pezzullo. "After that, it was like swimming with the current. Sure, Dante and I had differences of view, but never again was there a question of a rift."[26]

CHAPTER 5

Early U.S.-Haitian Relations

"Independence is the worst and most dangerous condition they [Haiti] can be in for the United States."

—President JOHN ADAMS, 1799

From their beginnings, the United States and Haiti have had an intense relationship defined by often-contradictory pushes and pulls. Like most relationships between people or peoples, it has had to navigate the magnetic fields of their respective expectations and fears. In the case of Haiti that fear has been foreign domination and dependency; in the case of the United States the central fear has been and continues to be concerns about race.

At the end of the eighteenth century, the two colonies shared a yearning for independence, which they encouraged in each other with arms and even men. When the American colonies rebelled against their English rulers, the French colonists of Saint Domingue aided them with clandestine shipments of weapons and ammunition. In 1779 Admiral Charles-Hector d'Estaing sailed from Saint Marc to command the siege of Savannah, in which six hundred mulatto and Negro troops fought courageously against the British. In 1781, another Saint Domingue fleet defeated Lord Cornwallis at Lynnhaven Bay in Florida. By cutting off Lord Cornwallis's escape by sea, the Saint Domingue fleet helped bring about the British army's decisive surrender at Yorktown.

U.S. president John Adams returned the favor in 1800 when black general Toussaint l'Ouverture appealed for help against the mulatto General Rigaud. The second U.S. president responded by sending warships loaded with ammunition and over two thousand muskets. Aided and strengthened by supplies from the United States, Toussaint l'Ouverture was able to push his campaign; and after months of battles and thousands of casualties, Rigaud and his mulatto troops were defeated.[1]

Prior to and during Saint Domingue's bloody slave revolt, the newly independent American states offered refuge to hundreds of white plantation owners and their families. Into the cities of Boston, New York, Philadelphia, Baltimore, Charleston, and New Orleans streamed exiles from the island, bringing wild tales of terrorism, burning, killing, and looting.

According to the historian Winthrop Jordan, "White refugees came from Haiti, bringing many slaves with them. That year (1793) saw the growth of a peculiar uneasiness, especially in Virginia, where many refugees had segregated."[2]

American slaveholders had real reasons to fear the example set by slaves in Saint Domingue. In 1800, black slave Gabriel Prosser fomented a slave uprising in Virginia that he claimed was inspired by Toussaint l'Ouverture. And in 1822, Denmark Vesey, who had been a slave in Haiti, led what has been described as "the most elaborate insurrectionary project ever formed by American slaves." Vesey allegedly told his co-conspirators that a large army was arriving from Haiti to join their cause. He said: "We must unite together as the Saint Domingue people did, never to betray one another, and to die before we would tell upon one another."[3]

Independent Haiti's first leader, General Jean-Jacques Dessalines did not help quell U.S. fears. After defeating the French in 1804 and declaring himself Emperor of Haiti, Dessalines launched a brutal campaign to eradicate the last vestiges of colonialism from the island. Stabbing, beheading, and disemboweling its way across Haiti, his army left a trail of thousands of white and mulatto dead. At the end of the slaughter Dessalines rejoiced: "I will go to my grave happy. We have avenged our brothers. Haiti has become a blood-red spot on the face of the globe!"[4]

Haiti was declared a sanctuary for escaped slaves and for any person of African or American Indian descent. Emperor Dessalines offered slave ship captains bound for the United States forty dollars for each African they brought to the island.[5]

Like his predecessor Toussaint L'Ouverture, Dessalines was not interested in restoring his people to a rural African way of life. Instead, he was determined to create a modern black state with an economy geared to trading on the world market. Betraying his vow to his people on Independence Day "to live free and independent and accept death in preference to the yoke," he established what was in effect a state serfdom. All men and women, except for a small group of administrators, were assigned by the state to serve either as soldiers or laborers "attached to the plantation." And Dessalines and his army ran the state-controlled two-thirds of the country's plantations with an iron hand.[6]

But he soon came into conflict with both *anciens libres* (those who were freed before the revolution—mainly mulattos) and *nouveau libres* (those who gained their freedom during the revolution—mostly black). In October 1806, as his army tried to crush a rebellion in the South, Dessalines was ambushed, stoned, and torn to pieces by rebel officers. His headless corpse was put on display in the *Place du Gouvernement*.

Now the new nation found itself divided according to economic priorities. The *anciens libres* in the South elected the educated and refined mulatto Pétion, who instituted a land distribution program that though widely popular failed economically.

The North, on the other hand, supported the self-taught black General Henri Christophe. According to the historian Michel-Rolph Trouillot: "Christophe's kingdom flourished economically, mainly because he imposed his own feudal version of militarized agriculture with an iron hand."[7] He forced his subjects to work long hours on plantations, but rewarded them with a modestly prosperous and secure state.

Within three years he established a state printing press, a judicial system called the Code Henri, a sovereign court with feudal seneschalships, and a system of public education, all supervised by a Royal Chamber of Public Instruction.

Christophe declared himself "King Henri I of Haiti, Sovereign of Ile de la Tortue, Ile de la Gonâve and other adjacent Islands, Destroyer of Tyranny, Regenerator and Benefactor of the Haitian Nation, First Monarch of the New World." And within the space of a day, he created a hereditary nobility with four princes, eight dukes, twenty-two counts, thirty-seven barons, and fourteen knights. They lived in splendor in a series of French-style palaces, the greatest of which was Sans Souci, which was designed by the king himself as a Versailles of the New World. King Henri's absolutism and grandiloquence were legendary and later served as the inspiration for playwright Eugene O'Neill's famous *Emperor Jones*.

Eventually Christophe's subjects grew weary of his severity and his army divided and mutinied. Isolated from his countrymen, half paralyzed by a stroke, Christophe learned that an insurrection had been organized against him by the mulatto General Jean-Pierre Boyer, who had become president of the South after Pétion's death from yellow fever in 1818. "No King! No Nobility! No Tyranny!" yelled his rebellious subjects. Deafened by the noise, Christophe calmly retired to his bedroom and shot himself in the head and heart.

General Jean Pierre Boyer, an ex-slave who had lived for a time in France, ruled for the next twenty-three years over a sort of republican monarchy maintained by the army. He also reunited the two halves of the country and underwrote the political and economic preeminence of the mulattos by restoring land that had belonged to them during the colonial period. In early 1822, he led the Haitian army into the Spanish colony in the eastern part of Hispaniola, where he abolished slavery. But his efforts to revive the plantation system failed, undermined by Pétion's land reforms and the peasantry's unwillingness to work for wages. With negligible export earnings, the central government went broke.

This marked the death knell of the plantation system. It also marked the end of the government's ability to control the types of crops planted. Sugar exports, which had totaled 163 million pounds at the height of the colony, shrunk to only two thousand pounds by 1825.

Former slaves simply abandoned the land they had been forced to work and started their own small farms in more remote districts. As the labor force atrophied, large landowners rented out their holdings, then retreated to cities to further their careers as merchants or government officials. This largely mulatto, French-speaking, and well-educated group became the country's elites. Their wives and daughters wore the latest Parisian fashions; and they often sent their sons abroad for higher education.

As the colonial infrastructure of roads decayed and were not rebuilt, the gap between this urban elite and the blacks in the countryside widened. Their respective economic and political goals, beliefs and even languages diverged. In the hard to reach countryside, ex-slaves developed a society derived from the ancestral traditions that they had brought with them from Africa.

Haiti's political and economic decline was exacerbated by the refusal of the United States and much of Europe to formally recognize its independence. French foreign minister Charles Tallyrand summed up the feelings of most European leaders when he wrote: "The existence of a Negro people in arms, occupying a country it has soiled by the most criminal acts, is a horrible spectacle for all white nations."[8] And the youthful United States, whose economy was dependent on slavery, kept the new Haitian republic at arm's length. Senator Robert Hayne of South Carolina expressed the sentiments of slave-owning states when he said: "We never can acknowledge Haiti's independence. . . . The peace and safety of a large portion of our union forbids us even to discuss it."

Political antagonism to the new black republic was given precedence over U.S. mercantile interests, which initially had been very strong. In 1790, while Saint Domingue was still a colony of half a million people, it was the United States' second major trading partner behind Great Britain. Since the French forbade the importation of rum and molasses in order to protect French brandies, Saint Domingue planters turned to the United States. Thereafter, rum and molasses were traded along the New England coast for refuse fish that was otherwise of little value. Distillation became the chief industry of many towns from New York to Boston. According to the historian Lowell Montague: "The trade was so voluble that it came to be regarded as the foundation of New England prosperity."[9]

By 1810 United States exports to all of the French West Indies (including Haiti) amounted to a paltry $109,000, only 2 percent of the value of goods sold to the Toussaint l'Ouverture government in 1800.[10]

It wasn't until 1862 that President Abraham Lincoln formally recognized Haiti, writing: "If any good reason exists why we should persevere in withholding our recognition of the independence and sovereignty of Haiti . . . , I am unable to discern it."[11]

But formal recognition by the United States and Europe did not bring political stability. In 1843, dissident blacks in the army revolted after accusing President Boyer of both corruption and treason. He fled to Jamaica, a presidential route taken sixteen years later by Faustin Soulouque. But before Soulouque crowned himself Emperor Faustin I in 1849, one black president drank himself to death, another was overthrown, and the one-eyed General Jean-Baptiste Riché died of an overdose of drugs taken to increase his strength. In fact, from the overthrow of Boyer to the U.S. occupation of 1915–34, only one of Haiti's twenty-two presidents served out his term in office. Three died natural deaths, one was blown to pieces, one was torn to bits by a mob, two were assassinated, and fourteen more were driven from Haiti by revolts.

Candidates for the office assembled armies of *cacos* (literally "birds of prey"), part-time guerrilla fighters recruited from peasant villages in the mountains. These brigades then marched on Port-au-Prince to do away with the incumbent president. "These Haitian revolutions proceed habitually by fixed rules, somewhat like a game of checkers," wrote William Seabrook in *The Magic Island*.

First attempts were not always successful, and second and third tries were common. "The forces of arms, preferably turned against Port-au-Prince, remained the principal asset in the race for the presidency," wrote the Haitian historian Michel-Rolph Trouillot.[12]

Each successive ruler left the country in worse condition, with its fundamental problems still unresolved. At a time when European powers were looking to expand their empires, Haiti's political and economic instability made it an easy target. Increasingly, warships were called in by foreign merchants to help collect unpaid debts. On more than twenty occasions from 1849 to 1915, U.S., French, and German troops arrived to claim from the vaults of the Banque Nationale d'Haiti large sums owed to their merchants.

The United States, eager to protect its hegemony over the Caribbean, watched developments in Haiti with growing concern. On four separate occasions between 1884 and 1891 the State Department warned European powers to stay out of Haiti. An Anglo-German-Italian attempt in 1902 to forcibly collect debts from the government of Venezuela and the impending bankruptcy of the Dominican Republic in 1904 caused President Theodore Roosevelt to update the Monroe Doctrine. According to the Roosevelt Corollary: "If a nation keeps order and pays its obligations, it needs fear no interference from the United States." But "chronic wrong-doing, or an impotence which results in the loosening of the ties of civilized order" would, in the Caribbean at least, result in a visit from the United States in the role of international policeman.

This was not an empty threat. By 1915 the United States had intervened in Colombia to create Panama for a future canal (1903) and in Cuba (1906). Marines landed in Honduras (1907), Nicaragua (1910, 1912), and Mexico (1914). And they would take over the Dominican Republic from 1916 to 1924.

Although Haitian leaders resisted U.S. interference, they continued to flirt with economic and political disaster. In 1911, 1913, and twice in 1914, German merchants extended loans to the Haitian government to be repaid by customs receipts.

Days after ship traffic through the Panama Canal began in August 1914, World War I erupted. Immediately, U.S. strategic concerns in the Caribbean mounted. In February 1915, the German government declared unlimited submarine warfare against neutral ships carrying cargo to its enemies Britain and France. On July 27, 1915, a German submarine torpedoed the U.S. freighter *Leelanaw*, creating near-hysteria in the United States. The day before, Haitian President Guillaume Sam, after hearing rumors of an impending coup, gathered all his political opponents and had them thrown in jail. They were to be executed if the uprising took place.

Sam had it coming. One French diplomat described him as "authoritarian, vindictive, pitiless towards foes, cruel to those whose existence, rightly or wrong, he considered a menace to his authority."[13] Shortly after midnight a group of *cacos* opened fire on the presidential mansion, slightly wounding Sam. Sam gave the order to "do the necessary," whereupon 187 helpless members of the country's elite families were shot, stabbed, disemboweled, and dismembered. Their wailing relatives led mobs that screamed for Sam's blood.

As nervous officials in Washington monitored these events, the U.S. Navy ship *Washington* carrying 330 marines pulled within a mile of Port-au-Prince. Radiograms flew back and forth to Washington. At 6 P.M. on July 28 Admiral William Caperton gave the order to land the marines. The decision had been made, according to a State Department spokesperson, "in order to seize the opportunity to end, once and for all, dangerously chaotic conditions in Haiti."[14] The U.S. Marines would stay for nineteen years.

CHAPTER 6

UN Sanctions

"They'll come and kill my children!"

—YANNICK CÉDRAS

It's safe to say that every foreign policymaker in the U.S. government was familiar with the phrase: Those who don't know history are condemned to repeat it. But the past history of U.S.-Haitian relations was not something that seemed to interest them in early 1993. Instead, White House policymakers were hell-bent on scoring a quick foreign policy victory for their new president by restoring deposed Haitian president Jean-Bertrand Aristide to power and stemming the flow of Haitian refugees. They imagined they could accomplish this without taking into consideration the tangled, tortured political culture of the second-oldest independent country in the hemisphere. Anyone familiar with Haiti could tell them that they were dead wrong.

U.S. special advisor Lawrence Pezzullo, who had been appointed in March, had clearly communicated the resolve of the Clinton administration to the various factions in Haiti. Supporting Pezzullo was an intelligent, energetic young Haitian desk officer, Nancy Jackson, a secretary, and a very strong deputy named Michael Kozak. Kozak had been sitting in bureaucratic limbo in a tiny office in Central American affairs after his appointment as ambassador to El Salvador had been blocked by the conservative senator Jesse Helms and the liberal senator Christopher Dodd, both of whom didn't approve of the way Kozak had helped resolve the Contra mess in Nicaragua.

An outgoing, let's-roll-up-our-sleeves kind of guy with a square boxer's body and face, Kozak was pleased when sometime in late March 1993 the new assistant secretary for Inter-American Affairs, Alexander Watson, asked him to join the Haiti Working Group. They toiled in a shabby suite of offices on the State Department's fourth floor with outdated Wang word processors, cracked glass partitions, desks that dated back to the fifties, and peeling paint.

Watson soon augmented the Haiti Working Group's staff with Richard Brown, a former ambassador to Uruguay, who was brought in to run the office and deal with sanction issues. Kozak and Pezzullo handled communications with Aristide, the Haitian military, the UN, and the White House. Nancy Jackson dealt with Haitian country issues, which meant coordinating with the embassy in Port-au-Prince. A young officer named Kenneth Merten, who had served in Haiti and spoke Creole, was named staff assistant. His job was to get papers through the maze-like State Department bureaucracy.

Both Lawrence Pezzullo and UN special envoy Dante Caputo had come to understand that personal security was a central concern of all Haitians, and that concern had to be addressed if a transition to constitutional government was going to succeed. Therefore, in concert with their staffs and agencies of the U.S. government, the two diplomats set out to develop a series of initiatives that would address these fears head on. The centerpiece was a UN "blue beret" military and police mission. The military component would include trainers to begin the restructuring of the FADH and Seabee units to engage in public works. The police mission would be divided between monitors who would accompany FADH units assigned to police duties and trainers from the U.S. Justice Department who would initiate the training of the new police force.

U.S. Marine general Jack Sheehan, who had served in Haiti in the late seventies and who knew General Cédras, was given the task of drawing up the plan for retraining the FADH. A no-nonsense Irish Catholic from Boston who was now operations officer at the Atlantic Command in

Norfolk, General Sheehan presented the outline of his plan to Pezzullo and Caputo in early April. It called for reducing the FADH from a 7,000-man to a 2,500 or 3,000-man force. Their training would be geared toward civil engineering and civic action, with a small coastal patrol and air rescue capacity. According to Sheehan's blueprint, a separate police force would be created under a Justice Department International Criminal Investigative Training Assistance Program (ICITAP), which had worked successfully in both Panama and El Salvador.

In early April 1993, General Sheehan and Pezzullo presented the plan to President Aristide and his advisors at his office in Georgetown. Pezzullo remembers General Sheehan going through the whole scenario with diagrams. When Sheehan finished, President Aristide looked pleased. "It's beautiful," he gushed. "General, you make me very happy."[1]

General Sheehan then flew to Haiti, where he presented the same plan to the FADH General Staff. President Aristide, meanwhile, was briefed about the Justice Department's ICITAP.

Under the ICITAP scenario, the Haitian police would be separated from the military and put under the jurisdiction of the justice ministry. A civilian police chief would be chosen along with an advisory board, which would supervise the creation of a police academy. All candidates for the academy would be carefully screened. During their six months of training they would learn how to keep order while at the same time ensuring individual rights.

Although President Aristide continued to complain about the pace of the negotiations, he did express his "optimism" about both training programs in a letter to Special Advisor Pezzullo the last week of April. That same week Pezzullo and Alex Watson traveled to UN headquarters in New York, where they raised the possibility of sending *gendarmes* (civilian police advisors) to accompany the military on their policing functions. These *gendarmes*, recruited from French-speaking countries, could act as observers and then blend into the ICITAP training program. Dante Caputo and UN undersecretary-general for political affairs Mig Goulding both liked the idea. Caputo suggested putting the military trainers under a U.S. commander and placing the *gendarmes* under a Canadian Mountie commander.

Caputo had already begun lining up support in the UN Security Council for the resolution needed to create such an international military/police constabulary force. If passed, this would be the first time the UN authorized introducing troops into a country that was not engaged in civil war or that did not pose a threat to international peace. In order to quell any potential opposition from Latin American countries (especially Brazil) wary of outside military intervention in their hemisphere, Caputo traveled to Venezuela on May 1. According to Caputo, Venezuelan president Andrés Pérez enthusiastically endorsed the plan and offered to send his foreign minister to talk to the president of Brazil.

Meanwhile, NSC director Tony Lake, still fearing the possibility of a bloodbath, asked the Defense Department to investigate the feasibility of deploying U.S. troops. They were tasked to study four contingencies: (1) a contingent of 500 Seabees; (2) a contingent of 1,800 men with Armored Personnel Carriers; (3) 5,000 U.S. military personnel; and (4) 15,000 U.S. soldiers. Pezzullo learned of the Defense Department planning from Chargé Chuck Redman, who heard about it from the CIA station chief in Port-au-Prince.

The CIA station chief understood that if rumors of such contingency plans reached the ears of the FADH high command, all diplomatic efforts might be squashed. His fears were justified. On May 9 a *Miami Herald* article announced that "a U.S.-backed proposal to create a multinational force of about 500 police officers for Haiti is expected to be taken up by the Security Council soon."[2] Reprinted in Haiti, the article raised a furor. Political and military leaders across the ideological spectrum condemned the idea as a disguised form of foreign intervention that many said conjured bitter memories of the nineteen-year U.S. military occupation of Haiti that ended in 1934. "If they invade us ... when the first cannon shot is heard, the cities will disappear and the nation will rise up," FADH chief of staff Phillipe Biamby told reporters, sounding a lot like Toussaint l'Ouverture two hundred years earlier.[3]

When UN secretary-general Boutros-Ghali learned of the Defense Department contingency plans in early May, he threatened to withdraw from the Haiti negotiations, charging that the United States was using the UN as a "Trojan Horse" to deploy a U.S. invasion force. UN special envoy Dante Caputo once again raised the red flag of "back channels." It fell upon U.S. special advisor Pezzullo to allay UN fears. He warned the NSC and the White House again that signals from them that did not support the policy of diplomatic negotiation could be misconstrued.

Chargé Chuck Redman tried to soothe the waters in Port-au-Prince. In meetings with General Cédras and the FADH general staff, he assured them that the UN police force would consist mainly of Canadian, French, and Caribbean officers and would take place "only with the agreement of President Aristide and all other responsible sectors."[4] Redman explained that the international police would work side by side with their Haitian counterparts and "be a visible sign of the commitment of the international community, and, we hope, have a dampening effect on the violence."[5] He also made it clear that the UN gendarmes would only be armed with side-arms and would not perform law-enforcement functions.

Following an exhaustive U.S. interagency review and approval by the UN bureaucracy, an aide mémoire carefully outlining the role, size, and deployment of the military and police trainers was presented to President Aristide by Caputo, Pezzullo, and Kozak on the morning of May 20, 1993. After getting what they hoped would be President Aristide's swift approval, Caputo, Pezzullo, and Kozak planned to travel to Haiti the next morning to deliver the same aide mémoire to General Cédras. Assuming that they would succeed on both fronts, UN secretary-general Boutros-Ghali was ready to request Security Council authority the following week to organize and deploy the police and military forces.

But the 9:00 A.M. meeting in Aristide's Georgetown office didn't go well. The deposed Haitian president accompanied by his ambassadors, Jean Casimir and Fritz Longchamps, and former prime minister Préval, read the aide mémoire and said they wanted to make some changes.

"It's against my constitution to invite in armed forces from a foreign power," explained the Haitian president.

"But this isn't an occupying army," Pezzullo argued. "These are train-ers. You've had trainers in Haiti for the last forty years. We've carefully read the article in your constitution. There's nothing in there that pre-vents the kind of training/observer mission that we're talking about. But if you want to add a phrase that states these personnel are going in exclu-sively as trainers, we have no objection."[6]

That's when Ambassador Casimir started saying things like: Why don't you put sub-paragraph D after sub-paragraph E? Mike Kozak recalled.

Kozak would go off into another room and make the changes only to have Casimir raise another objection: Why is D after C?

After Pezzullo, Caputo, and Kozak accommodated everything, Casimir said that he was just asking questions and didn't suggest that they change it.

"We were all getting dizzy," Pezzullo remembered. "Here was a program that they had agreed to earlier and now they were mincing words."[7]

Before they broke for lunch, Aristide said that he wanted what was contained in the aide mémoire, but couldn't sign it, because if he did, he could be impeached.

Mike Kozak couldn't believe his ears. "This is a guy who has been thrown out of his country," he remembered thinking. "The Parliament has voted him out of office and he's worried about being impeached?"[8]

Aristide then returned to the position he had taken earlier: that the Haitian Constitution prohibits the president from inviting in foreign troops. Mike Kozak, who had spent years as a legal advisor to the State Department, took the floor. "Mr. President, I actually took the time to read your constitution last night," he said, "and I couldn't find that article."

President Aristide immediately protested, telling Kozak that it was stated clearly in the constitution.

"Well, show me where," said a confounded Mike Kozak.[9]

Soon Longchamps, Casimir, and Aristide were tearing through a copy of the Haitian Constitution, but they couldn't find the article. Aristide claimed that the prohibition was implied.

At around 12:30, with their brains well scrambled, the diplomats agreed to break for lunch while Aristide's people redrafted the aide mémoire to their specifications. When Pezzullo, Kozak, and Caputo returned an hour later they were presented with a document that Pezzullo characterized as "redrafted by some Machiavellian nut." The paper began with a long dissertation about war crimes committed by the military.

"This wasn't intended as a diatribe against the FADH command," said a frustrated Pezzullo. "This is part of an attempt to get them to agree to leave. Why are you calling them names?"

"Well, after all, we have to get those things into the document," answered Casimir.[10]

Caputo was upset. "What are you talking about? This document isn't designed to be an attack on the military. It's an attempt to take a major step in getting them to relinquish power. That's the important issue. Don't you understand?"[11]

Caputo, Pezzullo, and Kozak argued with Aristide and his advisors into the evening, trying to get the Haitian president to sign some version of the aide mémoire. Around seven in the evening, a bleary-eyed Caputo pulled Pezzullo aside. "Larry," he said, "this is crazy. Let's leave it here and go see the military and keep our position neutral."[12] Caputo then asked President Aristide not to take a public position on the aide mémoire until the diplomats had tested the FADH's position. Aristide gave his word.

The next morning the three wrung-out diplomats boarded an American Airlines flight to Port-au-Prince. Before descending on the FADH general staff, the team met to discuss their prospects. U.S. chargé Redman, who had been meeting regularly with Cédras, was upbeat and predicted that the general would sign. At one point, Pezzullo asked Caputo's deputy, Leandro Despouy, for his assessment.

"They're going to say 'no,'" Despouy replied. "Because if you ask people on the street, taxi drivers, clerks at the hotel, they'll tell you Cédras won't sign. And I agree with them."

Redman was annoyed by Despouy's assessment: "If Cédras doesn't sign, [de facto prime minister] Bazin will."

"The only way to get Bazin to say 'yes' is if we go to him and threaten to undermine him if he doesn't sign," said Despouy.

Redman didn't approve of Despouy's tactics. "We can't do that," he countered.[13]

What the five diplomats didn't know was that hours before the diplomats met with the FADH general staff on May 23, Radio 16 December, a pro-Aristide radio station based in south Florida, broadcast a statement from the deposed Haitian president expressing doubt that the plan for the deployment of an international security presence was "for the good of the people." By the time Pezzullo, Caputo, Kozak, Redman, and Despouy entered FADH headquarters on the Place des Héros, the statement had reached the ears of the FADH command.

General Cédras had assured Chargé Redman only days earlier that he would sign the aide mémoire. After all, the military training mission was something he had himself proposed back in early April. But Monday morning, May 23, General Cédras looked over the aide mémoire and said that he couldn't sign it, that he didn't have the authority to approve the entry of troops into the country, that it was against the constitution. He told the diplomats that they would have to get the aide mémoire approved by the Parliament.

Pezzullo wasn't in the mood for a new round of excuses. "Come on, General," he shot back. "Who are you trying to fool? How many times have you had training missions in here?"[14]

Leandro Despouy said that Chuck Redman and Cédras, who up to that point had maintained a very cordial relationship, started trading accusations. Redman, an ex-Air Force officer, was incensed. "He started screaming at him," remembered Despouy, "saying: 'You have to sign this!' "

Perhaps Cédras's behavior had something to do with the Haitian character. "Haitians never say no," noted novelist Herbert Gold, who had lived in Haiti during the fifties and has returned several times since. "Ask him to dinner and you had to judge by the way he said yes whether he meant yes, no, or maybe-if-convenient. Each person told the truth that really mattered to him—that he sincerely wanted you to like him—but the signposts in discourse were as meaningless as the random numbers sometimes attached to houses on the road. . . . Some believed this intermingling of yes-no-maybe was a relic of the slave times." After all, a slave couldn't say no, but he could pretend to forget, drag his heels, or follow another master. "It was a smiling, most agreeable method of resistance."[15]

"Haitians are hard to read," said a State Department officer who had served in Haiti and Africa. "In Somalia, for instance, people are ardently anti-American and they come right out and tell you that to your face. But in Haiti, people at first seem friendly and deferential. It's only after you try to get things done that you see the depths of their distrust of *blancs*."[16]

Mike Kozak looked at his watch and realized that it was five years to the day that General Noriega and his general staff in Panama had backed out of a similar proposal. "Actually, I knew a group of guys like you in Panama," he started. "A lot of them were nice guys, soldiers who had the interests of their institution at heart. But when they still had the opportunity to influence events, they stalled. They fooled around and events overtook them.

Today, all those Panamanians are dead or in jail. I know that for a fact. And that's where you're going to end up if you continue to stall."[17]

Pezzullo was equally blunt. "You're leaving the international community with no other alternative, but to impose sanctions," he announced. "We don't want to do that, but you leave us no other choice."[18]

The meeting ended with Cédras urging the diplomats to talk to Bazin. Although they all expected such a discussion to be fruitless, they spent the rest of the day late into the evening trying to convince Bazin to sign. They got nowhere. As Pezzullo, Caputo, and Kozak were preparing to return to Washington, Despouy told them: "The only way to advance this is to get Bazin out of the way."

Pezzullo said: "If you think that by getting rid of him we can advance our cause, go ahead."

Caputo agreed. "Why should we defend him?" So Despouy began as he said "to make a series of alliances."[19]

"I started talking to a few ministers to try to get them to withdraw their support from Bazin," Despouy explained.[20] As he made his inquiries, he learned that the French Socialist Party was financing one of the parties (PANPRA) that supported Bazin. Despouy, who had worked with the French Socialists during his years in exile, traveled to Paris to see what could be done. He learned that the party supporting Bazin was really part of the Socialist International Party and quickly convinced them to cut all financing to PANPRA.

When the Haitian ministers from PANPRA still wouldn't resign, Despouy got the Socialist International Party to send a representative to Port-au-Prince. The next morning Despouy sent a coded message to Dante Caputo: "Yesterday there was a lot of agitation and at night the boat took two more hits. The boat is taking on water and will sink soon."[21]

A total of five ministers resigned. Noon the next day Bazin was on the radio officially throwing in the towel. "A change in government is necessary on account of the pressure and threats," he explained. "I was in an impossible position."[22]

While President Aristide shared some blame for torpedoing the initiative, Pezzullo and Caputo agreed that the FADH in particular had to pay a price. They agreed to press for stricter international sanctions against the de facto regime. The OAS voluntary sanctions had been only moderately effective. Back at UN headquarters, Caputo found a willingness among the Four Friends—the United States, Canada, France, and Venezuela—and the UN secretariat to push for mandatory sanctions. Pezzullo was also able to get interagency approval for stricter sanctions against shipments of petroleum products and the supply of arms and weapons.

The new international resolve showed itself at an OAS General Assembly meeting that opened in Managua, Nicaragua, on June 7, 1993. At the meeting OAS secretary general Baeno Soares announced that "the departure of Bazin opens a new opportunity to find a resolution to the crisis."[23] Pezzullo and Kozak attended as members of the U.S. delegation. They drafted a paper that outlined the U.S. position to unilaterally suspend the visas and freeze the personal assets of both military and civilian members of the de facto regime. In addition, they cosponsored a resolution that empowered the OAS to publicize the violations of the voluntary sanctions by member states.

The night after they introduced the resolution, Special Advisor Pezzullo, his deputy Mike Kozak, and UN/OAS special envoy Dante Caputo met for dinner at Los Ranchos, a popular Managua brasserie. As they sipped beer, Caputo opened up. "This has been an education," he said. "Living through the Reagan years I had the worst impression of the United States. But I've got to be careful politically. In Argentina they're writing stories that I'm a pawn of the United States."[24]

What Caputo didn't talk about were the problems he was having with his own staff. It was common knowledge on the thirty-eighth floor of UN headquarters that Haitian Jean-Claude Aimé, chief of cabinet to the secretary-general, was close to the Haitian military. Having served ten years as the gatekeeper to top offices of this premier international organization, Aimé had wide access to information and considerable bureaucratic power. On the other side of the political spectrum, one of Caputo's deputies, Francesc Vendrell, was openly sympathetic to the Aristide camp and continued to pass them sensitive information.

Complicating Caputo's mission was the fact that he was reporting to two organizations—the UN and the OAS. "The bureaucratic jealousy between the two was considerable," said Pezzullo. The Organization of American States felt that Haiti, as a member state in crisis, fell under their jurisdiction. The interest of France and other European countries, however, had brought the issue to the attention of the UN.

From Port-au-Prince Caputo's deputy, Leandro Despouy, reported that the threat of increased sanctions was already having an effect. When Pezzullo met Greg Craig, a Washington lawyer representing the wealthy Haitian Mev family, Craig said: "It's gone too far. The wealthy families may have supported the coup, but now they're being sucked dry."[25]

Realizing that the international community was more committed than it had ever been to Aristide's return, the Haitian millionaires began in Despouy's words "trying to find a way out for themselves." "They realized," said Despouy, "that the best strategy was to provoke a dialogue, a compromise between Aristide and the military. They wanted Aristide to accept a position that could pacify the country. They didn't want the angry Aristide who had been deposed."[26]

And their wishes carried weight. It was common knowledge in Haiti that business leaders were still paying a good percentage of the FADH's salaries. The difference was garnered from smuggling, including the trafficking of illegal drugs, and whatever the military could skim from state-owned businesses like the cement plant, the flour mills, the port and airport, and the electric company.

In the first days of June, Leandro Despouy, who had charmed his way through many doors usually closed to Western diplomats, began to notice that certain people close to the FADH were starting to seek him out.

One of these was a doctor who had lived in exile for many years in Mexico. He was friendly with politicians on all sides of the political spectrum and, most importantly, with General Cédras's political counselor, who was reputed to be the fattest man in Haiti. While Despouy never actually spoke to Cédras's political counselor directly, he would talk to the doctor, who would relay what Despouy said back to the counselor. According to Despouy, it was always: "Leandro, I spoke to him. . . . He said that what you said is possible. If you proposed such and such, then maybe . . ." All the conversations were very oblique.

"It was a very Haitian role to be playing," explained Despouy. "You see, Caputo didn't get along with Cédras. Pezzullo and the United States had taken a very strong position, and Redman was still pissed off about the training agreement. This left room for me to act as the conciliator."[27]

At one point in early June the doctor told Despouy to talk to Cédras's wife, Yannick. He said: "If you talk to her, she'll explain the rules of the game."

A few nights later, the Cédrases invited the tall Argentine over for dinner. In the relaxed setting of their modern, tastefully furnished home, the dialogue began. At first, Raoul Cédras did most of the talking, explaining his position.

Despouy listened sympathetically, always making sure to acknowledge Cédras's short, attractive wife. With her carefully plucked eyebrows, high cheekbones and almond-shaped eyes, Yannick Cédras hardly seemed the dragon lady that people described. One Haitian woman who knew Yannick and had been an associate of Baby Doc's extravagant wife, Michéle Bennett, felt the two women had something important in common. "Both were wildly ambitious," she explained. "And it was clear they ran the show."[28]

Even in the privacy of his home, Raoul Cédras was somewhat shy and seemed tired of politics and intrigues. He spoke mannered French, blurting out certain words to disguise a stammer, and sounded more like a victim than a protagonist in Haiti's latest political drama.

"We have been in this situation since independence," expounded the general. "The politicians have neglected the country, only taking care of their own interests. This explains the lack of structure."

He believed firmly in reincarnation, he said, and described his country as "decrepit and rootless." He also had a passion for skin diving, which he did every weekend at his beach house about an hour's drive from Port-au-Prince. "The political problems are all around," he said grinning wryly, "the slums, the ragged women, the starving children . . . Then splash! You are alone in the water, in the world of water, of peace, of fish, of shipwrecks."[29] According to some accounts, he had told friends that the treasure sunk around Haiti could "solve all of Haiti's problems and change the whole balance of power at home and abroad."[30]

When Despouy found himself alone with the general's wife, the conversation became more direct. She didn't talk philosophically about history or the paradoxes of life. She was much more instinctual and seductive. According to the rumor mill in Port-au-Prince, she had many female and male lovers, including her husband's chief of staff, Phillipe Biamby.

According to Despouy, she said: "An angel told me that there may be a way to save my husband. Either that or we have to establish a strong government here and resist."

"I came here to talk about finding a solution," offered the Argentine.

"The only solution for my husband here is a knife in his back," said Yannick batting her long lashes.

"That's not a solution," countered Despouy.

"We will never be able to live here in peace," Despouy recalled that she said sadly.

"It depends on how we work this out."

"The people will kill us."

"You'll be protected."

"No. They'll come and kill my children."

"That's why we have to find a solution that protects your whole family."

"That's not what Pezzullo and the United States want," she said. "They want to kill me, my husband, and our children."

"No. No," said the Argentine. "We want a Haiti where everyone can live in peace."

"Including us?"

"Including your family."

"You know we can't live here if that devil, Aristide, returns."[31]

After several nights of dinner, drinks, and conversation in the Cédras's comfortable Petionville home, General Cédras turned to Despouy and said: "If at some point I'm going to talk to someone from the Aristide side, we can speak here in Port-au-Prince. I could talk to the Presidential Commission."

This was the opening Despouy had been waiting for. He seized it, saying: "I don't believe you."

The general repeated the offer.

"Then why don't you say this publicly?" asked Despouy.

Cédras thought deeply for a moment, then slapped the table and said he'd do it tomorrow. And he did.

Once the idea of a negotiation had been broached, the question became: How, where, and when?

At UN headquarters, the United States had joined with the other Friends (Canada, France, and Venezuela) in drafting a request to the Security Council to impose mandatory sanctions against shipments of petroleum products and the supply of arms and weapons to the de facto regime in Haiti. If passed, Security Council Resolution 841 would go into effect on June 23 with the intention of strengthening the voluntary embargo that the OAS had invoked after President Aristide was forced out of office in September 1991. The Friends requested that the sanctions fall under Chapter 7 of the United Nations Charter, which up until that time had been reserved for actions against states that posed a threat to international peace or were engaged in civil war. Haiti fit neither category. But the Friends wanted to dramatize the depth of the international community's resolve.

Back in Washington, Pezzullo struggled to hold the Clinton administration to its commitment. While the threat of new sanctions was already having an effect in Haiti, the sanctions themselves were in jeopardy.

Special Advisor Pezzullo remembers a conversation in Under Secretary for Political Affairs Peter Tarnoff's office the second week of June. Deputy national security advisor Sandy Berger was on the phone expressing reservations about the resolution that would soon be put before the UN Security Council. "Sandy, we've committed ourselves here," explained Pezzullo. "We've had conversations with the Four Friends, the White House has already issued a presidential statement, we've got to move."[32]

Berger wanted to know what the resolution was going to say.

"I don't know exactly," answered Pezzullo. "The resolution is going to be written in New York. It's a cooperative effort. We're one of the leaders, so we will have a hand in drafting the resolution."

Sandy wanted to have another meeting.

"Sandy, for goodness' sake," countered Pezzullo, "we've already agreed to this. Why are we backing off?"

The following day, June 6, Pezzullo stopped in Tarnoff's office. "I'm going to New York to meet with Caputo and the Friends and get this thing moving," he announced.

Tarnoff put in a call to Sandy Berger, who told Pezzullo not to make any commitments.

Pezzullo couldn't understand why Berger was dragging his heels. The next morning he hopped on the Metroliner to New York. As soon as he arrived at the U.S. UN Mission, Tarnoff and Berger called and asked if he could delay the drafting of the resolution.

"Why are you putting this off?" asked a frustrated Pezzullo. By this time Pezzullo had become familiar with the way issues were dealt with at the NSC. "No matter how many meetings you had," he explained later, "you never knew what had been decided. You recommended something and no one objected, then, questions would surface later and they'd want to hold another meeting."[33]

"The White House and Sandy Berger in particular were calling, changing words, moving commas; it wasn't serious," recalled one State Department officer tasked with drafting the resolution. He remembered one call from Richard Feinberg from the NSC, who asked: "Why do we have to impose sanctions when they're going to hurt people? Why don't we do something like bombing the oil storage tanks in Port-au-Prince?"

"Sure," answered the officer, "if you're willing to barbecue half the people in Port-au-Prince."[34]

Back in Port-au-Prince, Caputo's deputy Leandro Despouy was dining with the Cédrases practically every night. Despouy had elicited from the general an agreement in principle to negotiate with Aristide's people. Finally, on the night of June 15, Despouy told the Haitian commander: "You have to negotiate directly with Aristide."

In typical fashion, Cédras backtracked, saying he'd have to think about it and that he'd have an answer tomorrow at dinner.

The general's wife, Yannick, called Despouy in his room in the Montana Hotel the next afternoon to confirm. "You know, tonight the UN is voting on the resolution," she began. "But let's not cancel the dinner."

"Of course," Despouy answered, somewhat embarrassed. "I have nothing to do with the vote."[35]

It proved to be a night to remember. According to Despouy, Yannick left the table several times during dinner to go upstairs and follow the progress of the resolution. The special session of the Security Council was broadcast live on CNN. As they were finishing dessert, Yannick rejoined them. Her husband looked up from his plate and asked: "What happened with China?"

They were hoping that China would veto the resolution. China considered President Aristide their enemy ever since the Haitian president officially recognized Taiwan in 1991.

"I don't know yet," Yannick answered. Then, turning to Despouy, she asked: "Don't you want to watch?"

The tall Argentine followed Raoul and Yannick upstairs. Despouy sat in a big armchair. Seated on either side of him were the Cédrases' two sons and daughter. They all watched as though their fates were being decided many miles to the north in New York. As the resolution passed, the camera panned to Dante Caputo, who had a pleased smile on his face. General Cédras leaned forward and pointed angrily at the TV. "That's who I'm supposed to negotiate with? Look at him! Look at his face! He wants to destroy me!"

Despouy, summoning all of his diplomatic tact, tried to explain: "No, Raoul," he said, "you're misinterpreting. It's just a diplomatic maneuver."

When Despouy looked down at his watch it was 11:30. Some nights he had stayed and talked with the Cédrases until two or three in the morning. "But not tonight," he remembered thinking. "I'll go back to my hotel and try to pin him down tomorrow."

As Despouy stood to say goodnight, the Haitian general took him by the arm. "Wait, let's take a walk around the garden." Just as they were stepping out the front door a huge explosion shook Port-au-Prince. General Cédras looked frightened. "Soon soldiers were running everywhere and screaming into walkie-talkies," Despouy recalled. "They were in a panic and the usually composed Cédras looked very concerned."[36]

After five or ten minutes, when nerves seemed to calm, the Argentine diplomat turned to the Haitian general and said: "I'm sorry, Raoul, I think I'll go now."

"No!" the general answered abruptly.

Despouy put his hand on the Haitian commander's shoulder. "No, it's okay. There's no problem."

The general told him sternly that he couldn't leave. There was anger in his voice.

"Are you taking me hostage?" Despouy asked half in jest.

"No," Cédras answered, "but we have to check the roads to make sure everything is clear."

So Despouy went back into the house and left the commander of the FADH barking orders to his soldiers on a portable radio. He found Yannick sitting on a sofa in the living room. They talked until 3 A.M., when the general returned. "She's in agreement," Despouy announced in French.

"About what?" asked the general.

"About negotiating directly with Aristide," said Despouy.

"After all, it's for the best," added Yannick.[37]

Despouy realized something important that night: it was easier to get Cédras to agree to something if he broached the subject first with his wife.

When Despouy finally got to his car some time after three in the morning, General Cédras still looked concerned. "I'm going to give you some soldiers to protect you," said Cédras. "I'll give you escort cars front and back."

The Argentine declined the offer, but Cédras insisted. "You have to understand that there are people who don't want this dialogue to happen. We have to be careful."

As he drove away, Despouy thought to himself: "Clearly the bomb had to do with the passage of the UN resolution. . . . And the Cédrases had been so fearful, as though they were expecting someone to attack them. . . ." The bomb had been a message. But from whom? Colonel François?

CHAPTER 7

The First U.S.
Occupation

"The little fellow does what he can; the big fellow does what he wants."

—a Haitian proverb

"In the beginning we were glad to see the marines," recalled Haitian teacher Franck Henniques years after the first U.S. occupation of Haiti ended in 1934. But that sentiment would soon change.[1] And, Jim Crow racism and U.S. insensitivity to Haitian culture would inspire a virulent black nationalism that would open the portals to the strange and macabre dictatorship of François (Papa Doc) Duvalier. "What they [the U.S.] had unwittingly inspired," wrote the Haitian anthropologist Michel Rolph-Trouillot years later, "was a return to Africa."[2]

But on the first day of the occupation, July 28, 1915, no one seemed to anticipate what lay ahead. Occupying troops found the country in a deplorable state. "In the streets were piles of foul-smelling offal," one wrote. "The whole project was filthy."[3] Bridges were broken; the railroads worked sporadically. Telephone and telegraph lines had been inoperable since 1911. In the customs houses, chunks of rocks served as weights. And many of the country's 1.5 million citizens were hungry. Contributing to the problem was the fact that *cacos* still controlled the mountain passes used by peasants to transport food to the coastal towns and cities.

Initially, President Woodrow Wilson worried whether or not the United States "had the legal authority to do what apparently we ought to do."[4] But soon he ordered the marines to take charge. Martial law was imposed on September 3 and the Haitian army was disbanded. Hoping to maintain a semblance of diplomatic cooperation, President Wilson had his State Department draft a treaty, which made Haiti a virtual protectorate. According to the terms of the "Haitian-American Convention" promulgated on September 16, 1915, and ratified by the U.S. Senate in February 1916, the United States assumed the right to police Haiti and control its public finances for ten years.

U.S. Rear Admiral William B. Caperton ordered about twenty-five hundred marines to fan out throughout the country and set up local headquarters outfitted with cars, trucks, and even airplanes. A Marine Corps officer was placed in charge of each district with instructions to keep order, collect taxes, arbitrate disputes, and distribute medicines. The fact that most of the U.S. Marines didn't speak either Creole or French and tended to be chosen from southern states, because in the words of one officer "they know how to deal with darkies," didn't make for a smooth transition.[5] From the start U.S. racism began to undermine the success of the occupation.

"There are some fine-looking, well educated, polished men here, but they are real nigs beneath the surface," wrote marine colonel Littleton W. T. Walker to a superior officer.[6]

One of those polished, educated men, Philipe Sudre Dartiquenave, was handpicked by the United States to become the country's next president.

In the countryside, resistance to the U.S. occupation was tenacious. To the north and in the center of the country, just north of Port-au-Prince, officers of the disbanded army, landowners, and peasants formed centers of armed resistance. Hoping to quickly put an end to the skirmishing, Admiral Caperton dispatched more U.S. Marines. Violence escalated. "We hunted down *cacos* like pigs," wrote Major Smedley Butler.

The strongest *caco* movement appeared in 1918 under the leadership of a charismatic landowner and officer in the disbanded army named

Charlemagne Peralte. In late 1919 with the help of a Haitian informer, marine captain Hermann Hanneken led a nighttime raid into Peralte's mountain camp. A marine shot the surprised *caco* leader twice. In order to establish proof of Peralte's death, marines propped his body against a board and tied him so that his arms hung limp and his head hung to one side, as if he had been crucified. The photograph they took, which was intended to demoralize the *cacos*, ending up securing the martyrdom of Charlemagne Peralte.

With the end of armed resistance, a new program known as "Operation Uplift" was launched to turn Haiti, in the words of Major Butler, into "a first-class black man's country."[7] In the next decade more than one thousand miles of roads and 210 bridges were built. A modern telephone system was installed. The tax system was overhauled and the currency stabilized by fixing it to the dollar. Hospitals and clinics were established throughout the country to combat malaria and yaws. American doctors were brought in to train Haitian doctors, and some Haitian doctors (including François Duvalier) were sent to the States to study. And the Service Technique was created to give formal instruction in field crop management and soil conservation.

Nearly all of Operation Uplift was paid for out of Haitian funds. During the prosperous 1920s, when the world price of coffee was high and U.S.-enforced stability allowed small businesses to flourish, Haiti's government revenues ranged between eight and ten million dollars a year, almost twice what they had been before the occupation. But with the onset of the Great Depression in 1928, coffee suffered drastically on the world market. Haiti's U.S. financial advisors, eager to get as much of the U.S. loan paid off before the Haitian economy collapsed, raised taxes.

Haitian resentment grew. University students protested vociferously and began to attack elite Haitian culture. "Educated Haitians who had based their pride and culture on careful emulation of white culture, only to be scorned and humiliated as 'negroes' by white invaders, now began to search for an indigenous black culture," explained the historian Hans Schmidt.[8] The new movement called *negritude* took root in Haiti after Jean Price-Mars published an ethnological study, *Ainsi parla l'oncle*, which explored and romanticized African folklore, language, and religion.

Finding their cultural voice, young Haitians formed national unions and met with U.S. representatives of the new National Association for the Advancement of Colored People (NAACP). "How should one confront the all-powerful invader if not by a moral resistance in order to safeguard the ancestral heritage and the cultural and intellectual patrimony of the nation?" asked the Haitian poet Jacques Romaine.[9] As the French philosopher Jean Paul Sartre, a champion of *negritude*, explained: "If he [the black man] is opposed for his race and because of it, he must first become aware of his race."[10]

In October 1929, when stipends for fieldwork were raised and stipends for work in the city reduced, students boycotted the Service Technique's agricultural school in Port-au-Prince and stoned the director's house. Student anger blossomed into a general strike that was joined by customs officials, store owners, and businessmen.

Three months later, on December 6, 1929, hundreds of peasants arrived in the town of Les Cayes to take part in the nationalist demonstrations that were still disrupting Haiti. Armed with rocks and clubs, they chanted: "Down with taxes! Down with poverty!" When a scuffle broke out, marines tried to disperse the crowd. According to eyewitnesses, some marines fired into the air, while others fired on the crowd killing as many as twenty-two and leaving fifty-one wounded.

The killings sparked a worldwide protest. Recently elected president Herbert Hoover, who had just launched his Good Neighbor policy, quickly dispatched a commission to Haiti to decide "when and how we withdraw."[11]

Nearly five years later, on August 15, 1934, an estimated ten thousand Haitians crowded the Port-au-Prince docks to watch the end of the longest U.S. occupation in history. Encouraged by the new, nationalistic president Stenio Vincent, Haitians went on a wild binge of destruction, tearing up bridges and badly needed telephone lines. Vincent responded by declaring martial law and suspending the constitution, thus becoming the first post-occupation authoritarian.

Not surprisingly, most historians and social critics came to regard the occupation as a failure. In the words of President Hoover's own commission, the United States had failed "to understand the social problems of Haiti."[12] Haitian anthropologist Michel-Rolph Trouillot was even more blunt, concluding: "It improved almost nothing and complicated almost everything."[13] In his opinion, U.S. racism only reinforced color prejudice in Haiti, which paved the way for the *noirist* rhetoric of François (Papa Doc) Duvalier.[14]

As the marines were departing in August 1934, François Duvalier, the twenty-five-year-old son of a Port-au-Prince schoolteacher was quietly receiving his medical diploma. The introverted and nearsighted young medical intern's growing interest in the negritude movement motivated him to join a nationalist literary circle known as *Les Griots* (a Guinean word meaning bards).

Duvalier, together with the black lawyer and voudoun priest Lorimer Denis, started to define his political philosophy in a series of pamphlets, essays, and articles. Citing Nazi ideologist Alfred Rosenberg, Duvalier and Denis argued that the political solution to Haiti could only be accomplished by saving the nation's soul. In real terms, this meant wresting power from the old mulatto elite and entrusting it in the black masses who embodied the African culture and religion that was the true character of Haiti. "All revolution, if it is to be profound and durable must have as its object the redemption of the masses," wrote Duvalier and Denis in 1946.[15]

But the political aspirations of Duvalier and others were thwarted. Not only had the mulatto elite consolidated and extended their own political and economic power during the U.S. occupation, but the new U.S.-trained Haitian army known as the *Garde d'Haiti* had emerged as a major political force. Conceived of as disciplined, hierarchical, and nonpolitical, the Garde quickly became the kingmaker of Haitian politics.

With the exception of reformist Dumarais Estimé, who was forced out of office by the Garde, Haitian regimes after the U.S. occupation were either military or military backed. In 1957 a fiery labor leader named Daniel Fignolé was installed as provisional president. "Under my administration Haiti will have true democratic government," said Fignolé in his inaugural address.[16] But when Fignolé started reassigning officers, the military high command swung into action. Nineteen days after Fignolé took office, the army chief of staff General Antonio Kebreau personally kicked in the door to the president's office in the middle of a cabinet meeting. "Ti-Coc, ou caca (Little cock, you're shit)," General Kebreau announced.[17] Fignolé was arrested and whisked away into exile in New York with his family.

With Fignolé out of the way, the presidential campaign of 1957 developed into a race between François Duvalier and his aristocratic mulatto rival, Louis Déjoie. The fifty-year-old, whispery-voiced Duvalier, always neatly dressed in a black suit, white tie, black shoes, black homburg, and thick-rimmed glasses, had the manner of a conservative country doctor. But his dress and unblinking eyes were immediately recognizable to most Haitians as the personification of Baron Samedi—the feared voudoun *loa* (or god) who guarded the gates to the graveyard. A longtime student and champion of voudoun, Duvalier was reputed to be a full-fledged *houngan* (priest) and also a member of secret societies like Bizango that practiced black magic. "Voudoun," he had written, "explains the origins of life by asking for symbols to show the play of cosmic forces. And doesn't science daily evolve towards an ever clearer conception of the universality of that cosmic force?"[18]

During the campaign, Duvalier actively sought the endorsements of powerful *houngans* and in certain sections of the country used vodoun temples as local campaign headquarters. Superstitious and deeply paranoid, he was also convinced that the number twenty-two could confer on him strong and sinister powers.

On Sunday, September 22, 950,000 Haitians went to the polls in an election organized by the army. Among reports of intimidation at the polls and ballot stuffing, 679,000 votes were cast for Duvalier versus 266,992 for his mulatto rival. Subsequent investigation revealed that in La Gonaive a few hundred inhabitants had cast 18,000 votes for Duvalier.

On October 22, 1957, Duvalier received the presidential sash from General Kebreau and pledged "to guarantee the exercise of liberty of all Haitians" and "to reconcile the nation with itself." Compared to Daniel Fignolé, the awkward, soft-spoken country doctor seemed harmless to the elite and to the army. Though he had appealed to disenfranchised and uneducated blacks, his real intentions were slow to become clear. Chief and foremost was his desire to consolidate power, which he did with a cold-bloodedness and irrationality that convinced Haitians of his unfathomable power.

The collection of strong-arm men, bombers, saboteurs, and toughs known as *cagoulards* that he had assembled during his presidential campaign formed the core of Duvalier's repressive machinery. Led by a slender man who dressed in elegant suits and sunglasses named Clement Barberie, these "hooded ones" as they were called, were soon roaming the streets at night and dropping in unannounced on the political opposition. The more fortunate were merely humiliated in front of their families and beaten, or thrown into the notorious Fort Dimanche. "A doctor must sometimes take life in order to save it," wrote Duvalier in *Memories of a Third World Leader.*

Then the mad doctor set out to "Duvalierize" the army. Diabolically exploiting the vanities and jealousies of its officers, he sowed dissent, advanced black officers only to emasculate them by going around them, and purged his allies. But it was the Dade County Sheriff's Invasion of 1958 that sealed the army's fate and established the true terror of the Duvalier regime.

On the night of July 28, 1958, a group of mulatto former officers, together with several U.S. mercenaries, including three ex-deputy sheriffs from Miami and Buffalo, disembarked from a fifty-five-foot fishing boat called *Molly C* at Montrouis opposite the island of La Gonvaîve. Traveling to Port-au-Prince on a commandeered tap-tap, they seized the Dessalines Barracks adjacent to the National Palace, only to be overcome by charging soldiers. Two rebels who managed to escape were hunted down and torn to pieces by the mob. Their severed heads and limbs were paraded triumphantly through the streets and later presented to the president.

Later that day, Papa Doc was photographed in his fatigues and helmet, brandishing a Colt .45. He had become in the words of one of his own generals: "an implacable monster, unpitying in everything that concerned his power."[19]

In the aftermath of the Dade County Sheriffs Invasion, or the "Pacquet Affair" as it was called, antiaircraft guns were installed on the front lawn of the Presidential Palace, a state of siege was imposed, and the legislature voted President Duvalier emergency powers. Also, a red neon sign was installed on the Camps de Mars that proclaimed: "I am the Haitian Flag, One and Indivisible. François Duvalier."

Deciding he could no longer trust the army, Papa Doc decided to organize his own personal gang and terrorist unit, named Volunteers of National Security but known almost exclusively as the Tonton Macoutes. These bogeymen—literally Uncle Knapsacks, or devils who steal souls and carry them in their bags into oblivion—were Duvalier's version of the brownshirts, except the Macoutes usually wore blue jeans, t-shirts, and sunglasses.

Black and recruited from the most disadvantaged classes (including women), the Macoutes were suddenly elevated into positions of power over even the richest, lightest-skinned merchants. In return for their loyalty to Papa Doc, they could seemingly rob, extort, torture, and murder at will.

But the Macoutes were more than just mobs of thugs. By cleverly infiltrating them through existing structures of authority, Papa Doc was able to multiply their power. In the countryside, for example, the *chef de section* was often the local leader of the Macoutes. If possible, he was also a *houngan*, a *bocur* (witch doctor), or both. Thus, Duvalier's political terror was extended into the mystical, subterranean realm of vodoun and black magic.

The American novelist Herbert Gold traveled to Haiti in 1963 and captured the mood of a night spent in a Port-au-Prince hotel. "The electricity went out. The stillness over the city was like an invisible hand, stilling its heartbeat, zombifying the living. Life was temporary, a loan that can be withdrawn without notice, which is a truth we all know but now eerie recognition of it made people whisper and hide in the dark."[20]

Reality seemed permanently twisted through the warped lenses of the paranoid, maniacal dictator who in June 1964 had himself elected president-for-life. "Duvalier is the professor of energy," declared the *Haiti Journal*. "Like Napoleon Bonaparte, Duvalier is an electrifier of souls, a powerful multiplier of energy."

Meanwhile, the country slipped further and further into poverty and despair. With intellectuals and professionals continuing to leave, the poorest country in the Western Hemisphere had the dubious distinction of staffing hospitals and schools all over Africa and North America. The rotting carcass of a country they left behind was picked over by an increasing number of vultures. "Duvalier revolutionized Haitian politics," explained sociologist Anthony P. Maingot, "and in the process widened and deepened the structure of corruption."[21] In the private sector, the old mulatto elite, which had been removed as contenders for the beneficence of the state, continued its old practices of avoiding taxes, corrupting public officials, and expatriating capital. Meanwhile, the circle of corruption widened to buy the loyalty of the new black elite.

And the costs of the kleptocracy were passed on to consumers. As a result Haiti's state electric company charged the highest rates in the Caribbean, and state telephone rates were exorbitant. The cost of shipping cargo on Air Haiti, the national airline, was higher than any other carrier in the region. In the early 1970s sugar from Florida, where workers were paid $6.50 per hour, sold for less than sugar from Haiti, where workers earned less than 25 cents per hour.[22]

By January 1971, President-for-Life François Duvalier was deteriorating fast. Racked by diabetes and heart disease, he named his fat, slow-witted nineteen-year-old son, Jean-Claude, to succeed him. "We all know," Papa Doc told his people, "that Caesar Augustus was nineteen when he took Rome's destinies into his hands, and his reign remains 'the Century of Augustus.'"[23] On April 21, 1971, Papa Doc died of heart failure. Few expected Jean-Claude to last out the year.

CHAPTER 8

Governors Island

"I am fed up!"

—UN/OAS special envoy DANTE CAPUTO to a reporter on
Governors Island

The night of June 16, 1993, had been a turning point in the effort of
the international community to restore President Jean-Bertrand Aristide
to power. Hours after the United Nations Security Council passed a ground-
breaking resolution imposing a tough economic embargo against the
de facto military government of Haiti, UN/OAS envoy Leandro Despouy
secured a commitment from FADH commander General Raoul Cédras to
hold face-to-face talks with the president he had ousted back in 1991.

One would have thought that policymakers at the White House
would have been patting one another on the back. This time the second-
guessing started after Special Advisor Pezzullo's deputy, Mike Kozak,
received a call from the commander of the U.S. Coast Guard. The Coast
Guard, which had ships deployed around Haiti to pick up refugees bound
for Florida, was calling to confirm its role in enforcing the Security
Council embargo against shipments of oil and arms into the country.

Kozak, who had helped draft the implementation of the U.S. embargo
against the Noriega regime back in 1988, organized a meeting with
officials from the Treasury Department and the Coast Guard for the

following afternoon. Everyone agreed to follow the same standard operating procedures that had been used in the past—the Coast Guard would stop and inspect all ships leaving or entering Haiti.[1]

Hours after the meeting, Kozak got a panicked call from the deputy national security advisor Sandy Berger, who accused Kozak of usurping the power of the president and giving orders to the Coast Guard. Sandy Berger seemed to be arguing against implementing the UN resolution that had just been passed. "The White House wanted the sanctions so that they could appear tough," reported Kozak, "but they didn't want to be blamed for disrupting the economy of Haiti."[2]

Meanwhile, UN envoy Leandro Despouy continued to talk to the Cédrases in Port-au-Prince. Now that the FADH commander-in-chief had agreed to hold face-to-face talks with deposed president Aristide, the issues were timing, location, and making sure the two leaders were serious about resolving the crisis.

Characteristically, President Aristide met the news that General Cédras was willing to negotiate with him directly with suspicion and more demands. When Caputo and Pezzullo tried to convince him to release a statesman-like public statement indicating his willingness to enter negotiations, Aristide drafted a diatribe calling the FADH leadership "war criminals." According to Pezzullo: "We went through a period of two weeks with Aristide that was like water torture, especially for Dante Caputo."[3] In addition to training and equipping a personal security detail which the Swiss and U.S. governments agreed to undertake, President Aristide demanded all kinds of preconditions before he would agree to sit down with General Cédras.

In Dante Caputo's mind it came down to a simple equation: "President Aristide was ready to ask us to take all the responsibility, but he didn't want to take any himself." Talks with the ousted president reached a critical point on the early morning of June 23. Pezzullo vividly remembers the four-hour phone conversation between President Aristide, Mike Barnes, and himself in Washington and Dante Caputo in New York. Aristide was not budging, demanding at one point that the entire military command step down before they started the negotiations.

After hours and hours of back and forth, Pezzullo started to lose his patience. "Mr. President, if a transcript of this conversation were ever released, people would never understand why the president would refuse to sit down with his military commander to work out a solution for his country," he said. "I don't think you could ever explain it."[4] Shortly thereafter Aristide finally agreed to face-to-face negotiations with General Cédras.

No sooner had President Aristide and the diplomats agreed to the wording of a public statement, than Aristide's public relations firm McKinney & McDowell issued a press release stating that he was meeting General Cédras on the condition of the "immediate departure of the high command and chief of police." Dante Caputo, who had read the joint statement to the press, quickly condemned this public duplicity and threatened to resign unless Aristide issued an immediate retraction. After extended telephone conversations with lawyers from the Aristide camp offering various explanations, the McKinney & McDowell press release was disavowed.

When UN special envoy Caputo suggested the next day that negotiations get under way as early as the end of the week, Aristide said he was traveling to Hollywood to attend a dinner that had been organized by Barbra Streisand.

"Your country is suffering under the military dictatorship and sanctions we just imposed at your behest," said Caputo. "What's more important, Mr. President, an homage from Hollywood or the future of your country?"[5]

President Aristide didn't answer, but he did go to Hollywood where he was feted by Robert De Niro, Susan Sarandon, Danny Glover, and others.

After June 24, the only sticking point was the venue. The first suggestion was a neutral site like the Bahamas or Aruba.

Back in Port-au-Prince, UN diplomat Leandro Despouy continued holding his nightly dinners with Raoul and Yannick Cédras. After the twenty-fourth they started taking on the undertones of a farce. "Caputo and Pezzullo changed the site seven times," remembered Despouy with a smile.

"First they said: 'Leandro, Aruba. . . .' I arrived at the Cédrases's house and said: 'Raoul, we have found a place that's ideal. No people to bother us, peaceful, beautiful, no distractions. . . .'"[6] But a few days later Pezzullo and Caputo called to say that Aristide didn't want to travel outside of the country for security reasons. So the site was changed to Puerto Rico.

When Despouy proposed Puerto Rico, General Cédras worried that once he entered U.S. territory, he could be arrested. His chief-of-staff Phillipe Biamby had been tricked by U.S. officials back in 1990 and ended up spending six months in a Manhattan jail.

After trying unsuccessfully to convince the general's wife, Yannick, Despouy got back to Pezzullo and Caputo and they decided together to try New York City. General Cédras had indicated that New York City was the only place in the States he would consider going because there he would be under UN jurisdiction.

When Despouy met with the Cédrases the next night and mentioned New York, the general asked: "Leandro, why didn't you tell me from the beginning that you wanted to bring me to New York?"

Despouy went to work: "Well, you see there were complications. But can you imagine this meeting at the palace of the UN. It's the perfect location right in the center of Manhattan, the greatest city in the world."[7]

Cédras's eyes started to widen and he said: "Okay. I agree."

But when New York police and UN security personnel learned that Aristide supporters were planning a huge demonstration to greet the military delegation, they voiced concern. Caputo and Pezzullo became convinced that a meeting in Manhattan could turn into a media circus rather than a substantial, productive negotiation. Two days before the talks were scheduled to begin, Pezzullo and Caputo were on the phone again to Despouy. "Leandro, United Nations headquarters is impossible," Caputo said. "There's no hotel in Manhattan that will take Cédras and his party because of security reasons. We're moving the negotiations to Governors Island."

"Where is that?" asked Despouy.

"It's in Manhattan," said Caputo.

"An island in Manhattan?" asked a befuddled Despouy. "What are you talking about?"

Caputo explained: "There's no other site. Tomorrow I'm holding a press conference in the morning and I need to make the announcement. Call Larry Pezzullo by eleven P.M. to let him know if Cédras agrees."[8]

This time Despouy decided to take up the change of venue with Yannick first. "I had explained to her that at UN headquarters there were sumptuous conference rooms and special rooms with photocopy machines and telephones," Despouy remembered. "Now I had to call and tell her that there was a very special place in Manhattan that was reserved by the UN for special encounters, very special encounters of historic importance," Despouy remembered. "She was trying to find it on the map. I told her it was an historic annex and that's where a big part of the discussions would take place."

Yannick said she sensed a plot.

Despouy said: "No, Yannick, it's a marvelous place. It's the perfect site."

Finally, after what Despouy said were "many, many assurances on my part about the accommodations, the security, the availability of telephone lines, and so on," Yannick gave her assent.[9]

Caputo had also sent Despouy three points that he said were the keys to a successful negotiation. "I told Cédras in no uncertain terms, no tricks, or we'll blame it all on you," said Despouy. "Cédras made it clear that he would agree to step down, and that he would accept the return of President Aristide as well as an international military presence as outlined in the aide mémoire of late May."[10]

"This is work I had to do with Yannick, too," Despouy explained. Then everything had to be agreed to by a skeptical FADH general staff. As Cédras's wife, Yannick was particularly interested in her husband's accommodations and whether or not he would have a private phone, which he could use to communicate back to Haiti. Despouy assured her that he would. Yannick asked the Argentine diplomat to promise her one thing—not to negotiate with her husband on Sunday. She told Despouy that her husband should not be bothered on that day, that the diplomats could talk to him, but not negotiate. In voudoun, Sunday is a forbidden day.

Exhausted from days and nights of phone calls and negotiations, Despouy couldn't believe they were finally going to New York. Neither did the CIA, which continued to report to the White House that the Haitian military would never show up.

But there they were at Port-au-Prince International Airport on Saturday, June 26. "All the bourgeoisie showed up," remembered Despouy, who accompanied the delegation. "There were military bands with clarinets and honor guards and military salutes. It was spectacular."[11]

The delegation of thirty-six boarded the American Airlines jet late in the afternoon. Joining Cédras was his brother, a voudoun priest, press spokesman Serge Beaulieu, Colonel Dorelien from the general staff, and a former military officer named Serge Elie Charles, who was acting as Cédras's advisor. Absent were FADH chief-of-staff General Phillipe Biamby and police chief Colonel Michel François. Despouy took it as a good sign that Colonel François sent his older brother Evans to represent him.

"The military delegation seemed very much in our hands, very nervous," remembered Despouy. They peppered him with questions the whole flight: Where will we be staying? What are we going to do tonight? What will happen when we arrive?

Based on the information he had received, Despouy told them: "When we land a helicopter will be waiting for us. It will take us directly to the island where there's a great hotel."

The nervous chatter continued with General Cédras chiming in, saying he needed a telephone in his room—a private line so he could communicate with Haiti.

Despouy reassured him: "No problem, Raoul. Everything has been taken care of."

"They were expecting a five-star hotel," Despouy explained. "I told Dante that this is what they were expecting."

When the military delegation landed at Kennedy Airport after dark, a lone young female staff officer from the UN was there to meet them. "I couldn't believe it," remembered Despouy shaking his head. "She was asking: How many of you are there? She didn't know anything."[12]

The reception was like a pail of cold water in the face of the Cédras delegation, which had brought along a woman to handle protocol. "You have to understand those guys are very, very traditional and very formal," explained Dante Caputo. "They speak a very old French, very nineteenth century. And they behave like that."[13]

Back at the airport, "the young woman from the UN was acting lost," remembered Despouy. "Asking stupid questions. She was like a tour director telling everyone to sit, to give her their passports. It was a disaster."[14]

Finally, Despouy asked: "Where's the helicopter?"

The UN aide said she didn't know anything about a helicopter. Instead the generals and their advisors were crowded into three microbuses.

Despouy was practically sitting on General Cédras's lap. It was after ten o'clock when they arrived at the ferry that would take them to Governors Island. The delegation was quiet and suspicious.

"We arrived on the island at about eleven," remembered Despouy. "The island was completely dark. I mean, pitch black. There weren't any lights and it was quiet, almost eerie. There appeared to be a little house like a motel. It didn't look anything like the fancy hotel I had been describing. I wanted to hide under the seat. It was a little bungalow with no lights, nothing. I heard a voice say: 'You're here!'"[15]

Dante Caputo and Lawrence Pezzullo were standing on the steps of the Officers' Club. Caputo was dressed in blue jeans. He offered his hand to Cédras. "How are you, General? It's good to see you. Want a Coke?"

When Pezzullo greeted Leandro Despouy, the Argentine whispered under his breath: "Oh, my God, they're going to leave."

The military delegation was in shock. They couldn't believe what they were seeing. As Despouy showed them to their rooms, Pezzullo offered the delegates bottles of beer. The accommodations were in Pezzullo's words "nice, but very spartan."

Despouy described them as "rooms for cadets." They were simple barrack-like rooms and the delegation members had to double up. "Ambassadors were having to share a room with one another. And the worst part was that there were no telephones. So that night they couldn't communicate with Haiti."[16]

Despouy was distraught. "We've made a very, very bad impression," he said chiding Caputo and Pezzullo. "Tomorrow we're not going to be able to do anything with these people."

Caputo didn't seem to understand. He asked: "But, why?"[17]

"For Haitians, the way you speak and the setting is more important than what you say," Despouy later explained.[18]

As it turned out, Governors Island did prove to be an ideal setting. Nestled between the eastern tip of Manhattan and Brooklyn, the 175-acre island housed the largest Coast Guard installation in the country. Some four thousand Coast Guard officials and their families lived along narrow leafy streets in a quiet, cloistered community accessible only by Coast Guard ferry or helicopter. The island—purchased in 1627 by Dutch settlers from the Manahatas Indians for two ax heads, a string of beads, and some nails—also featured a hotel, beauty salon, bowling alley, nine-hole golf course, Burger King, and spectacular vistas of Manhattan and the Statue of Liberty. With its narrow cobblestone streets lined with chestnut trees, it seemed plucked from a bygone America.

The diplomats and military met Sunday for a buffet breakfast at the Officers' Club. As they crossed the street, the Statue of Liberty shone in the harbor.

Formal negotiations were scheduled to begin on Monday and the Aristide delegation had not arrived. But Dante Caputo was eager to get started. His deputy and fellow Argentine Leandro Despouy warned him to go slow.

"I want to hear Cédras repeat the promises that he made to you," said Caputo. "I want to make sure that this is clear so that tomorrow we can start the negotiation."[19] General Cédras had told Despouy and U.S. chargé Chuck Redman, in confidence, that he was carrying a letter of resignation.

Caputo and Despouy went over to show the general and Serge Elie Charles the conference room where the talks would take place. It was a colonial-style room with a large conference table and antique chairs. Caputo took this opportunity to go over the four points. "Will you agree to a change in the leadership of the FADH?"

Cédras answered: "No."

"Will you assure your own departure?"

"No."

"Will you let the international community monitor the transition so that both sides can't take revenge?"

"No."

"Will you allow President Aristide to return?"

"No."

Caputo was stunned. He went over the points again and again, but was getting nowhere. When they broke for lunch, Caputo reported to Pezzullo. "Larry, it was awful," Caputo said. "It's as if we had never talked."[20]

"There must be some misunderstanding," said Pezzullo, who suggested that they try again after lunch. But after lunch, the general didn't budge.

Dante Caputo was distraught. "Tomorrow I have no choice but to call a press conference and say that this is a waste of time," he told Pezzullo.

"I can't believe this," said the U.S. diplomat. He, Caputo, Despouy, and Chuck Redman were all sitting in Caputo's suite.

"Why did these people come here?" asked Caputo shaking his head.[21]

Despouy repeated what Yannick had told him about doing things on Sunday. He even called her that night in Port-au-Prince. All Yannick had to say was: "I told you not to talk to him on Sunday!"[22]

Chuck Redman suggested that he and Pezzullo try talking to Cédras in the morning.

"Fine," said Caputo throwing up his hands. "But I'm going to make a press statement at ten o'clock."

The next morning Pezzullo and Redman walked across the street to the Officers' Club to find General Cédras waiting in the conference room wearing a sportshirt and looking relaxed. Pezzullo did the talking, with Redman translating his words into French.

Pezzullo started: "General, my understanding is that we had come to an agreement and you had spoken to Chuck here and Leandro, and you said you were willing to step down as commander."

"Yes," answered Cédras. And he offered his written resignation.

"And you will accept the return of a constitutional government?"

"Yes."

"And you would accept the return of President Aristide?"

The general said he thought the UN was inviting the start of a civil war in Haiti, but he would agree to Aristide's return.

Pezzullo went down a list of thirteen points. Cédras agreed to all of them. At the end, Pezzullo stood and shook the general's hand.[23]

As the two U.S. diplomats left the building, Bob White and Congressman Joseph P. Kennedy II, who were standing across the street, hurried over. Both men had been named to Aristide's delegation.

"What happened?" asked Bob White.

"I can't believe this," answered Pezzullo. "The guy was as open and friendly and willing to cut a deal as I've ever seen him. And yesterday he was very difficult."

"What does it all mean?" asked White.

"I don't know," Pezzullo replied. "But it seems to me that this is a great opportunity. Get a team together and we'll sit down right away and get this thing worked out."[24]

Dante Caputo sat in his suite with Leandro Despouy and Hugo de Sela from the OAS as Pezzullo related what had he and Redman had just heard from Cédras. Caputo exclaimed: "This is extraordinary!"

After considering for a moment, the UN/OAS special envoy turned to Despouy and said: "Go see Cédras and see if he'll talk to me right away."[25]

Meanwhile, television and newspaper reporters were gathering on the steps of the Officers' Club in anticipation of Caputo's news conference. Word had already leaked out that the talks had failed.

Caputo and Despouy, then, went through the thirteen points with Cédras again. Sure enough, the general agreed with everything.

Caputo returned to his suite exclaiming: "This is unbelievable!" He quickly dictated a statement to the press, which read: "I have just received some indications that permit me to say that the negotiations are still continuing."[26] The press conference was canceled and the relieved diplomats went to lunch.

After the drama of the first thirty-six hours, other members of the Aristide delegation started to arrive. It included his lawyers, Mike Barnes, Ira Kurzban, Bert Wides; his U.S. advisor Bob White; his ambassadors Jean Casimir and Fritz Longchamps; Prime Minister René Préval; Mildred Trouillot (the future Mrs. Aristide); members of his Presidential Commission in Haiti, Father Adrien, Micha Gaillard, and Evans Paul; and U.S. congressmen Joseph P. Kennedy II, Charles Rangel, John Conyers Jr., and their staffs; and Haitian publisher Robert Malval. Malval had been told by Aristide that the delegation would include only Casimir, Longchamps, Father Adrien, and himself. But when he saw the size of the delegation, he wasn't surprised. "This is the priest part of the man," he later explained. "He feels he has to be in communion with the group. Without the group he cannot function. It turned the proceedings into a kind of chaos."[27]

The large forty- to fifty-person delegation gathered in the one-hundred-year-old Victorian Admiral's House. Only a dozen or so, including Bob White and Mike Barnes, actually stayed on the island. The rest left with President Aristide and his Secret Service detail every night, and returned with him every morning. President Aristide preferred to stay in a suite at the United Nations Plaza Hotel in midtown Manhattan.

After lunch Caputo and Pezzullo met with Bob White, Mike Barnes, Evans Paul, and Robert Malval in Caputo's suite. After Aristide's representatives read through the thirteen points Cédras had agreed to, Pezzullo said: "If you form a small delegation, we can arrange for you people to start talking."[28]

"I didn't think we were going to negotiate," Malval responded. "I thought this was all going to be worked out."[29]

"We've been trying desperately to get agreement on these things, that's why we're here," Pezzullo explained.[30]

The Aristide delegates left to consult. Hours later, at 11 P.M., Caputo, Redman, Pezzullo, Despouy, and de Sela were sitting in Caputo's suite when someone from Pezzullo's staff popped in to announce: "They've left the island." The next morning was the same. The Aristide delegation arrived at about 9:30 or 10, but said nothing.

At lunch in the Officers' Club that Tuesday, Pezzullo said to Caputo: "Dante, I'm going over and tell Aristide what happened yesterday. I want to make sure he knows what's going on."[31]

At the red-brick Admiral's House at the north end of the island, Pezzullo found Aristide's delegation standing and sitting in little groups, talking, lounging, gossiping.

President Aristide emerged from one of the bedrooms and invited the U.S. envoy upstairs. "I thought I should tell you to your face what happened," began Pezzullo, "because it's historic and they're two hundred yards away from here." Pezzullo reiterated the thirteen points that General Cédras had agreed to. Then, he added: "I think we've got the makings of a real agreement. We told your people this yesterday and since then we've heard nothing. If you don't want to meet with the military personally, that's your business. But you should get a delegation together."

The president listened politely and, showing no emotion, said thank you.

Pezzullo was trying to be positive. "We'll facilitate anything. We have rooms. Just let us know."

Aristide said nothing.[32]

When Pezzullo returned to Caputo's suite, the Argentine asked: "What did he say?"

Pezzullo said: "I gave him a full briefing, he thanked me, and that's it."

Caputo looked concerned. "I'm hearing things from different people," he said, "from Joe Kennedy, from Bob White. Bob White and Mike Barnes are talking to the press."

"What are they talking to the press about?" Pezzullo asked.[33]

Caputo showed him an article in the morning's *New York Times*, quoting Mike Barnes, who said: "We have been simply waiting. So far there has not been a trend. Nothing."[34]

The next morning, Wednesday, when a reporter from the Haitian newspaper *Le Novelliste* asked Dante Caputo how long the talks would last, he answered: "This is my last clean shirt and I'm not in the habit of wearing the same shirt two days in a row."[35]

Moments later the former Argentine foreign minister ran into Mike Barnes outside the Officers' Club. "Why don't you put some conditions out there?" asked the attorney and former congressman who was now representing Aristide.

"What conditions?" asked Caputo incredulously.

"We can't stay here without some conditions," countered Barnes.

Later, Barnes stopped by Caputo's suite to complain about the lack of a framework.

"A framework for what?" Caputo asked. "You people need to meet and negotiate. We'll go step by step. We know exactly what we want to accomplish."[36]

Meanwhile, Pezzullo was getting frantic calls from the White House demanding to know what was going on. U.S., UN, and OAS diplomats started to sense that Aristide and his representatives were trying to sink the negotiation. They weren't going to say anything that could be construed as obstructive, they were simply going to caucus and not sit down with the military until Cédras and his people grew impatient and left.

When they met to discuss the situation Wednesday night, Pezzullo, Caputo, Despouy, Kozak, Redman, and de Sela all came to the same conclusion: Aristide wanted what Dante Caputo coined "the Immaculate Conception." In other words, he wanted the international community to oust the military leadership and stabilize the security situation in Haiti for him, and then he would return without having taken any responsibility. "We're going to have to force him to take us seriously," said Caputo at one point.

The question was: How?

The diplomats had to be careful what they said because one of the men on Caputo's staff, Francesc Vendrell, was a not-so-subtle spy for Aristide. Several times he was overheard relating the diplomats' strategy to Bob White. It became a running joke that whenever Vendrell entered the room, Leandro Despouy would start relating stories about his grandmother.

As their discussions continued past midnight, Despouy said: "This will never work unless we give them an agreement."[37] That idea clicked in everyone's head. So the diplomats got to work drafting a skeleton proposal, which they would flesh out later and present to both sides.

Caputo and Pezzullo discussed the best way to present it. "The problem now is the time period," Caputo explained. "Aristide is going to want to go back to Haiti next week. If we don't get the international military mission in there before him there could be problems. So what I would like to do is call Mig Goulding in from the UN to tell them that it will take about four months to make the transition, or it won't work."[38]

The idea all along was to bring in dual international police and military training missions that could supervise the transition while they prepared to fulfill their longer-term training missions. An international military presence in Haiti was something that had been asked for by Cédras, Aristide, the Haitian business community, and practically every Haitian that U.S. and UN diplomats had talked to.

According to Pezzullo: "Mig Goulding came down and in his beautiful way told both sides that the transition would take four months. He told them, 'By the time we get it together . . . I don't want to give you any false hope, . . .' et cetera."[39]

All this transpired before noon on Thursday. Soon, Mike Barnes was in Caputo's suite saying that if President Aristide was given a date certain for his return, he would agree. Caputo answered: "Fine, let's set a date." He deliberately proposed November 30, knowing that whatever date he gave Aristide's side would try to move it up. Next, Caputo summoned the ambassadors of the Four Friends, who quickly went over the document, changed a few words, and said: This is great.

At 2 P.M. on Thursday the Four Friends ambassadors presented the draft agreement to President Aristide. Simultaneously, Leandro Despouy and Chuck Redman presented it to General Cédras.

By 3:30 that afternoon, the military sent out their spokesman, Serge Beaulieu, to announce that they would accept the agreement with a few grammatical changes. The press now waited for a reply from the Aristide camp. An hour later Ambassador Jean Casimir emerged from the Admiral's House to say that they were still studying it.

The military wanted to sign the agreement the next morning, Friday, so that they could catch the 12:30 flight back to Port-au-Prince.

Thursday evening, Bob White, Mike Barnes, and Congressman Joe Kennedy II appeared in Caputo's suite. Mike Barnes said that they had hoped that the international community would change the leadership of the FADH before President Aristide returned. Pezzullo pointed out that once General Cédras resigned, the president could appoint a new commander-in-chief, who could then reassign FADH officers anyway he wanted. Article 264 of the Haitian Constitution provided that only the commander-in-chief could make changes in the military command. Mike Barnes wanted to know how a legitimate government could be formed under the guns of the same army that destroyed it.

"It's going to take cooperation from both sides," Pezzullo explained. "That's why we're here. If the two sides want to find a way out of this crisis, we can help. The international community is pledging $1 billion in economic assistance over three years to kick-start economic recovery. But the political will has to come from them."[40]

Congressman Kennedy asked the special advisor what other commitments they might get from Cédras.

Pezzullo explained that the military had already yielded the four main points: setting a date for Aristide's return; restoring constitutional government; replacing the commander-in-chief and, through his replacement, restaffing the high command; and inviting an international military force to ensure a peaceful transition. Caputo pointed out that Aristide would be the first president in the Western Hemisphere to be restored to office after a coup.[41]

As the meeting ended, Joe Kennedy said he thought it looked like a good agreement and he was going to advise the president to sign.

Pezzullo replied: "Good. We're waiting. If you can get him to agree this evening, we'll sign the agreement tomorrow morning."[42]

Kennedy, White, and Barnes left for President Aristide's hotel suite in Manhattan, where Kennedy and White pressed the president to sign.

Kennedy vowed that he would stand by Aristide no matter what he decided. Congressmen Conyers and Rangel concurred.

Robert Malval passed a note to Kennedy asking if President Clinton would strongly support the accord.

Yes, the congressman answered.

That was enough to satisfy Malval. But, according to Bob White, the majority of Haitians were not convinced. "It was a big gathering," remembered White. "Aristide sat there and listened to all these Haitians, some of whom spoke with great feeling and eloquence. But it really didn't have a lot of relevance to the problem at hand. There were times when people were crying. It got that emotional. It was not a pleasant walk in the park."[43]

Robert Malval found himself arguing for the agreement against Aristide's advisors and die-hard members of Lavalas. "I stood up to those guys," he remembered, "and I told Aristide he didn't have any choice. If he didn't sign, the U.S. would let him go. I said: You have no right to keep people back home waiting."

When Ambassador Casimir argued that Aristide shouldn't sign, because the agreement was some kind of U.S. trick, Malval turned on him. "What are you suggesting, we start our own private army and have some sort of Bay of Pigs?" Malval asked. "What is the alternative?"[44]

One Haitian stood up and with his voice shaking with emotion shouted: We are the sons of Peralte! We can never accept this!

"Then how many people are being trained?" asked Malval. "You must have a camp somewhere that I don't know about."

"You talk like that because you're bourgeois," snapped one member of Lavalas.[45]

Friday came and the Aristide delegation moved to the Admiral's House on Governors Island. Still, they gave no answer. Meanwhile, the military was growing anxious. Sometime in the afternoon Dante Caputo received two letters from Aristide's U.S. lawyers. One was a document they wanted Caputo to sign to guarantee the accord. Another for General Cédras's signature pledged that Police Chief Michel François and the entire military command would resign and leave Haiti.

Caputo read the two letters, shook his head, and handed them to his deputy, Leandro Despouy. "Leandro, tell Aristide I'm not going to sign this, but tell him in the nicest way possible."[46]

On his way over to the Admiral's House, Despouy was cornered by Aristide's American lawyer, Bert Wides. "He started telling me he had gone to Harvard, that he was the guy who started the Watergate investigation, that he started oversight of the CIA, that he wrote the Voting Rights Act. Next, he was trying to convince me that Pezzullo and Kozak were agents of the CIA. It was psychological warfare," concluded the Argentine. "I thought the man was deranged."[47]

Getting free of Wides, Leandro Despouy entered the Admiral's House carrying the two letters. The tall Argentine was escorted upstairs to a small bedroom where Aristide was sitting with Father Antoine Adrien, who greeted the UN/OAS envoy with great affection.

"I had the feeling that the mood was in my favor," remembered Despouy.

President Aristide read the letter addressed to Dante Caputo, sighed, and said that since Caputo has put himself at the center of everything, he should take some of the responsibility.

"But Caputo is helping you," offered Despouy. "Don't you think you should be taking some of the responsibility yourself?"

As President Aristide read the letter asking for Police Chief Michel François's resignation, his face relaxed. Aristide told Despouy to try to get Cédras to sign the agreement, not the letter. He said the agreement was more important.[48]

Despouy was intrigued. Aristide's U.S. attorneys had been insisting that Colonel Michel François and the rest of the high command be removed. But François's retirement did not seem to be a priority for Aristide.

Friday passed and the Aristide delegation returned to Manhattan without saying a word. During the afternoon President Aristide received calls from Secretary of State Warren Christopher, Venezuelan president Carlos Andrés Pérez, and UN secretary-general Boutros Boutros-Ghali, all urging him to sign.

Robert Malval recalled one emotional scene that took place late Friday afternoon. "Michael Barnes, who had been going back and forth between Caputo and Pezzullo, came back and announced: 'I'm afraid this is the best we can get.'" Ambassador Casimir started to weep like a kid.

"It was like a Greek tragedy," said Malval. Then Mike Barnes started to cry. "Imagine a weeping lawyer. It was very repugnant."[49]

Friday night the discussions continued at President Aristide's suite in the UN Hotel. "We spent the whole night discussing what kind of trick Cédras and the U.S. might pull," said one presidential commission member who was there. "It was clear to most of those present that Aristide was going to sign."[50]

Around midnight Pezzullo received a call from Peter Tarnoff at the State Department, who said that the White House wanted to know the status of the talks. "Peter, Aristide's people are trying to piss off the military and blow up the negotiation," reported Pezzullo. "I can't do anything. I tried to talk to Aristide, but he's closeted with all his advisors. I think we've got to get out the guns."

Tarnoff suggested that Pezzullo talk to Tony Lake.

Minutes later Pezzullo was explaining the situation to the president's national security advisor. "What do you want me to do?" asked Lake.

"Try to get to President Aristide," said the special advisor. "I've tried to get him on the phone; I tried to meet with him when he was here. But he left without telling us what his thoughts were and I can't get through."[51]

Neither could Lake when he called President Aristide at his suite in the United Nations Hotel. He was told that the Haitian president was sleeping. Mike Barnes got on the line instead and tried to open up the negotiation. Lake told him to talk to Pezzullo.

At 1:30 A.M. Lawrence Pezzullo received a call from Barnes. "It was a very heated exchange," remembered Pezzullo. "Mike was getting very emotional and I got nasty with him, too."[52]

"You're deliberately trying to screw this thing up," said Pezzullo at one point. "I don't care what else you want to call it, but you're deliberately trying to take it down."

Barnes accused Pezzullo of not being a friend to Aristide.

"You should be ashamed of yourself," fired back the special advisor. "What the hell are we doing here if your president doesn't want this to work?"[53]

According to Pezzullo, Barnes had no specific objections except that he wanted the military to resign before they signed the agreement.

"Read the agreement," said Pezzullo. "It contains a very specific formula for the military to leave power."

Barnes said he would confer with President Aristide.

"The military has to leave tomorrow," Pezzullo added. "History is going to show that you people avoided responsibility at a critical time."[54]

Pezzullo got off the phone at 3:00 A.M. At 6:00 A.M. he was awakened by Caputo, who said that Mike Barnes had just called to say that Aristide would sign.

"Thank goodness," groaned a groggy Pezzullo. "When?"

"They're going to be here in a little while."

By 9:00 A.M. Aristide and his representatives still hadn't shown up. Instead, his U.S. lawyers called again to introduce changes to the agreement that in Caputo's words "were unacceptable to Cédras and logically impossible to implement."[55]

Barnes proposed moving Cédras's resignation up to the date that the new prime minister was confirmed by the Haitian Parliament. Caputo said that he wouldn't recommend doing everything at once. Then Barnes complained that the proposed arrangement left the military with all the power. "I don't have the ability to magically erase the army," replied Caputo.

Barnes asked if they could have more time. But Cédras and his delegation had to leave the island by 11:30 A.M. if they were going to catch the 12:30 P.M. flight back to Port-au-Prince. And General Cédras was determined to catch that flight. Pezzullo had already checked to see if they could buy some time by ferrying the military delegation to Kennedy Airport by helicopter. But there were no helicopters big enough to accommodate them on Governors Island and it would take too long to fly one in from another military installation.

Robert Malval received a phone call from the French ambassador sometime around 10:30 A.M., who asked: "Where's Aristide?" Malval explained that he thought President Aristide was waiting for an invitation from the White House. "Both Aristide and Cédras are egomaniacs," he later explained, "and I think both of them expected the historic handshake to take place at the White House, not Governors Island."[56]

By 11:00 A.M. journalists had gathered in the first floor of the Officers' Quarters expecting to witness the signing of the agreement. CNN and all the major news outlets were ready. General Cédras, Lawrence Pezzullo, and Dante Caputo stood in a small room no more than ten yards away.

"I'm not going to sign if he's not going to sign," insisted the grim-faced Haitian commander-in-chief.[57]

"At eleven everything was blocked," remembered Caputo. "It seemed impossible." Shortly after eleven Caputo received a phone call from Mike Barnes. Barnes was trying to convince Caputo that he had agreed to guarantee the removal of the entire high command of the FADH. The ploy didn't work.

Meanwhile, General Cédras kept looking down at his watch saying: "I have to leave. I have to leave." Pezzullo was pacing back and forth.

Caputo put his hand over the receiver: "Wait, just one minute, General."

"No, I have to leave," repeated Cédras.[58]

Caputo tried to get President Aristide to come to the phone. But the Haitian leader continued to speak through his U.S. lawyers, which made the UN/OAS special envoy remember the pictures of the U.S. Marine officers on the walls of General Cédras's office back in Port-au-Prince.

Cédras said he was leaving.

Caputo pleaded: "Please, General, I need one more minute."

At exactly 11:29 A.M. Barnes said that President Aristide would sign. Caputo, who had been staring at his watch, exclaimed: "Oh, my God, we made it!"[59]

"Frankly, up to the last minute," remembered Bob White, who was with President Aristide that morning, "I thought it could go either way. The sense was that the U.S. was forcing Haitian democrats to make a pact with the devil." Although White, Mike Barnes, and Haitians Micha Gaillard, Robert Malval, and Evans Paul were urging President Aristide to sign, it was the radical conspiracy-theorists led by Bert Wides and Jean Casimir who seemed to be winning. As Bob White put it: "Bert Wides has a whole conspiracy theory that he was repeating over and over about what the United States government is all about. He was in effect a comfort to those Aristide advisors who believed in conspiracy and that you could only expect the worst from the U.S. government."[60]

Dante Caputo asked Pezzullo to leave him alone with Cédras. "General," he said, "before you sign the agreement you have to sign this letter saying that you will resign on October 15."

"The scene was very unusual," remembered Caputo. "Cédras was sitting there looking at the letter. The letter says: 'I will retire by October 15, 1993.'" The UN special envoy handed him a U.S. government pen. Cédras quickly signed the letter and threw the pen to the floor.[61]

Then the two men walked out together. The setting was very formal. Caputo stood on one side of the general with UN undersecretary-general for political affairs Mig Goulding. Pezzullo was on the other side with Hugo de Sela from the OAS. CNN was broadcasting live. Pezzullo leaned over to Cédras and said: "I want you to know that I admire the way you've comported yourself. You should be proud, your military should be proud and so should your country." There was a glimmer of appreciation in Cédras's eyes as the two men shook hands.[62]

The general sat down before the agreement and Caputo handed him a fountain pen. Cédras started reading the two-page document. Cédras's face looked as if it were carved of stone. "Green with anger" is the way Pezzullo described it. There was a very long pause. "We're on live television, General," said Caputo trying to smile.

Cédras signed and quickly left. "It was clear from the faces of his delegation that they looked upon this as a defeat," concluded Caputo.[63]

There was no celebration on Governors Island. Instead, Dante Caputo went into an extraordinary ten-hour meeting with Aristide's lawyers Mike Barnes, Bert Wides, and Ira Kurzban. He was joined off and on by Mig Goulding and Hugo de Sela. "It was incredible," remembered Caputo. "Barnes was screeching: 'Everything is going to be destroyed!' At one point he broke down and started crying. All the time Bert Wides was weaving wild conspiracies. He was shouting, attacking people. He was seeing conspiracy all around, saying that this was all a CIA and State Department plot. He was trying to intimidate me, saying I was going to be charged with being part of a CIA conspiracy, of destroying Haiti."[64]

Barnes and Wides once again tried to get Caputo to sign side letters. "They kept pushing letters under my face typed on United Nations stationery, demanding that I sign," said Caputo. They claimed they were "interpretations" of the agreement.

Caputo refused, explaining that he had no authority to commit the UN to anything without the approval of the Security Council.[65]

Throughout the afternoon and evening Pezzullo fielded calls from the White House. President Clinton, who was playing golf, stopped at each tee to check with Tony Lake. Has he signed? asked the president.

Not yet, answered his national security advisor.

Finally, at 11:30 P.M. President Aristide appeared. He waited in the small office where General Cédras had signed his resignation earlier that morning. First, he called in Caputo to thank him. Then, he summoned Pezzullo.

Together they entered the big room where the press had gathered with Mig Goulding, Hugo de Sela, Leandro Despouy, Mike Kozak, and the Four Friends ambassadors. Aristide, on the advice of a *houngan*, refused to sign the same piece of paper that Cédras had signed.

Afterward he made a brief statement: "To all of the international community, peace and love. Peace and love to all the Haitian people." Then everyone shook hands.

Pezzullo went into a nearby room and called the White House. Then, he and the rest of the diplomats retired to the Officers' Club for a celebratory scotch. Vendrell, who had spied unabashedly for Aristide, congratulated Pezzullo, saying: Larry, good work.

"It was specially difficult because we were dealing with people we couldn't trust," replied Pezzullo.

Vendrell sat up. What do you mean? he asked.

"Well, you know that guy Bert Wides, he works for the CIA."[66]

According to Caputo, Kozak, and Despouy, who were all there, Vendrell turned white and visibly shook. When he left minutes later, the diplomats shared a belly laugh that, according to Pezzullo, "was worth all the aggravation."

The next morning, the U.S. special advisor got up early and caught the Metroliner back to Washington. When Dante Caputo returned to the fuchsia and gold apartment he was subletting from an Indian diplomat in Manhattan, he weighed himself and discovered that he had lost fifteen pounds. For the last few days he had been living on adrenaline, cigarettes, and an occasional scotch.

CHAPTER 9

The Fall of Baby Doc

"Let the flood descend. . . ."

—Father JEAN-BERTRAND ARISTIDE, 1990

Ask a Haitian to explain the turbulent political climate in his or her country and chances are he or she will tell you that the country is still emerging from the creepy graveyard of Papa Doc Duvalier. "Think of us as a whole society suffering from battered-wife syndrome," said the daughter of an army colonel who fled the country in the early sixties.[1] By the time Papa Doc's moon-faced son inherited power in 1971 at least half a million Haitians were living in exile.

Jean-Claude (or Baskethead, as he was called by his schoolmates) was the youngest president in the world when he became President-for-Life at nineteen. Initially regarded as a lazy affable playboy with no stomach for turning Haiti into a nation of zombies, he seemed content to play with his expensive cars, chase young girls, and party. He left the details of running the country to his domineering mother, Simone (known inside Haiti as "Mama Doc"), his beloved sister Marie-Denise, and a circle of ex-ministers and other Duvalierist "dinosaurs." Prominent among them was Simone's longtime lover and Papa Doc's trusted advisor and bagman Luckner Cambronne. All this was done with the repressive state apparatus, represented by the mirrored sunglassed faces of the Tonton Macoutes, firmly in place.

After thirteen brutal years of Papa Doc, the outside world responded warmly to the less repressive and friendlier façade of the Jean-Claude regime. Thousand of exiles, including light-skinned businessmen from the old elite, began to drift back after years in exile. With them came tourists, mainly from the United States. By the end of the seventies luxury cruise ships regularly called at Haitian ports and a Club Méditerrané was welcoming visitors to secluded beaches at Montrouis. By 1977 an estimated 167,260 foreigners had visited Haiti.

Hoping to encourage political and economic reform, U.S. aid grew consistently from $4.3 million in 1971, to $9.3 million in 1974, to $35.5 million in 1975. With U.S. support, Jean-Claude created the Léopards, an elite counterinsurgency unit, to respond to internal threats. Also, in 1972, the Military Academy, which had been closed since 1961, was reopened and a politically well-connected class graduated in 1973. At the head of the class was Raoul Cédras. Graduating below him were Phillipe Biamby and Himmler Rebú—all personally selected by President Jean-Claude Duvalier.

Whether out of indifference or a genuine feeling of openness, President-for-Life Jean Claude let other independent power centers that his father had undermined regain some of their strength. As the seventies progressed, mulatto elites, the Roman Catholic Church hierarchy, and urban intellectuals all felt their influence grow.

In the meantime, old-guard Duvalierists took advantage of Baby Doc's lax control to enrich themselves. The venality of their schemes was often astounding. But for sheer originality nothing matched the Audubon stamp scandal of 1975. Hatched by Jean-Claude's sister, Nicole, his ambassador to Spain, General Claude Raymond, and other insiders, the scam involved producing fake Haitian stamps and selling them to international collectors.

Meanwhile, a short, soft-spoken seminary student, Jean-Bertrand Aristide, was studying at the Salesian Seminary in Cap Haitien. Only a year younger than the dictator, he had impressed the elders in the Catholic Church with his quick mastery of French, Latin, Greek, English, and Spanish. Born in the southwestern town of Port-Salut, where his father managed a modest farm, the young Aristide had moved to Port-au-Prince with his older sister and mother after his father died at an early age. "We had no fixed residence and I have no shortage of memories of moving," he explained.[2] His mother was one of the informal traders and sellers of goods Haitians call a *Madam Sara*.

While at the seminary, the eighteen-year-old Aristide expressed objections to the use of Latin, which he felt disrupted communion. At the same time, he was reading the works of modern Haitian and South American writers and of liberation theologians Gabriel Marcel and Leonardo Buff. The themes of active engagement against social and political injustice resonated deeply in the young Haitian's mind. "In what we call theology of liberation," he later explained, "we look at what is going on and ask ourselves, what would Jesus do? . . . People are hungry, people have no jobs. Jesus would say, I don't agree with this situation. I'm going to change it."[3]

Had Haiti's economy continued to grow, Jean-Bertrand Aristide's call to action might have fallen on deaf ears. But as the seventies ended, Haiti's economic fortunes began to totter. And when the economy waned, so did the popularity of Jean-Claude Duvalier.

In early 1982 pathologists at Jackson Memorial Hospital in Florida found evidence of toxoplasmosis in a dead Haitian's brain. It was, according to David Black in *The Plague Years*, "a clue from the grave, as though a zombie, leaving a trail of unwinding gauze bandages and rotting flesh, had come to the hospital's Grand Rounds to pronounce a curse." Then an article in the *New York Times* reported that thirty-four Haitians in Florida and Brooklyn had various rare diseases associated with the Acquired Immune Deficiency Syndrome (or AIDS). An alarm was set off around the world. Soon Haiti was officially listed by the Atlanta Center for Disease Control as one of the "four H's" at high risk of AIDS—homosexuals, heroin addicts, hemophiliacs, and Haitians.

The Jean-Claude government responded by closing down Port-au-Prince's gay bars and hotels that catered to a mostly foreign clientele. But the fear of AIDS scared off tourists, two-thirds of whom came from the States. Seventy thousand Americans had visited Haiti during the winter of 1981–82. The following season that number plummeted to ten thousand. By the mid-eighties cruise ships stopped going to Haiti altogether.

But the event that clearly accelerated Jean-Claude's decline from power was his marriage to Michèle Bennett. The daughter of a mulatto coffee exporter, Michèle had previously been married to the son of Alix Pacquet, the man who had tried to overthrow Jean-Claude's father. Divorced and the mother of two sons, the long-haired, vivacious mulatto Michèle was a twenty-seven-year-old secretary in her father's export business when she was invited to have lunch with the young Duvalier in late 1979.

Less than a year later, on May 27, 1980, they were married in a ceremony that cost an estimated three to seven million dollars, which qualified it for a listing in the *Guiness Book of Records*. Afterward the newlyweds entertained friends, family, and officials at a lavish reception. An underground painting by artist Edouard Duval-Carrié showed Baby Doc in a white wedding dress standing on rocks with a tail emerging from his dress shooting himself in the head.

To old-time Duvalierists for whom *noirisme* remained an important cause, the light-skinned, corrupt Michèle was a rude slap in the face. And she wasn't the type to underplay her role, insisting on attending all cabinet meetings with her husband and redecorating the palace with the finest Egyptian art, African elephant tusks, gold and lapis lazuli bathroom fixtures, and furniture copied from European palaces.

She adorned herself with closets full of Valentino, Givenchy, and other *haute couture* clothes. And she ordered her jewelry in bulk. A single order from Spritzer & Fuhrmann came to $200,000. To accommodate her baubles she needed a mobile five-foot vault and floor-to-ceiling suede jewelry boxes.

"Of course I spend money on clothes," she said indignantly to journalist Bella Stumbo. "How do you expect the First Lady of Haiti to look?"[4]

Nobody seemed to like her, not the army, not the Duvalierists, not the peasants, not the Macoutes. But this didn't stop her family from taking advantage of their connection to the Palace to enrich themselves. Her father, Ernest Bennett, quickly extended his interests into almost every sector of the country. A BMW dealership, coffee and cacao exports, and Air Haiti—which he used to transship Colombian cocaine—were only some of his businesses.

Routinely skimmed by the Bennetts and other Duvalier cronies were the Finance Ministry, Tobacco Authority, State Lottery, the State Gambling Commission, State Automobile Insurance, the phone company Teleco, Electricity of Haiti, Cement of Haiti, National Bank of Credit, the Tax Department, and the Flour Mill.

Meanwhile, drought, crop failures, and famines were becoming chronic. Trying to escape the misery of the countryside, desperate men and women started taking to the sea in boats. Between January 1980 and September 1981, 23,000 Haitians entered Florida illegally. For all of 1981 an average of 1,259 arrived each month. Categorized by the U.S. government as economic refugees ineligible for residence, these Haitians were jailed until deportation orders could be processed.

In 1980 Congress threatened to cut off aid to Haiti unless its government took steps to halt the exodus. On November 17, 1980, the Duvalier government responded with a decree making it illegal to organize "clandestine departures." But the incoming Reagan administration pressed the issue further. After an exchange of letters with the Haitian foreign ministry, President Ronald Reagan issued Proclamation 4865 ("High Seas Interdiction of Illegal Aliens") and Executive Order 12324 ("Interdiction of Illegal Aliens").

Henceforth, the United States would patrol the waters between the two republics and intercept and return to Haiti any illegal immigrants, using force if necessary. The resulting Haitian Migrant Interdiction Operation (HMIO) run by the Coast Guard employed a full-time Coast Guard cutter deployed in the Windward Passage and air and helicopter support flying out of the Guantánamo Naval Base.

The late seventies, Jean-Bertrand Aristide noted in his autobiography, "was a time of more and more active militancy." As programming director of the Catholic radio station Radio Cacique, Father Aristide found ways to tweak the regime with commentaries on the Bible, stage pieces, short plays, and quotes from the Bible itself. He had learned, he wrote, that "the gospel in its raw form could act like a stick of dynamite."[5]

Aristide was not the only seminarian who felt politically out of step with his superiors. "A small group of priests resisted the Pharisees who held the reigns of command," he wrote. "It was a group whose numbers and audience was growing even faster." What Aristide described was the birth of the *ti legliz* or the "little church" of liberation theology. "We used to meet in the late 1970s, not entirely secretly, like children who hide out in order to commit little acts of mischief, but trying not to attract much attention from the hierarchy."

A grassroots movement was gaining strength in the *ti legliz*, peasant groups, the urban poor and even in the ranks of the military. Meanwhile, conditions were getting worse.

In the National Palace Jean-Claude and Michèle staged opulent costume balls where the President-for-Life, dressed as a Turkish sultan, handed out fabulous jewels as door prizes. His wife ordered Télé-Nationale to broadcast these parties live, thinking that the masses would get a vicarious thrill watching their First Lady dance in a body-hugging dress festooned with expensive jewelry.

In March 1983 in return for restoring the right of Rome to name bishops and archbishops (a night wrested away by Papa Doc), the Vatican agreed to honor Haiti with a papal visit. Jean-Claude and Michèle lavished millions on the Pope's reception.

Upon arriving at the newly redecorated François Duvalier Airport, Pope John Paul II read his speech in Creole as millions listened on television and radio: "There must be a better distribution of goods, a fairer organization of society, with more popular participation, a more disinterested conception of service on the part of those who direct the society. Things have got to change here!" It was a stunning repudiation of the Duvaliers and everything that they stood for.

On January 8, 1985, after tours of study in Greece, Israel, and Quebec, Father Jean-Bertrand Aristide returned to "a country in a state of general mobilization for change." Seven months later, when schoolchildren in Gonaives took to the streets to protest against the hunger and misery in their lives, three students were shot to death by Macoutes and policemen.

Protests erupted almost daily throughout December and into January. On Independence Day, January 1, 1986, Father Aristide addressed an expectant crowd of parishioners at St. Jean Bosco. Using the national soup of vegetables, potatoes, and a stem of plantains as a metaphor, he asked: "Should we put in potatoes?"

The crowd answered: "Yes."

"Should we put in okra?"

"Yes!" shouted the crowd.

He went down a whole list of ingredients until he came to the stem of plantains, which in Haiti is called a *regime*.

"Should we put in the *regime*?" asked Aristide.

The crowd rose in unison and shouted: "No!"[6]

A month later the colorful priest had his first brush with martyrdom. It was January 31, and once again he was preaching in St. Jean Bosco. "The gentleman was about to draw his revolver during the Eucharist celebration," Aristide remembered. He was a Macoute named Stephan Joseph and was disarmed by the parishioners before he could fire a shot. "They beat him unmercifully after disarming him," wrote Aristide. "If he fulfilled his contract, a passport and visa for leaving the country awaited him."[7]

At the end of January, the Reagan administration refused to certify that the Jean-Claude regime was "making progress" in protecting human rights. Day by day the pressure mounted on the Duvaliers to leave. Depressed and strung out on drugs, Baby Doc prayed for a miracle.

Meanwhile, seething, hysterical mobs surged through the streets looting property and killing any of the Duvalierist henchmen they could get their hands on. The *déchoukaj* (or uprooting) had begun. The Duvalier's hillside vacation home in Fermathe was stripped of its expensive furniture. Carved doors were ripped off their hinges. Tiles and bricks were smashed. In Petit Goave mobs overran the house of a Macoute, hacked off his legs, and paraded his limbless torso through the streets.

One week later U.S. ambassador Clinton MacManaway Jr. was summoned to the National Palace, where the exhausted dictator asked if he could have a plane to fly himself and his family into exile. He left on a U.S. Air Force C-141 with his mother, his wife, their four children, and seventeen aides.

"I have never seen so much rejoicing in the city," wrote Father Aristide several years later. "The symbol of the dictatorship was on its way to join others in the garbage cans of history, but the foundations were not going to disappear from one day to the next."[8]

Via radio and television Haitians learned that their new rulers were five men called the National Council of Government. Their new president was the gruff, bullheaded General Henri Namphy, who vowed that his government would ensure "a firm, just and good transition to democracy."[9]

It sounded good, but the distrust and problems were deep-seated. The Haitian popular movement—unions, peasants, students, teachers, political parties, and the *ti legliz*—wanted Duvalierism pulled out by the roots. Houses were looted down to their foundations; statues were pulled down; and graves were desecrated.

The most savage manifestation of *déchoukaj* was replayed over and over as crowds of poor Haitians hunted and beat to death members of the Macoutes. Often all that remained were a few charred bones and a blackened patch on the street.

"I stood and marveled at the justice of the people," said Father Aristide, who had clearly emerged as one of the leaders of the unarmed revolution. "Our consciences should be clear. These Macoutes were Satan, Satan incarnate."[10]

On April 26, 1986, popular movement leaders, including Father Aristide, organized a memorial march for the victims of Duvalier's torture chamber and prison, Fort Dimanche. When marchers pushed past army barricades into the forbidden grounds of the prison, panicky soldiers fired back with live ammunition and tear gas.

The Fort Dimanche killings proved to the popular movement that the Namphy government was, in the words of Father Aristide, nothing more than "Duvalierism without Duvalier."

An increasingly disillusioned General Namphy announced presidential elections to be held in November 1987. But this did little to stem the street riots, strikes, and demonstrations that threatened to shake the country apart. Then, in early 1987, the Constitutional Assembly, which had been working quietly since the fall, presented the nation with a document that seemed to capture the spirit of the movement in the streets. To guard against the centralization of power, the new constitution called for the direct election of a president and a bicameral legislature, and a prime minister chosen from the majority party in the legislature.

The most revolutionary articles, however, were those dealing with elections. A Provisional Electoral Council (CEP) consisting of nine members—one each chosen by the Catholic Church, the Protestant churches, the government-appointed Consultative Council, the Supreme Court, the human rights organizations, the Association of Haitian Journalists, the National Council of Cooperatives, the university, and commerce and industry—would have absolute authority on election issues and operate completely independently of the government. Most controversial was Article 291, which empowered the council to disqualify from political office for ten years anyone who was "known for having been, by his excess zeal, one of the architects of the dictatorship."

Significantly, Father Aristide opposed the new constitution and urged his followers to vote against it. Why? He felt that the Haitian people were falling into "a trap that would lead them into sham elections directed by the U.S. government and the Haitian army, and into a continuation of the downward political spiral begun when the United States supported François Duvalier's rise to power."[11]

Despite Aristide's misgivings, Haitian enthusiasm for their new constitution was confirmed on Sunday, March 29, 1987, when over one million people showed up at the polls to vote 99.8 percent in its favor. Foreign observers noted that many poor Haitians waited in line for hours to vote for the first time. Former U.S. ambassador Bob White called it "a model election."

But putting the new constitution into practice proved much more daunting. As the popular Haitian saying goes: "Constitutions are made of paper, bayonets are made of iron."

In August, Father Aristide and several other priests from the *ti legliz* traveled to Pont-Sondé to say a mass in memory of peasants slaughtered by local landowners. "The priest had scarcely introduced me," Aristide wrote, "when the Macoutes moved in, their guns turned on the podium. . . . The killer hesitated, appeared to waver, and lowered his gun. In a kind of televised slow motion, he walked clumsily backward, as if he were paralyzed. . . . Am I invisible, insensible to bullets? One might have thought so."[12]

In this swirling maelstrom of violence and uncertainty, presidential and senatorial candidates tried to spread their message throughout the countryside. As Sunday, November 29, 1987, approached, the violence intensified and grew more specific. The headquarters of candidates Marc Bazin, Leslie Manigat, Silvio Claude, and Grégoire Eugène were stoned and shot up; the printing house that was running off the ballots was burned. Graffiti appeared overnight that read: "A bas CEP, Vive l'Armée" (Down with the CEP, long live the Army). Night after night machine-gun fire could be heard coming from the "hot" slum neighborhood of Carrefour Feuilles.

"Bloody Sunday," as it came to be called, began and ended in eerie silence. At daybreak men and women lined up silently to wait for ballots that often never arrived, only to be harassed or shot at by Macoutes. In downtown Port-au-Prince, Macoutes machine-gunned unarmed voters in the courtyard of the Argentine-Bellegarde school. After emptying their guns, they hacked off limbs and heads with machetes as terrified men and women burrowed under benches and hid behind whatever boxes or protection they could find. Journalist Geoffrey Smith arrived as the Macoutes fled. He found the two women who had been running the elections; their faces had been shot half off, and they lay in a mess of blood and election pamphlets. "There was such an ambiance of palpable evil and fear," he reported.[13]

By midmorning thirty-four people had died and the streets of Haiti were deserted. The United States announced that it was cutting off all aid to the Namphy regime.

General Namphy's solution was to "put an end" to the Election Council and call for new, rigged elections for the following February in which his handpicked candidate, political science professor Leslie Manigat, would emerge the winner. But four months after he was elected, Manigat found himself and his family on a plane for Santo Domingo. His mistake: trying to rein in the army by putting General Namphy under house arrest.

On Sunday, September 4, 1988, as Father Aristide was administering communion at St. Jean Bosco church near La Saline slum, a young man surged toward him brandishing a .38 revolver. Parishioners quickly disarmed him.

The following Sunday thousands of people in white crowded the nave once again to hear Father Aristide. Twenty minutes into the mass, as he was reading from the Gospel of Matthew, armed henchmen wearing red armbands and chanting "*Jodi-a, se jou malé*" (Today is an accursed day) closed in on the church. Then the doors burst open and two dozen howling, wild-eyed men attacked the crowd with gunfire, machetes, and clubs. Father Aristide clung to the microphone, frozen. "A group of young people were trying to drag me to the altar to avoid the shots," he remembered.[14]

"People were clawing at the doors, hiding behind the altar, diving under pews, anywhere," said a woman in the congregation. "It seemed to go on forever."[15]

Father Aristide was whisked away by supporters to an inner courtyard as the church was set on fire. At least thirteen parishioners had been killed and another seventy-seven wounded. That night Hurricane Gilbert swept across the island extinguishing the embers of St. Jean Bosco and washing away the blood.

For days afterward the country was in shock. Soldiers of the Presidential Guard arrested General Namphy at the Palace and forced him into exile. The ti soldats (little soldiers or enlisted men) then turned over the presidency to Papa Doc's former aide-de-camp General Prosper Avril.

But popular movement leaders didn't trust Avril, either. "A general leaves. A general returns," said Father Aristide in a radio broadcast. "And then what? And, then, nothing . . ."[16]

Eager to please the United States, General Avril agreed to implement a high-profile anti-narcotics campaign against FAHD officers involved in the transshipment of Colombian cocaine. On April 2, 1989, when General Avril fired four officers for their involvement in drug trafficking, a contingent of Léopards took him prisoner. The coup leader, Colonel Himmler Rebú, supported by Guy François and Phillipe Biamby, offered the chief-of-staff, Hérard Abraham, the presidency. "Their timing was terrible," remembered Abraham, who turned them down.[17]

Sensing that they were losing control of the situation, the three men agreed to release General Avril in return for safe passage to the United States. When their plane landed in Miami, they were detained by customs officials, who arrested the three officers for violating U.S. customs' laws. They remained in a Manhattan detention center for six months.

Back in Haiti, the popular movement demanded an accelerated timetable for democratic elections. In early 1990, Haiti's major political parties proposed a provisional government to be led by a member of the Supreme Court and nineteen-member Council of State, which would include representatives from all sectors of "civil society."

On March 10, 1990, following a pre-dawn meeting with U.S. ambassador Alvin Adams Jr., General Avril resigned. General Hérard Abraham recalled the army to its barracks and transferred power to a provisional government headed by a little-known Supreme Court judge named Ertha Pascal-Trouillot. Trouillot promised early, internationally supervised elections. Father Aristide remained skeptical. "The driver's gone," he said in a taped message to radio stations. "But the truckload of death is still among us."[18]

The eloquent Salesian priest had ridden the crest of the popular movement a long way, surviving three assassination attempts and constant harassment. Before the end of 1990 Father Aristide would ride the popular movement all the way to the Presidential Palace, proving the novelist Herbert Gold's observation: "Haiti is the land of unlimited impossibilities."[19]

CHAPTER 10

The New York Pact

"All Haitians are paranoid."

—Prime Minister ROBERT MALVAL

The ink was barely dry when Aristide's advisors started complaining that the Haitian president was "not at all comfortable" with the terms of the Governors Island Agreement.[1] They wanted the United States and the international community to forcibly remove the high command of the Forces Armées d'Haiti (FADH). The UN/OAS special envoy Dante Caputo called it "the immaculate conception" scenario. The international community was to simply erase the political problems of Haiti and guarantee President Aristide's safety.

Article Eight of the documents signed by General Cédras and President Aristide on July 3, 1993, read: "The Commander-in-Chief of the Armed Forces of Haiti has decided to avail himself of his right to early retirement and the President of the Republic shall appoint a new Commander-in-Chief of the Armed Forces of Haiti, who shall appoint the members of the General Staff, in accordance with the Constitution." Therefore, President Aristide could appoint a new commander in chief who could in turn appoint a new general staff loyal to him (the president)—thereby replacing the officers he considered disloyal.

To clarify this point, Dante Caputo sent a letter to General Cédras, President Aristide, and the UN Security Council stating that it would be considered a violation of the Governors Island Agreement if "the general staff of the Haitian armed forces refuses to accept decisions made by the new commander-in-chief." This was the *only* commitment adopted by the Security Council as a criterion for verification of the Governors Island Agreement.

Article Seven called for "the adoption of a law establishing a new Police Force and appointment, within this framework, of the Commander-in-Chief of the Police Force by the President of the Republic." This meant that President Aristide would be able to reassign the man who had organized the coup against him: Lieutenant Colonel Michel François.

Still, President Aristide and his advisors complained that "we were astonished to learn that members of the high command could stay in the army as long as they accepted posts outside of Haiti. We never understood that they could remain in the army."[2] According to Cédras's predecessor, General Hérard Abraham, it was safe to say that many of the old general staff officers would retire of their own volition.[3]

Upon his return to Washington from Governors Island, Pezzullo was congratulated by Secretary of State Warren Christopher. He also received an invitation from Robert Toricelli of the House Foreign Affairs Committee to appear before his subcommittee on InterAmerican affairs. "I'm not accustomed to complimenting the State Department," said the Democrat from New Jersey, "but this is a great accomplishment. I frankly never thought it would happen, and everyone who ever talked to me didn't think it would happen."[4]

But the Aristide camp was already petitioning members of the National Security Council staff of the White House. Mike Barnes, who had managed President Clinton's winning presidential campaign in Maryland, complained to Nancy Soderberg and Sandy Berger "that it was a bad agreement, imposed on Aristide," according to Pezzullo.[5]

Days after returning to Washington, Mike Kozak received a call from Richard Feinberg, who headed the Latin American division of the NSC, asking him for an informal, one-on-one briefing with Nancy Soderberg. When Kozak arrived at Soderberg's office she was sitting with fourteen people. "I got sandbagged," he said, "I was immediately peppered with questions and, more than that really, complaints."[6]

Soderberg, echoing her boss Tony Lake, said that UN military force levels provided for under the agreement were not high enough to prevent a bloodbath when Aristide returned to Haiti. Kozak explained that this was an issue that had already been debated and resolved by the Clinton foreign policy team.

"My sense was that they were using the force level argument to broadside the agreement," Kozak said.[7] Soderberg wanted to know why Kozak hadn't stopped Aristide from signing the agreement.

Pezzullo and Kozak, still feeling some of the euphoria of their diplomatic achievement, were taken aback. They realized later that this was the first manifestation of a phenomenon that would gather momentum in upcoming weeks: Namely, that an alliance was forming between people from both sides of the Haiti issue in the White House, the CIA, and the Office of the Secretary of Defense to sink Governors Island. Conservatives at Defense and CIA had long argued that the political problem for President Clinton was the Haitian refugees, not President Aristide, whom they regarded as a bad risk and possibly a nut case. They favored coming to an understanding with General Cédras whereby he would accept the return of Haitian refugees and put a stop to the political repression in Haiti.

On the other side, Aristide enthusiasts at the NSC led by Soderberg felt that the United States should spare no cost, political or otherwise, to restore the deposed leader. His unreasonableness, in their minds, was evidence of his dedication to the poor people of Haiti.

Back in Port-au-Prince, General Cédras began the task of selling the Governors Island Agreement to his colleagues on the general staff. He had anticipated that his greatest challenge would come from the chief of police, Colonel Michel François, which is why he had included François's brother Evans François in his delegation to New York.

Immediately after returning to the Haitian capital on Saturday afternoon, General Cédras drove to his office, where he met with Colonel François. Cédras didn't know that François had already heard from a spy in Aristide's camp in Washington claiming that Cédras had promised in a secret side letter he signed with Dante Caputo to deliver François's head. Of course, this wasn't true. No secret side letter existed, despite the efforts of Aristide's lawyers to pressure Caputo to sign one.

According to a Haitian friend of the two military leaders, General Cédras tried that afternoon to convince François that no such letter had been signed. But Colonel François, based on what he had heard from his source in Washington, was filled with suspicion.

What was going on? Was Colonel François's spy double-crossing him? No, he wasn't. Then why did Aristide's aide believe that there was such a letter if no letter existed? Because, says Bob White, emotions and tensions were so high the last day at Governors Island that many in the Aristide camp came away convinced that they had elicited such a promise from Dante Caputo. In fact, many had been handed a fraudulent version of the agreement by Ambassador Casimir and Mike Barnes. Robert Malval was one of those who received the fraudulent text. It was not the version that had been signed by Aristide and Cédras but, instead, stated that Colonel François would resign on October 15.

Malval returned to Port-au-Prince convinced that this was a secret agreement that resulted from the last-minute negotiations of Mike Barnes. "It was a dirty trick to play on someone who had just been asked to be your new prime minister," Malval said years later.[8]

Without Colonel François on board, General Cédras knew that he was in trouble. An extremely cautious man by nature, Cédras had made the boldest political move of his career. "Remember, he's not a politician," said his predecessor General Abraham. On Sunday morning, July 4, he went on national television to explain why he had signed the Governors Island agreement. Speaking in Creole from behind his desk at military headquarters he said: "A prime minister and a government will be named soon, and the army will have no say in those decisions. . . . All the changes will be made according to the Constitution and army regulations. I have not accepted, and will not accept, that one single member of the army be removed."[9] Dressed in his military uniform that showed his three-star rank, General Cédras referred to "President Aristide" for the first time since the coup.

As UN/OAS envoy Leandro Despouy watched from his room at the Montana Hotel, he thought of the challenge ahead: How to achieve the political truce needed to implement the Governors Island Agreement. Article One of the agreement called for: "Organization, under the auspices of the United Nations and the Organization of American States, of a political dialogue between representatives of the political parties in the Parliament . . . in order to agree to a political truce and promote a social pact to create the conditions necessary to ensure a peaceful transition."

The problem was that the political class of Haiti was completely polarized. On one side were the Constitutionalists loyal to President Aristide; on the other was the Alliance, allied with the military. "There was no dialogue between them whatsoever," remembered Despouy.[10] Then there was the dilemma of how to deal with the pro-military members of the Senate who had been elected in sham elections the previous January 18 and were controlled by Colonel Michel François.

Even though François, through bribes and intimidation, exerted strong influence over the Alliance deputies in the Chamber of Deputies and among the January 18th senators, some Alliance politicians remained who saw the need for a political reconciliation.

With his tiny staff of three—which now included Juliette Remy and Max Duboyer—Despouy started holding talks with members of the Haitian Parliament at the Hotel Montana. Remy and Duboyer, who were both French, found themselves working every day until two or three in the morning. "These people would come and go in twos and threes," remembered Remy. "I would sit with one delegation in the lobby, while another delegation walked by. When they didn't talk politics the opposing groups were friendly, talking, making jokes. Then, the next minute they would be screaming at one another."[11]

As their efforts started to yield a delegation of parliamentarians from the two sides—Constitutionalists and Alliance—who were willing to travel to New York for talks, Despouy and Remy ran into the problem of how to pay for their tickets. "We were literally begging," remembered Remy. "There is no other word."[12] Finally, out of desperation, Max Duboyer lent the money to pay for the parliamentarians' plane tickets.

Despouy knew going into the talks that the normalization of Parliament depended on the resignation of the thirteen January 18th senators. To underscore this point, he held a press conference at the airport the day of their departure to New York. "I'm confident that the majority of the political forces in Haiti don't want the thirteen illegal senators seated in the future, so that, finally, they can have one unified Parliament and in this manner they can ratify the new Prime Minister."[13]

His remarks raised the ire of Police Chief François, who tried to prevent some of the delegates loyal to him from leaving for New York. But they left anyway. On Tuesday, July 13, 1993, two weeks after the signing of the Governors Island Agreement, fifty-six prominent Haitian politicians flew to New York.

It was a heady experience for Juliette Remy, who had joined Leandro Despouy only weeks before. Now she was on a jetliner surrounded by anxious Haitian politicians who battered her with questions about their accommodations in New York and how they would be received. Since the Constitutional (pro-Aristide) block had named their own presidents of both the Chamber of Deputies and the Senate—which at the time were both controlled by the (pro-military) Alliance—there were four presidents of the two houses of Parliament on the American Airlines DC-8. "These four men who could never agree on anything sat together and talked as though they were friends," recalled Remy.[14] Remy thought that UN officials had made all necessary arrangements. But when the jetliner landed at Kennedy Airport there was only one woman from the UN handing out badges to identify members of the delegations. To Despouy, it was an unwelcome replay of his experience two weeks before.

"We had requested separate minivans so the Alliance and Constitutionalist delegates could travel separately," said Remy.[15] Outside the terminal sat one bus surrounded by a huge crowd of pro-Aristide demonstrators. UN officials had provided no security.

As the delegates stepped out into the thick night air, pro-military senator Thomas Eddy Dupiton was recognized by the crowd, which grew more excited and pressed around him. A tall, dignified man of fifty-one who had once been a New York City messenger, Dupiton pushed back. Soon he and several demonstrators were throwing punches. Leandro Despouy had to step between them and escort the harried senator onto the waiting bus. There Dupiton sat fuming, surrounded by his political enemies, as the demonstrators outside kept up their chants. "Without meaning to and because they didn't understand the Haitian mentality, the UN had created an explosive situation that was in danger of destroying the whole reunion," said Despouy.[16] "It was very, very tense," added Remy.[17]

Upon arriving at the Helmsey Hotel on Forty-Second Street, Remy got on the phone and started asking UN officials for help. Another large, noisy pro-Aristide demonstration was gathering outside. "One official said he had a concert to go to and couldn't be bothered," she remembered.[18]

New York City that Wednesday was sweltering hot. With the Four Friends ambassadors in attendance, talks got under way in the basement of UN headquarters. "It started off as sort of a love-fest," said U.S. special advisor Pezzullo, who sat to one side with the other ambassadors.[19] Dante Caputo chaired the conference at the front desk with Leandro Despouy and Hugo de Sela by his side. The Constitutionalist and Alliance delegates were seated on opposite sides of room.

Caputo began by stating: "There is very little time to reach a political settlement," so we have to gets things moving."[20] He then invited delegates from both sides to make any opening remarks. Several took the floor.

"They were very eloquent," remembered Pezzullo. "They were saying that they were pleased that the international community was taking the time to help them."[21] Victor Benoit, who headed KONAKOM, which was part of the coalition that had sponsored Aristide's presidential campaign, spoke of the need to heal political wounds. Next, Evans Paul, mayor of Port-au-Prince and an Aristide supporter, said he had come in the spirit of reconciliation. Following Paul were a series of Lavalas (Aristide loyalists) parliamentarians.

The Lavalas delegates stated that they couldn't sit in the same room with the January 18th senators, who they felt had no right to be there.

Caputo broke in: "We came here to resolve things, not to make them worse."[22] Sensing that the emotional tenor of the meeting was turning, he called for a recess and retired to his office upstairs with Despouy and Pezzullo.

"This was all preplanned," Caputo said in the elevator, "The Lavalas people are already at it. And Bert Wides is giving them instructions. Let's call Aristide and tell him to stop."[23]

The Argentine diplomat reached President Aristide in his Washington office. Pezzullo, who was also on the line, remembered the Haitian president asking at one point: "How can you ask me to get involved?"[24]

"Mr. President, I'm asking you because these are your congressmen," Caputo responded. "We're not going to be able to get this done."[25]

Despite the UN/OAS special envoy's entreaties, Aristide made it clear that he wasn't going to help. Exasperated, Caputo sent all the delegates to lunch.

By the time delegates drifted back at two, the mood of the conference had turned sour. Caputo called Leandro Despouy, Mike Kozak, and Lawrence Pezzullo together and said: "I think the best thing we can do is break this up into a couple of working groups. One working group will meet with me this afternoon to starting working on the shape of the agreement. We'll leave the January 18 issue for later. The reason we invited these 18th of January senators in the first place is so that they could agree on the decision, so it wasn't imposed on them."[26]

Leandro Despouy remained downstairs with the eighteen to twenty Constitutionalist delegates who were to make up the working group to deal with the January 18 issue. Meanwhile, Dante Caputo escorted the first working group of Alliance delegates upstairs. Juliette Remy, who worked with Despouy, reported that it took them seven hours just to convince the Constitutionalist members to start talking. "The pattern was that every time you were going to start something, you didn't start working," she recalled, "you talked about how you were going to proceed and the problems they had in talking."[27]

While the second group argued about whether or not they should start talking, Caputo was making rapid progress upstairs. "At first they were guarded," Caputo reported later, "then they started to talk to one another. After awhile they were calling each other by their first names. What was most illuminating is that someone at one point said: 'This is a time for us to heal old wounds and come together.'"[28]

While Caputo broke for dinner, the second working group was still in the basement of UN headquarters meeting with Leandro Despouy. He deliberately didn't offer them anything to eat or drink. Nor would he call a recess. It was only out of hunger and exhaustion, reported one delegate at the meeting, that the Constitutionalist group agreed at 3 A.M. to formally engage the issue of the January 18th senators.

"It was like a boxing match or a game of chess," said Juliette Remy. "You had to get them to the point where they had to give up."[29]

It was clear to international observers that Haitian politicians had no experience whatsoever in compromise. "All they had in mind was revenge, revenge, revenge," said one French diplomat.[30]

Thursday morning the first working group produced a draft agreement that called for a political truce in Parliament for six months and the ratification of a new prime minister appointed by President Aristide. During that period Parliament would consider and pass a series of laws submitted by President Aristide designed to alleviate the political crisis and fulfill the commitments he had made at Governors Island.

At first glance it looked like President Aristide and his allies in the Parliament were getting exactly what they wanted. But according to Lawrence Pezzullo, "After Thursday morning we started to get into the same stupidity with the Lavalas group."[31] It was a replay of Governors Island. The Lavalas delegates, who included a majority of the Constitutionalists, went into caucus and didn't talk to anyone. As they met alone the Alliance delegates grew nervous. Meanwhile, Aristide's lawyers, Bert Wides and Ira Kurzban, lobbied for more precision in the agreement and for "guarantees." This dynamic continued throughout Thursday and into Friday.

At one point on Friday, July 16, Ambassador Pezzullo joined the Lavalas caucus. Two delegates, Senators Firmin Jean-Louis and Turneb Delpé, told him that they wouldn't sign the pact until the January 18th senators turned in their special license plates. Firmin Jean-Louis told Pezzullo that he should inform President Clinton that this was an important issue.

"You mean to tell me that you think that the President of the United States should be concerned with a problem over license plates for Haitian senators?" Pezzullo asked in amazement.

"Certainly," answered the Lavalas senator without a hint of humor.[32]

The delaying tactic went on into Friday. Meanwhile, discussions with the January 18th working group continued. Pezzullo described the talks as "strident at times, but good." All present, observers and participants, agreed that Leandro Despouy was the key. Mike Kozak remembers hearing delegates say: "Wait a minute. Let's listen to Professor Leandro."[33]

Then, Despouy explained: "If you look at your Constitution, Article 167 says that in the event of a dispute a commission can be formed to hand down a ruling. The Constitution is not specific, but the way I read it, this commission would be similar in composition to other Constitutional commissions with someone from the Senate, someone from the Chamber of Deputies . . ." and so on.[34]

Early Friday morning the January 18th senators agreed that they would not take their seats while the Constitutional Commission deliberated on the validity of the January 18 election. They understood that the ruling of the commission, which would be dominated by Aristide partisans, was a foregone conclusion. But this gave them a dignified way to step aside.

The wording of the final agreement was pretty much in place. In addition to providing for a special Constitutional Commission, the agreement called for a political truce of six months "to guarantee a smooth and peaceful transition." President Aristide was invited to "appoint as soon as possible a new Prime Minister of national concord," while members of Parliament pledged "to ensure the confirmation of the new Prime Minister selected, in accordance with the Constitution, without delay." The parliamentary blocs would also "undertake to ensure that the following laws are passed, on the basis of an emergency procedure." These laws to be submitted by the president or prime minister concerned, among other things: (1) establishing a police force separate from the armed forces; (2) passing an amnesty law for people involved in the September 1991 coup d'état; and (3) establishing a compensation fund for victims of the coup. The most troubling provision as far as the Lavalas delegates were concerned had to do with the amnesty law.

UN secretary-general Boutros Boutros-Ghali, who was scheduled to leave that evening on a trip to the Middle East, asked the Haitians to conclude their talks by 2 P.M. so that he could be present for the signing. But once again the Lavalas delegates went into caucus, where they remained until 10:30 that night. The rest of the Constitutional and Alliance delegates waited. "There's no excuse for their behavior," one Alliance deputy told reporters from the Haitian newspaper *Le Nouvelliste*.[35]

Lavalas delegates complained that the international community was imposing a solution on them—a "prefabricated solution" said one deputy—and badgered Dante Caputo for more guarantees.

According to one Haitian who was there, the mood in the caucus shifted back and forth between a feeling that Lavalas could dictate the terms of the agreement to one of complete paranoia.[36]

U.S. special advisor Lawrence Pezzullo, Venezuelan ambassador Diego Arria, and the Canadian ambassador addressed the group at 11 P.M. Pezzullo spoke last. "Democracy is not created by cowards," he began. "No democratic system is built out of talking it to death. Somebody has to take a stand and do something. And this is the moment. You have the whole international community here to help you and for the life of me I don't understand what the problem is. You have a perfectly good agreement and you're insulting those people out there in the other room with whom, I assume, you want to build some comity. I think you're being ill-advised by some of your American lawyers here who don't know your country."[37]

Minutes after the U.S. special advisor left the meeting, he was rushed by Bert Wides, who screamed that he had no right telling his clients not to listen to his advice.

"Get away from me," said Pezzullo, who was standing with his back against a coffee bar. Bert Wides pushed closer.

"One more step and I'll cold-cock you," warned Pezzullo.[38]

Minutes later the Lavalas delegates emerged from their caucus ready to sign. It was almost 1 A.M. Saturday, July 17. Aristide lawyer Ira Kurzban continued to argue with Caputo about inserting new language. "Basically, he was asking for more guarantees from the Haitian military and the military wasn't there," Caputo said later.[39]

The three-page New York Pact was signed by all the delegates except Lavalas members Firmin Jean-Louis, Turneb Delpé, Jacques Rony Modestin, Alexandre Médard, Rindal Pierre Canal, and MRN leader Rene Théodore. Firmin Jean-Louis, who led the boycott and in the words of one diplomat "sold out to the highest bidder," was campaigning for president of the Senate.[40] According to another Constitutionalist delegate, he was getting his instructions directly from President Aristide. Turneb Delpé in a statement to the press said he didn't sign because "the pact was dictated by the UN and the countries who were friends of the Secretary-General—France, the United States, Canada and Venezuela." He went on to say that "the document opens the way to an indictment of President Aristide by the elected Parliament in the High Court of Justice."[41]

After the pact was signed the forty-odd delegates broke into applause. "It was an emotional moment," said one of them. "Nothing like this that required the cooperation of both sides had ever happened before."[42] They all thanked Despouy especially and said the pact would never have been realized without his understanding and patience.

"It was an important beginning," said one member of the Alliance.[43] Despite President Aristide's resistance, politicians on both sides of the political spectrum had agreed to build a democratic base for Aristide to govern.

"The whole thing was psychedelic," concluded Pezzullo. "I've never been through something like that where the people you're trying to help are the biggest impediments to getting it done."[44]

"Haitians have a talent for hiding behind legal mumbo-jumbo," said one diplomat involved in the negotiations. "They'll ask you to do something, but then they'll tell you why it should appear that you're holding a gun to their heads. They couldn't possibly be seen as complicit. So you assume all the responsibility and they can sit on the sidelines and criticize your actions. And you end up being criticized for what they asked you to do."[45]

With the signing of the New York Pact two main ingredients for the restoration of constitutional government and the return of President Aristide to Haiti were in place. "We are on track with a very concrete step in the implementation of the Governors Island Agreement," Dante Caputo told reporters at a press conference after the signing. "This marks the first step in the peaceful transition period in building democracy in Haiti."[46] But Father Antoine Adrien, coordinator of President Aristide's Presidential Commission, was less enthusiastic. "The weakness of the agreement," he said, "is that the military is still in power. There are so many possibilities and the situation is so complicated that something could happen to stop the process."[47]

Lawrence Pezzullo saw another problem. "Even though the Governors Island agreement and the New York Pact were important steps forward," he concluded, "the spirit had been drained out of them because of the palpable venom from the Aristide camp."[48]

After four long, difficult days of negotiations, Dante Caputo and Leandro Despouy from the UN, Hugo de Sela from the OAS, and Lawrence

Pezzullo, Mike Kozak, and Ken Merten from the U.S. State Department's Haiti Working Group were in the mood to celebrate. It was two o'clock on a Saturday morning and the only restaurant they could find that would serve them dinner was an Italian restaurant–karaoke bar on Second Avenue. As the diplomats wolfed down plates of pasta and drank beer, people got up and tried to sing "Feelings," "Yesterday," and "Send In the Clowns."

"We couldn't have found a better place," said Dante Caputo with a wry smile.[49] It proved to be a perfect metaphor for what lay ahead. Everyone— President Aristide, the Haitian military, and the Clinton administration— knew the melody by now, but none of them could sing the song.

CHAPTER 11

The Rise and Fall of Aristide

"If Haiti isn't a jungle, why then all these beasts?"

—folk singer MANNO CHARLEMAGNE

The presidential campaign of 1990 was borne on the wings of the popular movement that had gathered steam in the late eighties. This loose federation of priests, students, political parties, peasant groups, and union activists had protested, rioted, and suffered imprisonment, torture, and martyrdom for the right to have a voice in their own political future. Finally, in March 1990 with the resignation of General Prosper Avril, a man controlled the army who believed that fair, honest elections were the best hope for Haiti.

For years, as a professor at the Military Academy, General Hérard Abraham had preached that a professional military should stay out of politics. Now, this lean, distinguished-looking man of fifty worked with Provisional President Ertha Pascal-Trouillot to organize the transition to democracy.

The two of them fought against a deep strain of suspicion and treachery that ran through the Haitian political psyche. Even though Provisional

President Trouillot stated over and over that the sole objective of her government was to hold free, fair national elections, the popular movement labeled her a Duvalierist. Nor did it ease their fears when President Trouillot announced that she had no intention of remaining in office after the election.

When in an address to the United Nations, President Trouillot referred to "my spotless white dress" as a symbol of purity, Aristide said it was really covered with blood. As far as Trouillot's promise of early elections, Father Aristide answered: "Justice against the Macoute criminals must happen before elections." He wanted the provisional government "to take up its responsibilities. . . . The authorities have sufficient resources in hand to make judicial procedures."[1]

But did they? Not according to most observers and FADH commander-in-chief General Abraham. Struggling to build a legal, professional army out of the corrupt legacy of the Duvaliers, Namphy, and Avril, he wasn't about to make the arbitrary arrests demanded by leaders of the popular movement. "Was it a crime to be a Macoute or to have been associated with the Macoutes?" asked a Haitian historian. "If it was, at least 25% of the country would have been behind bars."[2]

In late June after thirteen people were killed in Port-au-Prince in political violence, the popular movement demanded arrests of Duvalierists and Trouillot's resignation. When the Council of State organized a meeting with representatives of trade unions and grassroots organizations to discuss a solution to the political crisis on June 21 at the Hotel Santos in Port-au-Prince, four armed men, two in army uniforms and two in civilian clothes, entered the lobby and opened fire with automatic weapons.

Witnesses of the shooting claimed that police officers made no effort to stop the killers. Father Antoine Adrien, head of Haiti's Holy Ghost fathers and a leading figure in the democratic movement, blamed *zenglendos*—thugs and soldiers thought to be on the payroll of the Duvalierists. Father Aristide went on the radio to chastise the U.S. ambassador Alvin Adams. "Speak of elections after justice, please," he said. "Let's begin by disarming the Macoutes."[3]

The Hotel Santos incident dramatized something that General Abraham had been struggling with for months: namely, that he commanded an institution that in addition to being highly politicized and corrupt was almost completely lacking in discipline. Determined to provide security for the upcoming elections, he formed the Security Coordinating Committee (SCC), made up of five colonels chosen carefully from the ranks of the FADH. To head the committee he appointed a colonel who had been one of his top students at the Academy and graduated first in his class, Colonel Raoul Cédras.

By the end of September 1990, the SCC, working with UN advisors, proposed a series of emergency measures. To thwart the activities of extralegal groups like the Macoutes and to supplant the weak police and judiciary, departmental military commanders were given broad discretionary authority in the conduct of their operations. Priority was given to the Port-au-Prince metropolitan area, where carefully selected units were instructed to respect the election laws as prescribed by the Provisional Electoral Council (CEP), to refrain from the use of arms, and to remain impartial and cooperate fully with the civilian CEP.

Another crisis shook the country in July when Baby Doc's former minister of interior and Macoute henchman, Roger Lafontant, returned to Haiti. Many believed that Lafontant, a physician who saw himself as a successor to Papa Doc, aimed to push the weak provisional government aside in a coup d'état.

The popular movement, enraged that Lafontant had even been allowed back into Haiti, called a general strike. When the government's chief prosecutor issued a warrant for Lafontant's arrest on charges of high treason, Lafontant's supporters took to the streets of Port-au-Prince threatening motorists and chanting "Long live Lafontant!" General Abraham argued that instead of provoking a showdown between the hard-core Duvalierists and the popular movement, which his weak, polarized military could hardly prevent, the best hope for Haiti was still free and orderly national elections.

In the midst of this latest crisis, the Provisional Electoral Council set December 16 as the date for the first round of presidential and parliamentary elections. "But what kind of elections would the Haitian people witness or take part in?" asked Father Aristide in his autobiography. "Would they be elections by machete and machine gun, the voters discouraged or forced to vote at gunpoint—or would ballots be stuffed?"[4]

Given the dashed expectations of the years since Baby Doc's depar-ture in 1986, Father Aristide and other Haitians had a right to be skep-tical. Then, on October 16, Roger Lafontant announced the formation of his own political party, disingenuously named the Union for National Reconciliation (URN). And he declared himself the party's presidential candidate.

An increase in murders and violent assaults, gasoline shortages, and frequent blackouts only added to Haitians' sense of foreboding. Also, a showdown was looming between the Provisional Electoral Council and Lafontant. "Are we headed for a repeat of the bloody '87 elections, or worse?" asked a commentator in *La Nouvelliste*. Would the CEP invoke Article 291 of the Constitution, which prevented "architects" of the Duvalier dictatorship from running for high office, and disqualify Lafontant?

With the possibility of full-scale political conflict building by the hour, Provisional President Trouillot continued to call for calm. Both inside and outside the country, she was mocked for being powerless and cor-rupt. "The body in the Palace, the head in Washington and the heart with the Duvalierists" read one less than flattering characterization of the first lady in a Port-au-Prince newspaper. "There is general agreement that Mrs. Pascal-Trouillot lacks the strength and courage to see through a non-violent election," concluded an analyst for the *Economist*.[5]

But Haiti is a country rich in irony. And the irony this time was that Lafontant's candidacy pushed Father Aristide to consider running for the presidency himself. Only a few months earlier, in June, Aristide had denounced "presidentialism, this incurable sickness" of Haitian politicians.[6]

"Unlike those who see Jesus as a divine being," Father Aristide explained, "I discern in him before anything else someone who was fully human. It is out of the human dimension that the divine in him is revealed. He was so human that he was God: I share that theological vision. That is why I finally agreed to discover and experience the complementarity between the priest and the president."[7]

On October 18, Father Jean-Bertrand Aristide declared his candidacy for the presidency of the republic. Being a practical politician who wanted his party to win, Victor Benoit, the leader of the democratic-socialist

KONAKOM party and the candidate of the popular movement umbrella group National Front for Change and Democracy (FNCD), agreed to step aside and let Father Aristide run under the banner of the FNCD. Aristide called his campaign *lavalas*—the torrent that scours everything in its way. Lavalas, he explained, "represented something quite different from the FNCD. The latter was a collection of a variety of movements and political parties. . . . Lavalas was much, much more: a river of many sources, a flood that would sweep away all the dross, all the after-effects of a shameful past."[8] While he pledged his love for the poor and promised to lift Haiti "from misery and poverty," he never presented a detailed description of his program of government.[9]

As his campaign symbol, Aristide chose a red rooster—representative of the voudoun *loa* Ogum, a liberator who believes in justice and is not afraid to use his sword.

Father Aristide's entry into the presidential race raised the stakes on both sides. CEP officials reported an enormous surge in voter registration, especially among the urban poor. Hundreds of UN and OAS observers led by former U.S. president Jimmy Carter were deployed throughout the country to help the CEP with the formidable task of organizing and supervising the elections. Statesmen around the world spoke of the need to avoid a repeat of the bloody elections of 1987.

In late November, the CEP excluded Roger Lafontant from the race on a technicality—he had not submitted his birth certificate to election officials. In effect, the gauntlet had been thrown down to the Duvalierists. The message delivered to them was clear: You will play by the rules.

As the December 16 date approached, pressure on the armed forces grew more intense. The candidates agreed that General Abraham and SCC commander Colonel Raoul Cédras were performing admirably. General Abraham later admitted that his subordinates kept coming to him and asking which candidate he was going to endorse. Over and over he reminded them that the FADH's role was to provide security and maintain a neutral, professional stance.

Speculation now centered on how well Father Aristide would fare against centrist candidate Marc Bazin. A former World Bank economist, Bazin pledged to put the corrupt, weak Haitian economy in order. Many international diplomats saw him as the candidate with the best chance to build a successful consensus government. Father Aristide, meanwhile, spoke darkly of apocalyptic violence and the need to cleanse the country of Macoutes. "I don't have to campaign," he told reporter Don Bohning of the *Miami Herald*. "It's the people who will do the campaigning."[10]

"Titid's not like the others," explained one market woman, "he does not have any woman, so he wouldn't be spending the country's money on fancy cars and diamond necklaces. He's pure."[11] But the business class distrusted him. "He is a cross between the Ayatollah and Fidel," groused one. "If it comes to a choice between the ultra-left and the ultra-right, I'm ready for an alliance with the ultra-right."[12]

Election day, December 16, 1990, passed without incident. Voters were asked to choose a president from among eleven CEP-approved candidates, 27 senators from 119 approved candidates, and 83 deputies from among 337 candidates, as well as municipal and local administrative councils. More than a thousand international observers were called upon to supervise approximately 14,000 election offices. A team of international observers visited each presidential candidate the morning of the sixteenth to assure them that the balloting was proceeding smoothly and to ask if they would respect the results if they didn't win. All answered affirmatively, except Father Aristide, who insisted that if he didn't win it followed that the elections were rigged.

After preliminary results were announced the next morning, thousands of Haitians took to the streets waving branches stripped from trees, singing, shouting, dancing with joy, and crowing like the rooster that was Aristide's campaign symbol. Father Aristide had won by a landslide! The official tally, announced eight days later, showed him garnering 67.5 percent of the vote, followed by Marc Bazin with 14.2 percent. OAS observer Henry F. Carey pointed out later that of 3,227,115 registered voters, only 1,640,729 (50.8 percent) had bothered to vote and over 300,000 ballots were lost.[13]

The enormity of what had happened took a few days to sink in. On January 2, François-Wolff Ligondé, the conservative archbishop of Port-au-Prince, expressed what many upper- and middle-class Haitians were feeling. "Fear is sending a chill down the spines of many fathers and mothers. Is socialist Bolshevism going to triumph?" he asked his congregation, which included many of the most influential people in Haiti. "Is the country heading toward a new dictatorship?"[14]

One week later, on the evening of January 6, 1991, the sound of automatic weapons fire and explosions jarred Port-au-Prince residents as they lay down to sleep. President Ertha Pascal-Trouillot was at home with her family when the driver of an armored personnel carrier (APC) knocked on her door and told her he was escorting her to the Presidential Palace. On the way the APC driver stopped to pick up another passenger, a balding, heavyset man whom Trouillot could not recognize in the dark. Only after arriving at the Palace did she learn that her companion was Roger Lafontant and that she had been taken hostage in a coup attempt.

Shortly before one, she was forced to go on the radio and in a quaking voice deliver her resignation. Following her came the raspy, baritone voice of Papa Doc's former Macoute henchman Roger Lafontant. He had assumed power as "provisional president," he said, in order to rescue the country from an election that he called a "masquerade" and "a scathing insult."

While Lafontant sat in the Palace, calling friends and army officers to rally support, word spread house to house throughout the poor sections of Port-au-Prince. An angry din of banging pots and shouting rose from all parts of the city. By 9 A.M. when General Abraham directed an assault on the Palace, his soldiers had to wade through thousands of Aristide supporters waving machetes and pick-axes and demanding Lafontant's head. After a fifteen-minute battle Lafontant and his men were taken into custody. Meanwhile, the furious mobs went on a rampage.

Before the army was able to restore order, mobs stormed the Vatican Embassy, seized the Papal Nuncio, and forced him into the street, where they stripped and beat him and his secretary. They sacked and burned the nunciature; sacked the home of Trouillot's interior minister; sacked and burned the residence of Archbishop Ligondé, who had managed to escape the country; and burned the 220-year-old wooden cathedral. They also vented their rage on the houses, stores, and businesses of suspected Macoutes. When the violence ended, by the afternoon of January 7, seventy to a hundred people had been killed. Many had been subjected to *Père Lebrun*, a practice named after a local tire advertisement, whereby a tire was placed around a victim's neck, filled with gasoline, and set on fire.

President-elect Aristide tried to calm the rioting throngs by calling for "vigilance without vengeance." He also telephoned General Abraham on the night of the January 7 and informed him that he was assuming power immediately. "No, you're not," answered General Abraham, who argued that Father Aristide would not only be violating the Constitution, he would also be interrupting run-off elections for the Senate and Chamber of Deputies scheduled to be held January 20.[15]

President-elect Aristide addressed his followers via radio on January 9:

Brothers and sisters . . . I note that you are at the same time happy and sad, happy because Roger Lafontant and other terrorists like him are in jail, and sad, because he and his accomplices are not in your hands.[16]

Less than a month later, on February 7, 1991, five years to the day since Baby Doc's flight into exile, Jean-Bertrand Aristide was sworn in as President of Haiti. In the days leading up to the event, his euphoric followers, the denizens of the *bidonvilles* of Port-au-Prince, proudly refurbished the city—cleaning, painting, stringing decorated plastic soda bottles across streets like Chinese lanterns, lining streets and paths with pastel-colored pebbles, and covering walls with murals. It was the moment of transcendence for the popular movement, which President Aristide celebrated with a torrent of extravagant prose: "Dear friends, ladies and gentlemen: I am greeting you, as you know, as an avalanche member [*l'avalassment*]. We walked as an avalanche; we arrived as an avalanche; we are continuing to organize ourselves as an avalanche, an avalanche of love which is covering our country . . . My heart is basking in this avalanche of love. That is why I cannot help myself from making to you a declaration of my love. . . ."[17]

More than a third of Haitians who had voted against the popular priest, listened with trepidation. They included most of the business class, many army officers, and most of the political parties. What kind of president would they be getting? they asked themselves. Would he be the man who said, "Titid and the people are one," and saw himself as a revolutionary prophet? Or would their new president transform himself into a politician who would use his popularity to build a consensus government and a country in which all Haitians who played by the rules could live in peace?

To some, including General Abraham, who stood to the right of Aristide on inauguration day, the new president revealed his approach later in his speech when he addressed the army. First, President Aristide spoke of a wedding between the Haitian military and the people. "Today, the wedding will be celebrated as it should be," he declared. "It will be celebrated in love, love that I feel for you, my brother Lieutenant General Abraham. Allow me to tell you before the whole world, before the Haitian nation, I love you. I love you very much, as much as I love the Haitian army." But Aristide's love didn't prevent him from then staging a *coup de théâtre* and asking the general "for an act of confidence." He wanted General Abraham to retire six officers, whom he went on to name, and promote eight others including Colonel Raoul Cédras to general chief of staff. "You can applaud," the new president added, "because what I am asking will be for the good of all of you."[18]

General Abraham did not applaud. That night in a private meeting with President Aristide, he tendered his resignation. President Aristide insisted that he stay on. Only, answered the general, if you support me in maintaining the independence and professionalism of the FADH. General Abraham went on to explain that the best security for Aristide's new government, or any democratic government for that matter, could be provided by an army that was strictly nonpartisan. President Aristide said that he too wanted a professional, nonpartisan military. But as General Abraham would see on other occasions, the new president had what another aide called "a double personality." He would appear perfectly reasonable and conciliatory when he spoke to you directly, but then take action through intermediaries that was much more radical and provocative.

Outgoing provisional president Ertha Pascal-Trouillot met at least two faces of her successor's psyche on the reviewing stand at his inauguration. After delivering a speech praising "the recent free elections" which "have given democracy true meaning in our country," President Aristide then handed Trouillot an arrest warrant. According to an eyewitness: "He praised her, came over and kissed her on both cheeks, and handed her an envelope, which she thought was a thank you letter."[19] She was being charged with conspiring with Roger Lafontant to thwart the elections.

Months later, when Mrs. Trouillot was placed under house arrest, President Aristide himself came to call on her, bearing a bouquet of flowers. She remembered that he had tears in his eyes when he told her how sorry he was that she had been arrested. "When he says things, he really believes them," said Mrs. Trouillot months later. "He could turn off that part of his brain that had me arrested in the first place."[20]

The day following his inauguration, President Aristide threw open the gates of the Palace to thousands of streets kids, beggars, and cripples. "Today, I'm here to say to you that you are human beings just as important as anyone else," he said addressing the ragged throng. "Rich and poor, we're all people, and we must love one another."

President Aristide stated in his autobiography that he envisioned a "direct" democracy rather than a representative one. "The democracy to be built," he wrote, "should be in the image of Lavalas: participatory, uncomplicated and in permanent motion."[21] He set out to govern without resolving, or even acknowledging, the contradiction between his vision of democracy and the constitution he swore to uphold.

From his first days in office, President Aristide was hearing two sets of voices. One, which featured local business leaders and U.S. ambassador Alvin Adams, urged him to build a consensus and to slowly and legally reform and rebuild the system. The other, which consisted of a tight circle of supporters, told him to scour the country in a flood of radical change, as promised under the banner of Lavalas.

Although President Aristide acknowledged the political logic of the first, he usually was swayed by the drama of the second. According to a longtime Haitian friend of his who was also a political ally, "Aristide is a zealot at heart who sees people and especially Haitian politics in terms of good and evil. Those who are on his side, the people's side, are good; those who resist him are evil or do so for evil reasons. And the drama of it excites him. That's why he likes to play the game, to make bold gestures. In his mind he's outsmarting the devil."[22]

President Aristide's approach quickly put him at loggerheads with both houses of Parliament. The party that had sponsored his campaign, the FNCD, had won only twenty-seven of eighty-three seats in the Chamber of Deputies and thirteen of twenty-seven seats in the Senate. Instead of working to build a coalition of support, Aristide jettisoned the FNCD—the left-of-center coalition of intellectuals and labor and grass-roots political leaders. "From the start we were shut out of the process," complained FNCD senator Jean Robert Martinez. "The President didn't even talk to me."[23]

In place of the FNCD, President Aristide began to rely heavily on Lavalas, an unstructured movement of affluent idealists and long-exiled leftists who had helped finance his campaign. "These folks came right out of another era," explained one diplomat. "Their political models were Paris in 1968 and the Cultural Revolution in China."[24] And they viewed the Parliament as an adversary. "For Lavalas, Parliament became a negation of the power the people gave Aristide," explained Jean-Claude Bajeux, a human rights advocate and Aristide supporter. "They reasoned that Aristide should have had all the power because he was the people."[25]

Thus, the stage was set for conflict from the first days of Aristide's presidency. From judicial appointments to ambassadorial nominations, he repeatedly bypassed the Parliament, whose advice and consent role was clearly established by the constitution. He also made sweeping reforms by decree, abolishing the rural *chefs de section* and eliminating over two thousand federal jobs in an effort to gain control over the government. But instead of reforming the system or creating something better in its place, he simply filled the old *chef de section* posts with Lavalas loyalists.

In June, when enlisted men and sailors rebelled against their officers, President Aristide personally intervened and seemed to take the side of the *ti soldats*—the enlisted men. Officers grumbled that he was deliberately trying to undermine their authority. They also pointed to the creation by President Aristide of a 200- to 300-man presidential security force, known as the SSP, which was to be trained by Swiss experts.

General Abraham, who had been on an inspection tour of rural units, returned to Port-au-Prince to meet with the president the first week of July. Although Aristide urged the commander-in-chief to stay on, General Abraham stated "that the President and his close advisors had created conditions which made it impossible for me to continue."[26] To replace the highly respected General Abraham, President Aristide chose General Raoul Cédras. But according to intelligence sources, President Aristide had to "pay General Cédras big money" to convince him to take the job.[27] Then, in what was perceived as an insult to Cédras and the army, President Aristide never made Cédras's appointment permanent and never formally submitted the general's nomination to the legislature as required by the constitution.

Three weeks later, the situation turned uglier. One afternoon, an officer loyal to Colonel Cherubin (President Aristide's new police chief), Captain Neptune, got into a confrontation with four teenagers in a supermarket parking lot. After shooting one of the youths in the arm, he called another officer, Lieutenant Salomon. Salomon—who earlier had been cashiered by Colonel Cédras for sadism—arrived on the scene and arrested the four youths and a bystander. He later claimed that the five men tried to escape and were shot. But he couldn't explain why they were found lined up on the ground with their hands tied behind their backs. According to the U.S. embassy, they had been beaten and electrocuted and shot at close range.[28]

General Cédras ordered an immediate investigation, which found that the youths had been wrongly executed and recommended that Salomon be tried for murder in a civilian court. Both Colonel Cherubin and President Aristide tried to intervene on Lieutenant Salomon's behalf. The Salomon case became a test of wills between the army, which was trying to maintain its independence from the president, and the police, which was increasingly dominated by Aristide loyalists.

The constitutional crisis reached a peak in August 1991 when legislators threatened to introduce a motion of no confidence against Aristide's prime minister Réne Préval. After the legislators refused to back down, a mob of over two thousand Aristide supporters surrounded the Parliament and threatened anyone who voted for the measure with Père Lebrun. That same week, the headquarters of the FNCD was sprayed with bullets, the offices of FNCD mayor Evans Paul were stoned, and the headquarters of a labor union loyal to the FNCD was burned by Aristide supporters.

Increasingly, President Aristide seemed to be relying on the mobs, sometimes appealing to them in terms that were shockingly incendiary.

During the circus-like trial of Roger Lafontant, which had gotten under way in July, tremendous crowds of *lavalassiens*, responding to direct calls from President Aristide, engulfed the courthouse brandishing tires and matches. When the ex-Macoute leader tried to take the stand to defend himself, the howling mobs surged toward the courthouse doors.

A week later, President Aristide addressed a group of secondary school graduates in Croix de Bouquets, a suburb of Port-au-Prince.

"In front of the courthouse, for twenty-four hours, Père Lebrun became a good firm bed [a Creole phrase for support]. Inside the courthouse, the Justice Minister had the law in his hands, the people had their good firm bed outside. The people had their little matches in their hands. They had gas nearby. Did they use it?"

"No!" shouted the students.

"But if things didn't go as they should, would the people have given Père Lebrun?" asked the President.

"Yes!" was the enthusiastic reply.

"That's why when you're learning," continued Aristide, "you will learn to write Père Lebrun, you will learn to think about Père Lebrun. You will have to use it when you must, the way you are supposed to and when you have to."[29]

Many Haitians were alarmed. What had happened to the priest who had promised "democracy" and "the perfume of love?"

By September, discontent with President Aristide had reached a critical mass in the army, the Parliament, and the business community. By the middle of the month, as the president prepared to leave for New York to address the United Nations, rumors of a coup were rampant.

High above the city in Petionville, the conspiracy had already begun. A group of wealthy businessmen from the Accra, Halloun, Shemali, Hamdal, and Bigio families had started to raise money for a coup in late July. They were joined by legislators and disgruntled FADH officers. One of them, Major Michel François, had once been General Abraham's executive officer and was now commander of the downtown police headquarters, known as the Cafeteria. The thirty-four-year-old François had been the man in charge of the security of Parliament back in August when Aristide had given his supporters orders to burn it down. "I stopped it!" he declared. From then on Aristide had "hated him," he said, and gave orders to General Cédras to have him transferred, but Cédras refused.[30]

Described by a colleague as a "hard-core right-wing officer" who "has a tendency to get the job done," François began to prepare for a coup d'état. The wealthy families put up money for food, at least one shipment of two thousand Uzis and Galil assault rifles, and money to pay for bribes. They even lent their trucks and jeeps. According to one report, key commanders received as much as five thousand dollars a piece. "The rich helped us because we saved them," Major François later explained.[31]

Fearing for the safety of their leader, thousands of pro-Aristide supporters met the president when he returned on Friday, September 27, from delivering his speech before the UN General Assembly. They engulfed his entourage in a protective sea as it made its way to the Palace. There the president addressed tens of thousands of his wild, cheering supporters in his most famous and controversial speech. His tone was defiant. He began with an appeal to the rich:

This money you have is not really yours. You acquired it through criminal activity. You made it plundering, by embezzling. . . . You made it under repressive regimes. . . . Today, seven months after 7 February, on a day ending in seven, I give one last chance. I ask you to take this chance, because you will not have two or three chances, only one. Otherwise, it will not be good for you . . .[32]

He went on to implore senators and deputies to "work together with the people" because "we prefer to fail with the masses than succeed without them." Then, he upped the ante:

If I catch a thief, a robber, a swindler, or an embezzler, if you catch a fake lavalas . . . If you catch someone who does not deserve to be where he is, do not fail to give him what he deserves. [crowd cheers] . . .
What a nice tool! What a nice instrument! [loud cheers] What a nice device! [crowd cheers] It is a pretty one. It is elegant, attractive, splendorous, graceful and dazzling. It smells good. Wherever you go, you feel like smelling it. [crowd cheers] . . .[33]

To those listening to their president there was no doubt that he was referring to the practice of vigilante justice known as Père Lebrun. Later, his apologists would claim that he was alluding to the constitution or, according to one, "it is entirely possible that, as in the past, he is being mistranslated."[34] But the speech was captured on videotape for all to see and hear.

During the night and into Saturday, shooting could be heard coming from Cité Soleil and Carrefours as soldiers fought off Aristide supporters who tried to disarm them. Several soldiers were necklaced as was former presidential candidate Silvio Claude, who had issued a statement condemning President Aristide's call to violence. On Saturday night, President Aristide said that he "called General Cédras to ask his feelings about the [coup] rumors, to which I still gave little credence. He supported me in my skepticism," President Aristide wrote in his autobiography, "and we laughed about it together."[35]

On Sunday, however, the revolt gathered steam. According to one U.S. embassy official, it was not well organized, "but a bit of a rolling ball that picked up speed and support." It started among soldiers of the *Engin Lourdes* mechanized unit and the downtown police headquarters, the Cafeteria.

President Aristide's suburban house in La Plaine came under fire late Sunday afternoon. "By evening there was no doubt about the rebellion," he wrote. "My house was surrounded and bullets were splattering against its walls. . . . That night was shattered by cries and by the incessant noise of automatic weapons."

The next morning, Monday, French ambassador Jean-Raphael Dufour arrived with an armored car and offered to escort the president to the National Palace. Before he left, President Aristide telephoned the commander of the national penitentiary and ordered that Roger Lafontant be executed in his cell.[36] "Along the route we were attacked several times," Aristide remembered. Finally, they reached the Palace and the company of presidential guards. President Aristide was convinced that these *ti soldats* would protect him. But in twos and threes they abandoned him until he was left alone in the Palace with several aides. Soon, another group of soldiers came bearing handcuffs. They seized the president, whose suit and head were splattered with a bodyguard's blood, and led him across the street to military headquarters. "They tied him up," a soldier was heard screaming over Army Radio. "All they need now is to throw a tire around his neck. My God, my God!"[37]

The scene was chaotic. General Cédras was watching from the balcony of military headquarters when he saw a soldier put his pistol up to President Aristide's head and prepare to pull the trigger. "But I shouted down to him to stop, to bring him upstairs instead," said Cédras.[38] Soon the general's office was teeming with enlisted men. "There was a great mass of them . . . rankers, the lot," he recalled. "I couldn't tell who they all were. They were enraged, ready to tear him [Aristide] limb from limb, because his mobs were burning them alive in outposts across town."[39] One U.S. official who arrived later to help negotiate with the soldiers to spare Aristide's life confirmed Cédras's description. "It's not true that the officers were in charge," he said. "It was very touch and go."[40]

"Aristide was here in this chair," said Cédras to a reporter as he reenacted the scene. "So I jumped in front of him to shield his body, and I told them not to touch a hair on his head. That's not the way we do things here any more." According to Cédras and others, Aristide was so frightened that he wept and vomited. "He humiliated himself," Cédras said later. "I think he can never forgive me for being present at that sad scene."[41]

President Aristide remembered it differently. "Cédras is pleased with himself," he wrote in his autobiography. "The officers drink to his health. There is the atmosphere of a macabre festival alongside the bloodied faces of my friends. I myself have my hands tied. They try to humiliate me. The military discuss my fate in loud tones. 'We ought to kill him.' They almost get into an argument about who will have the pleasure to do it."[42]

It was only after the intervention of the U.S., French, and Venezuelan ambassadors that Aristide's life was spared. Late Monday night he sat in the empty Port-au-Prince airport waiting for the plane that was being sent by Venezuelan president Carlos Andrés Pérez to fly him into exile.

Meanwhile, General Cédras was making a statement on nationwide radio. "Today, the armed forces find themselves obligated to assume the heavy responsibility to keep the ship of state afloat," he began. "After seven months of democratic experience, the country once again finds itself prey to the horrors of uncertainty. With all Haitians, we will bring the ship to port."[43]

Violence continued over the next few days as, according to a State Department report, "Haitian troops engaged in random shootings and selected killings of residents in poor neighborhoods who were suspected pro-Aristide organization leaders."[44] The Department of State's *Country Report on Human Rights Practises for 1991* concluded that "credible estimates placed the dead nationwide during this post-coup period at between 300 and 500."[45]

General Cédras still maintains that he knew nothing about the coup before it happened. But General Abraham, for one, finds that "impossible to believe."[46] Said a friend of Cédras: "He likes to play the part of the reluctant debutante."[47] Deposed president Aristide and his aides harbored no doubts about the general's complicity. "Cédras betrayed Aristide, pure and simple," said one close friend of the Haitian president.[48]

Whether General Cédras had conspired or not, President Aristide's eight months in office had shaken Haiti's political confidence to the core. Now the two men were being asked to help restore Haiti's political confidence. Neither man had shown a preference for statesmanship or compromise before.

CHAPTER 12

Reconciliation

"Haitians to an astonishing degree . . . live on their nerves."

—Haitian writer J. C. DORSAINVIL

The New York Pact signed by forty-odd Haitian politicians at one o'clock on Saturday morning, July 17, 1993, called for "a political truce to guarantee a smooth and peaceful transition." It was the first step toward implementing the Governors Island Agreement signed by President Aristide and General Raoul Cédras only two weeks earlier. It also marked an opportunity for the Haitian Parliament to take back some of the political initiative. Up until July 1993 the Parliament had been "pretty much of a vague unknown nonentity," according to a U.S. embassy official. During President Aristide's seven-month reign, it had been ignored and pushed aside.

Now, the international community was taking their constitutional role seriously. Dante Caputo's deputy, Leandro Despouy, together with his "collaborator" Juliette Remy, returned to Port-au-Prince at the end of July to help guide the legislators through the specific steps toward implementation of the New York Pact.

Specifically, the two political blocs—the pro-military Alliance and the pro-Aristide Constitutionalists—had to agree on a slate of new officers for the Senate and Chamber of Deputies. Once the two chambers were "normalized" they could ratify President Aristide's new prime minister and that prime minister's program of government. With those steps accomplished, the punitive UN sanctions imposed against the de facto military government in June would be lifted.

In July U.S. special advisor Lawrence Pezzullo and UN/OAS special envoy Dante Caputo both tried to convince President Aristide to agree to lift the sanctions sooner. They argued that now that Cédras had accepted President Aristide's return to Haiti, the economic suffering of the country could be spared. But President Aristide wanted the sanctions to remain. In fact, he asked that they stay in place until *after* his scheduled return to Haiti on October 30. In a letter to Special Advisor Pezzullo, Aristide's lawyer Mike Barnes argued that sanctions should stay in place as a "demonstration of outrage over the tragic circumstances in the country."[1]

The New York Pact also stated that once the new prime minister and his government were approved, the Parliament would consider and pass several new laws submitted to them by President Aristide dealing with amnesty for the leaders of the 1991 coup d' état and the creation of a civilian police force separate from the army.

Although diplomats in New York and Washington were speaking as though the normalization of Parliament was a foregone conclusion that would be accomplished in a few days, Leandro Despouy and Juliette Remy discovered that the reality was much more difficult. Together with Ellen Cosgrove, Lou Nigro, and the newly assigned chargé d'affaires, Vicki Huddleston, of the U.S. embassy, they began to develop a keen sense of the complex personalities and dynamics of the Haitian legislature.

First, it became apparent that Police Chief Michel François and FADH chief of staff Phillipe Biamby were working behind the scenes against the Governors Island Agreement. François was paying off members of the Alliance and using intimidation. Biamby's role was much more shadowy and ambiguous. Following the coup of September 1991, he had been brought back into the army by General Cédras because Cédras felt he needed someone like Biamby, who had rapport with the rank and file. To many soldiers, General Cédras had two strikes against him. First, he had been a protégé of President Aristide, rising from colonel to commander-in-chief of the FADH in less than seven months. Secondly, Cédras had never really commanded troops. "He was a loner and saw himself as an intellectual," said a fellow officer. "He didn't have the common touch."[2]

His rival, Colonel Michel François, a thickly built man of thirty-six, possessed the straightforward manner of a street kid who had made his way up the ranks. Common soldiers liked him and related to him easily. "You'll find his type in any man's army," explained Malval. "Ambitious, tough and capable of killing. Cédras is much more dignified and aloof."[3]

The newcomer, Phillipe Biamby, was able to exploit the rivalry between Cédras and François, both of whom were his friends. Biamby heard firsthand from François how Cédras had negotiated an honorable exit for himself at Governors Island and had pushed the blame for the coup onto François.

Although Biamby, in the words of someone who knows him, "is not a very intelligent man, or a good politician, he knows how to get around."

"He was the most sinister of the three," explained Despouy, "because he was the one who was always absolutely opposed to a solution to the crisis. When Michel François turned against the Governors Island Agreement, Biamby helped Michel and started intriguing against the agreement."[4]

And Biamby was in a perfect position to do so. His ties to General Cédras were personal and strong. Not only had they graduated together from the military academy, but Biamby was an intimate of Cédras's wife, Yannick. Friends reported that they had been lovers off and on for years. Both of their fathers had served prominently in the government of Papa Doc Duvalier.

Like many hard-core Duvalierists, Phillipe Biamby was an adept of voudoun with ties to the secret black magic society of Bizango. Unmarried and avidly interested in pornography, he was a physical fitness enthusiast who liked to brag about his stamina. "The guy was vicious in every sense of the word," explained Robert Malval. "Something that tells you a lot about him is that at the age of eleven he shot himself in the stomach in order to find out how it would feel."[5]

Back in April 1989, Biamby was a commander of the Presidential Guard that participated in an attempted coup against General Prosper Avril, and Michel François was under his command. When the plot failed, Biamby and his two coconspirators were sent into exile.

After the coup that toppled President Aristide, Biamby returned to Haiti. According to friends, he was down on his luck and gambling heavily. But he was still ambitious and asked his friends Cédras and François to let him back into the army. Convinced that Biamby could act as his enforcer, Cédras took him back, promoted him to brigadier general, and made him chief of staff of the FADH.

Michel François felt that by reinstating Biamby he was returning a favor. Back in 1986, François was a rebellious, young officer who was about to be thrown out of the service. Biamby intervened on his behalf and secured a scholarship for François to study in the United States.

The UN envoys Leandro Despouy and Juliette Remy didn't know all this in August 1993. But they were learning that those Constitutionalists who had refused to sign the New York Pact—Firmin Jean-Louis, Jacques Rony Mondestin, and others—were turning into the pact's greatest defenders. "The irony," noted Remy, "was typical of Haitians."[6] A man of fierce political ambition—and of "wildly uncertain character" in the words of one U.S. diplomat—Firmin Jean-Louis realized that the pact could help him.[7] Specifically, he wanted to be president of the Senate. By holding up the normalization and the lifting of sanctions he could get his way.

Back in Washington, President Aristide accepted an invitation offered by American businessmen with investments in Haiti to meet with the U.S. and Haitian private sector in south Florida a week after the signing of the New York Pact. Robert Malval, who had been asked by Aristide to organize the conference, expected it to fail. "Up to that point, the big families had been opposed to Aristide's return," he later explained. "To my surprise, not only did they accept, but people were fighting to get on board."[8]

The deposed president delivered a moving speech about the need for reconciliation. Then, he and M. Raymond Roy, head of the Haitian Chamber of Commerce, embraced each other on the podium. "I love you," President Aristide declared.[9] After watching these two scions of vastly different, and often hostile, sectors of Haitian society vow to work together, two Alliance senators who were sitting in the audience—Jutnel Jean and Serge Joseph—met with President Aristide and expressed their desire to switch parties. Other politicians intimated that money changed hands. Whatever their motivation, the switch of allegiances had major repercussions, because it changed the balance among the seventeen legitimate members of the Senate. Now the Constitutionalists (or FNCD bloc) held a one-vote majority.

The situation in the Chamber of Deputies was equally complicated since Colonel Michel François was pressuring Alliance deputies not to attend sessions of Parliament. "For days and days we were trying to get a quorum and those guys were too afraid," noted Remy.[10]

UN envoy Leandro Despouy started holding talks with the Parliamentarians in his room at the Montana Hotel. Within days it became clear that a compromise could be reached in the Chamber of Deputies. The Alliance, which held a distinct majority in the Chamber, was led by Antoine Joseph. Joseph, a forthright and honest man in his late thirties who was friendly with both Cédras and François, understood that the Governors Island agreement was the best hope for a political truce in his country. "He was one of the keys," said Remy, "even though he represented a generation that came from a Duvalierist background."[11] Joseph proposed that the majority party in the Chamber receive three of the five top offices. Under that arrangement the president, vice president, and first secretary would go to the Alliance. The second secretary and *questeur* (or treasurer) would go to the FNCD. On July 22, after a day of blatant delaying tactics by pro-Aristide deputies, Joseph defeated his FNCD rival, Pierre Canal Rindal, for the office of president and the Chamber was effectively normalized.

Leandro Despouy offered the same arrangement to the Senate. But since two Alliance members—Jutnel Jean and Serge Joseph—had switched parties giving the Constitutionalists a one-vote majority, the situation was much more volatile. The Constitutionalists, afraid that the two senators would be pressured to change their votes again, refused to sit in Parliament. Also, Firmin Jean-Louis was determined to secure the position of president even though he was widely disliked. The Constitutionalists put forward their own candidate, Jacques Rony Mondestin, for *questeur* (or treasurer). This put him up against popular Alliance member Julio Larosiliere, who already held that position.

U.S. special advisor Pezzullo felt it was time to put pressure on President Aristide. "We were getting good information that Aristide was using his people to block the process," Pezzullo explained.[12] With the help

of Mike Kozak he drafted a memo to the White House advising President
Clinton "to have a frank talk with the President [Aristide] about his intentions." The meeting took place on Thursday, July 22. President Aristide
was invited first to the State Department, where he met with Secretary
of State Warren Christopher and Special Advisor Pezzullo. "Christopher
was at his best," Pezzullo remembered. "Basically, the secretary told
Aristide that we expected full cooperation from him." President Aristide
"squirmed like a schoolboy as Christopher laid it out clearly," Pezzullo
reported. "Aristide realized he'd been caught."[13]

"But the White House let the ball slip," Pezzullo said. When he and
Christopher arrived at the Oval Office there were fifteen people in the
room. "It was the wrong setting for a dressing down," said Pezzullo. "It
would have been humiliating to Aristide for President Clinton to speak
candidly with so many members of the administration present."[14]

The Haitian president, sensing that he could turn the meeting his way,
diverted the subject to the recent increase in human rights abuses in his
country. President Clinton listened with concern. The campaign to play
the human rights issue had started two days earlier when Haiti's ambassador to the United States, Jean Casimir, had requested an urgent meeting of the OAS. UN international civilian mission chief Colin Granderson
reported to the U.S. embassy in Port-au-Prince that allegations that
human rights abuses had increased in recent days were unfounded.[15]

Having seized the initiative at the White House, President Aristide
waxed on for thirty minutes. Afterward all President Clinton could say to
reporters was: "I'm excited about this process. There's a major potential
for a victory for democracy here."[16]

Three days later President Aristide did name his candidate for prime
minister. The respected publisher Robert Malval struck most diplomats
as both a curious and welcome choice. An eloquent and sincere man,
the fifty-year-old Malval had been a longtime supporter of Aristide and a
member of his delegation at Governors Island. The problem was that he
had no political experience and was almost completely unknown by the
political players in Haiti. Malval, as was his style, made no secret of this
fact. "We are not a political bunch or a gang, my family," he told reporters
in accent-free English he had learned while studying at the University
of Miami. "But we have always had a dream, and that is the creation of a

state where rights are respected." He characterized his view of politics in two words: "tough and vicious."[17]

What Pezzullo, Caputo, Despouy, and most Western diplomats didn't understand was that in choosing Malval, Aristide knew he was getting a prime minister who could never steal his popularity. Not only was Malval an extremely cultivated man with fine manners and European tastes, he was also a mulatto. According to one U.S. diplomat: "He is practically white."[18]

Meanwhile, the political atmosphere in Port-au-Prince was growing tenser by the day. Senators, who had already received threats, had to wade through crowds of hostile police *attachés* sent by Colonel François when they arrived for reconciliation talks at the Montana Hotel. And the logjam continued. "There was complete stubbornness on the part of the Constitutionalists," said UN envoy Juliette Remy.[19] The man who had become key to her and Leandro Despouy's efforts to normalize the Senate was Alliance senator Julio Larosiliere. Larosiliere represented a bloc of four or five other Alliance senators who were willing to work toward normalization. Even though they didn't trust President Aristide, they believed in the return of constitutional government. The remaining Alliance senators, however, at the direction of Michel François, were trying to impede the process. Prominent among them were Eddy Dupiton and Bernard Sansaricq.

For three days and nights in early August, Haitian senators remained at the Hotel Montana in an attempt to break the deadlock. "We were meeting in the morning with the FNCD; meeting in the afternoon with the Alliance; meeting again at night with the Constitutionalists; and so on," remembered Remy. "There were literally a hundred politicians coming in, discussing, having fights in the hallways."[20]

"It is impossible to describe the climate of intimidation and lunacy," wrote Despouy. "The hotel had been transformed into the Parliament with groups of senators meeting in different rooms, afraid to leave for fear of being kidnapped."[21] The hallways were teeming with journalists; in the parking lot plainclothes "attachés" waited for a chance to intimidate anyone entering or leaving the hotel. Every three or four hours, Dupiton, Sansaricq, or some other Alliance senator would arrive to hold a press conference in which they would denounce the whole process as "a conspiracy of the international community." As for representatives of the Four Friends who witnessed the whole process, "they were getting completely fed up," said Remy. "They were saying someone has to be reasonable."[22] They would spend hours and hours waiting for meetings that sometimes didn't get underway until nine or ten at night.

Meanwhile, in Washington, President Aristide kept expressing his reluctance to involve himself in the Senate debate. On August 4 in a meeting with Father Adrien of Aristide's Presidential Commission, UN special envoy Dante Caputo threatened to call for an immediate lifting of sanctions if pro-Aristide legislators did not cooperate in normalizing the Senate.

Leandro Despouy and Juliette Remy still hadn't been able to convince Senator Thomas Eddy Dupiton to attend the talks at the Montana. On the evening of July 27 Dupiton was shot at from a passing car and wounded in the arm. From his hospital bed, the Alliance president of the Senate blamed "pro-Aristide forces." When he returned home a few days later, Dupiton seemed to soften his position. He would participate in the talks if the Constitutionalists were reasonable, he said.

Later that day, Saturday, August 7, Haitian senators finally seemed to reach a compromise. The president, vice president, and first secretary positions in the Senate would go to the FNCD; and the second secretary and *questeur* would go to the Alliance. It was the same arrangement that Despouy had proposed two weeks before.

But two Constitutionalist senators, Firmin Jean-Louis and Jacques Rony Mondestin, refused to accept the deal unless their personal demands were met. Adding to the drama, Jutnel Jean, one of the senators who had switched allegiances from the Alliance to the FNCD, suddenly disappeared. The Montana resounded with rumors: Jutnel Jean had been kidnapped; the Constitutionalists had spirited him out of the country to protect him; the Alliance had forced him to leave.

Hurrying back and forth between Dupiton's house and the Hotel Montana, Despouy quickly worked out the rest of the compromise. The Alliance would accept Firmin Jean-Louis as the new president of the Senate. In return, the Constitutionalists would accept Julio Larosiliere as *questeur*. If Jutnel Jean couldn't be found, one of the Alliance senators would refrain from voting.

A special session of the Senate was set to convene the next day at noon. That night and into the next morning, Leandro Despouy, Juliette Remy, and Max Duboyer sent out invitations signed by current Senate president Franck Léonard to all political figures, journalists, and diplomats. Since the eighty-five-year-old Léonard wasn't there, his signature had to be forged. By 5 A.M., the bleary diplomats were grabbing paper and envelopes without paying close attention to what they were doing. Inadvertently, they sent out some invitations, including those to General Cédras and the director for human rights of the UN Civilian Mission, Ian Martin, in UN envelopes.

The next morning Ian Martin was livid. According to Remy: "He screamed at us for sending out invitations from the Haitian Parliament in envelopes that read UN Civilian Mission to Haiti!"[23] Martin was convinced that the faux pas would provoke an international incident and compromise the independence of his mission.

Despouy had more immediate problems. Gathered at the Montana were Remy, several officers from the U.S. Embassy, and the Four Friends representatives. Everyone else—diplomats, journalists, and the leading political figures in Haiti—were at the Parliament. Despouy was awaiting word from Julio Larosiliere that the parliamentary session, scheduled for noon, would proceed as planned. It was already 11:30. Two hours later the entire Alliance bloc arrived at the Montana to say that Colonel Michel François's favorite senators, Dupiton and Sansaricq, were threatening to block the agreement that had been worked out the day before.

"The Four Friends representatives were completely fed up," remembered Remy. "They were saying that the normalization would never take place."[24] After quickly consulting with Despouy, Julio Larosiliere went to Parliament and announced that the meeting was being adjourned for three days.

"It was like a weird movie," remembered Remy.

Finally, Tuesday, August 10, arrived and Leandro Despouy and Juliette Remy traveled to Parliament for the big event. The modern, airy white building hadn't been occupied for weeks. The water and electricity had been shut off; the garbage hadn't been collected; the hallways hadn't been cleaned. "The smell of overflowing toilets was everywhere," said

Remy.[25] To add to the unwelcome atmosphere, assorted plainclothes atta-chés roamed the halls.

The main part of the building was taken up by the spacious Chamber of Deputies. The Senate chamber consisted of a small room on the first floor that had seats for about forty guests. On that incredibly hot Tuesday morning the room was packed to overflowing with hundreds of diplo-mats and journalists. Politicians and ambassadors sat on the floor near the president's bench. Diplomats were leaning against the walls. One industrial fan moved the thick tropical air.

"It's time for the last act of the comedy," remarked a passing sena-tor.[26] As diplomats and reporters waited and wilted, secretaries and senators could be seen running back and forth. Over the wailing fan, bits of loud discussions drifted in from the hallway. An aide rushed in and whispered into Despouy's ear: "Dupiton and Sansaricq are threatening a boycott!"[27]

The tall Argentine diplomat tried to appear nonplused. For the meet-ing to progress, Dupiton had to resign and eighty-five-year-old Franck Léonard had to be fit enough to preside. Months before under less try-ing circumstances Léonard had gotten so upset that he suffered a heart attack and collapsed.

"You couldn't have asked for more drama," said one U.S. Embassy officer.

After an hour and a half of waiting in the dense heat, Léonard strode in, picked up the gavel, and called the session to order. The remaining six-teen senators hurried in behind him. They seemed to want to get things done. "Good," thought Despouy. "Finally!"[28]

But as the elderly provisional president took attendance, he called out the names of the illegal January 18 senators by mistake. The Constitu-tionalists stood en masse and walked out of the room. "It was a complete collapse," recalled Remy.[29]

After another hour of senators and secretaries scurrying back and forth, Despouy didn't know if he should laugh or cry. He didn't dare leave the room for fear that people would think he was giving up. Again, Franck Léonard strode into the room and read the list of senators. This time he excluded the illegals. Next, Thomas Eddy Dupiton took the floor and delivered a dramatic speech, which was a preamble to his resignation.

Prime Minister Robert Malval seated next to OAS Secretary-General Baena
Soares in late November 1993, a week before Malval submitted his resignation.
(Photo courtesy of Editions Regain/Kursteen Malval and Alice Blanchet)

President Aristide and Haitian Ambassador to the U.S. Jean Casimir arriving at OAS headquarters in Washington, D.C., November 1993. (Photo courtesy of Trina Vithayathil and Alice Blanchet)

President Aristide addresses the press as Ambassador Casimir, Minister of Foreign Affairs Claudette Werleigh, OAS Secretary-General Baena Soares, and U.S. Ambassador to the OAS Harriet Babbitt look on. (Photo courtesy of Trina Vithayathil and Alice Blanchet)

Prime Minister Malval addresses the press in Port-au-Prince. U.S. Ambassador to Haiti William Swing stands second from the right. (Photo courtesy of Trina Vithayathil and Alice Blanchet)

U.S. Special Envoy Lawrence Pezzullo congratulates Prime Minister Malval at Malval's installation at the National Palace in Port-au-Prince, September 2, 1993. (Photo courtesy of Editions Regain/Kursteen Malval and Alice Blanchet)

UN-OAS Envoy Leandro Despouy greets Prime Minister Malval at Malval's installation, September 2, 1993. (Photo courtesy of Editions Regain/Kursteen Malval and Alice Blanchet)

UN-OAS Envoy Dante Caputo with Prime Minister Malval at Malval's installation, September 2, 1993. (Photo courtesy of Editions Regain/Kursteen Malval and Alice Blanchet)

General Raoul Cédras, General Jean-Claude Duperval, and other FAHD leaders at Prime Minister Malval's installation, September 2, 1993. (Photo courtesy of Editions Regain/Kursteen Malval and Alice Blanchet)

Prime Minister Malval greets his new Minister of Justice Guy Malary at the National Palace, September 2, 1993. (Photo courtesy of Editions Regain/Kursteen Malval and Alice Blanchet)

Prime Minister Malval, former Prime Minister René Preval and Senator Firmin Jean-Louis listen as President Aristide speaks, Washington, D.C., September 1993. (Photo courtesy of Editions Regain/Kursteen Malval and Alice Blanchet)

Prime Minister Malval with President Bill Clinton at the White House, January 1994. (Photo courtesy of Editions Regain/Kursteen Malval and Alice Blanchet)

General Raoul Cédras and his wife Yannick, August 1, 1994 (Photo courtesy of Bill Gentile/ Zuma Press)

FAHD soldiers at a FRAPH rally in Port-au-Prince, October 27, 1993 (Photo courtesy of Les Stone/Zuma Press)

Along the way he lacerated the international community and in highly nationalistic language warned that *blancs* (white people) were taking over the country. Remy and Despouy, who were following a written text of the speech, kept asking themselves: "How is this going to work?"[30]

The attacks grew more personal as Bernard Sansaricq took the floor. Pointing to Despouy, "he started accusing him of all sorts of terrible things," remembered Remy. Sansaricq, meanwhile, worked himself up into such a lather that he couldn't finish his speech. As the Alliance senator stormed out of the room, all eyes turned to Léonard. The eighty-five-year-old provisional president appeared lost. "This poor man didn't know what was going on," said Remy. "We're all thinking that he must propose the people who had been agreed upon for the different posts."[31]

After an uncomfortable silence, Despouy got Julio Larosiliere's attention. "He's forgotten what to do," whispered the Argentine in French.[32] Larosiliere quickly refreshed Léonard's memory, and seconds later the provisional president stood to nominate Firmin Jean-Louis for the new president of the Senate. Then, Jean-Louis's FNCD compatriot Jacques Rony Mondestin rose to his feet. He started to denounce the compromise, saying that he hadn't been informed.

At that point another Constitutionalist senator took the floor and for several minutes the two men were shouting at the same time into separate microphones. Suddenly, a moderate from the Constitutionalist group stood and in a deep, booming voice proposed that they move to the next step. An eerie silence fell over the hall. All eyes turned again to Léonard, who now had to tell the senators to vote for a new president. Once again, he was lost. After what journalists described as "an extraordinary silence," Alliance senator Ebrané Cadet seized the initiative. A huge, extremely animated man who later condemned the international community, he felt that it was time for the Parliament to act. "I propose that we nominate Senator Firmin Jean-Louis by acclamation!" boomed the senator. One by one the other legislators stood and clapped their hands.[33]

"It came as a complete surprise," said Despouy.[34] Firmin Jean-Louis stood, puffed out his chest like a rooster, and walked proudly to the bench, where he asked Léonard to step aside so that he could proceed. With the new president elected, the senators went on to approve the other officers by acclamation. And Julio Larosiliere was elected *questeur*. "It all turned out fine," said Remy, who was immensely relieved. "Even the television reporters only transmitted the good part of the proceedings, so everything came off well."[35]

It was the end of a remarkable process that received scant attention in either New York or Washington. "Once Parliament was normalized," concluded Remy, "there was a sense of optimism in the country that the transition to constitutional democracy could really work."[36]

The very next day Antoine Joseph and Firmin Jean-Louis, presidents of the normalized Chamber of Deputies and Senate, traveled to Washington to consult with President Aristide about the composition of his new "government of national concord" as outlined in the New York Pact.

Chamber of Deputies president Antoine Joseph stressed to Aristide that the new government needed to be as inclusive as possible. Joseph even proposed that several moderate Duvalierists be included in the new cabinet. Leandro Despouy, Juliette Remy, Mike Kozak, and Vicki Huddleston all felt that a broad-based, technically qualified cabinet was key to political reconciliation.

When Robert Malval spoke to President Aristide, Aristide said, according to Malval: "Let's keep the cake small. If we have a small cake and give one slice to every party, they'll be happy. If the cake is too big, they'll want more. We'll enlarge the cake after my return on October 30."[37]

Like Joseph, Malval tried to convince Aristide to bring in some opposition figures "to balance things." "I tried to get him to appoint a man like Raymond Roy [president of the Chamber of Commerce] as minister of foreign affairs. I told Aristide bluntly, your people in Washington with Ambassador Casimir handle 99 percent of foreign policy, so the appointment will be largely honorific. I mean, the man was eighty years old."[38]

But Aristide argued that the appointment of Roy would be an insult to Ambassadors Casimir and Longchamps. When Malval proposed other names, President Aristide turned them down, too.

When the appointments were finally announced, most international observers were disappointed. Although several of his choices were capable individuals—in particular Marie-Michele Rey for minister of finance, Victor Benoit for minister of education, and Guy Malary for minister of justice—almost all of them were close sympathizers if not members of Lavalas. At first glance, Aristide's one concession to the military seemed to be the appointment of General Cédras's brother-in-law, Rene Prosper, as minister of interior. But Prosper and his sister, Yannick, weren't even on speaking terms. So what appeared to some as a concession was perceived by the Cédrases as a personal dig. At least Prosper, a former colonel, was respected within the ranks of the FADH. That wasn't the case with Aristide's appointment for minister of defense, Jean Belliote, a well-known homosexual who lived in terror of the FADH general staff.

"The thing [the new government] is Lavalas times Lavalas," concluded one U.S. Embassy official. "It is a catastrophe that risks repeating all the mistakes of the past."

"If this Cabinet was named by Aristide," warned Senator Julio Larosiliere, "he chose it so it would fail."[39]

"If President Aristide was serious about returning to Haiti under the terms of the Governors Island Agreement and reconciling the country, the signals were all wrong," concluded Leandro Despouy.[40] On August 25, Robert Malval and his program of government were approved by the Chamber of Deputies and the Senate. Two days later the UN Security Council voted unanimously to lift the sanctions.

Robert Malval gamely tried to put the best spin on the new government. "In 1991 we had a government of friends of the president," he said in an interview. "Now we have the political allies of the president, what I would call the small concord." Malval, in accepting the position of prime minister, said he would serve only to the end of the year. At that time, he explained, President Aristide had assured him that he would appoint "a government of large concord."[41]

The upshot was that Malval—a man who had no popular support in Haiti—was being saddled by a government that owed its loyalty exclusively to President Aristide. "Aristide never trusted giving anyone that much authority," observed Pezzullo. "If you're not Machiavelian and very conspiratorial, you can't follow the thinking of the man."[42]

Nor did President Aristide seem to be willing to expend any political capital to explain how the transition would work. During the brief debate over Prime Minister Malval's program of government, extremist legislators on both sides raised the specter of the international military and police training missions as a ploy by foreign governments to take over Haiti. Even though President Aristide had formally agreed to invite the international police and military missions, he seemed to be doing nothing to dispel the fear and disinformation spread by some of his Lavalas supporters.

In order to stem this xenophobic tide, Mike Kozak of the Haiti Working Group and Jan Stromson from the Justice Department were dispatched to Port-au-Prince in mid-August. On the morning of August 19, they briefed members of both houses of Parliament. "Once it was explained to them," reported Mike Kozak, "they said: 'That's no problem.' It was clear right away that neither General Cédras nor President Aristide, who had asked for the trainers as part of the Governors Island Agreement, had done anything to explain it to their partisans."[43]

UN envoy Leandro Despouy was in Washington on August 30 for the swearing in of Robert Malval. The new prime minister made a short, heart-felt statement in which he said: "You can kill us, but you will never kill the dream of the people of Haiti."[44]

What struck Despouy as odd was the fact that "no one on Aristide's side or among the crowd of diplomats acknowledged the difficulty of having arrived at the ceremony. It wasn't their ignorance about our efforts that bothered me," explained Despouy, "but the ease with which these people judged that future events would fall into place."[45]

Three days later, on the afternoon of September 2, 1993, Robert Malval was formally sworn in as prime minister in a ceremony at the National Palace in Port-au-Prince. UN/OAS special envoy Dante Caputo and U.S. special advisor Lawrence Pezzullo both flew in for the occasion. "The mood at the Palace was very joyous," remembered Pezzullo. The crowds outside were waving and excited. The city was calm. Jammed together in the Palace public rooms were General Cédras, the high command, the parliamentarians, the diplomat corps, the press, and the Haitian business community. "It must have been 180 degrees in the reception room," said Pezzullo. "I came out soaking wet down to my shoes."[46]

The military arrived with automatic weapons and steel helmets. "I thought Cédras looked like a jerk," commented one diplomat.[47] "If you're looking for subtlety with these people, forget it," said another.[48]

Following the ceremony and Malval's speech, dignitaries were invited upstairs to personally congratulate the new prime minister. The order was determined by the chief of protocol: UN envoys, then the OAS, the

Four Friends ambassadors, the members of Parliament, and so on. The military commanders were eighth. After waiting for five to ten minutes, they turned and walked out.

According to Malval's niece and administrative assistant Alice Blanchet: "It was programmed ahead of time, because their spouses were invited and didn't show up."[49] Whether the officers were looking for a pretext to be insulted or not, the message was clear: The transition was not getting off to a smooth start.

Pezzullo saw further evidence of this later at a reception he attended at U.S. ambassador Charles Redman's residence. Minutes after he arrived, UN special envoy Dante Caputo wandered over with his forehead scrunched into a scowl. "I understand that Malval met with the military command this afternoon and it didn't go well."[50]

Later Malval summoned Pezzullo into a study and confided that he was having trouble talking to the military.

"Do you want me to give you some advice?" asked the diplomat with many years of experience dealing with military officers who had inserted themselves into politics. "Number one: Don't ask the military their opinion. Give them orders. Next time you go see them, make sure you have an order. You're the prime minister. Don't give them the impression that they have anything to do outside their role as protectors of the law."

Malval, who was already feeling the burdens of office, nodded. "That's good advice."

"Number two," continued Pezzullo. "Get the new commander-in-chief of the FADH named quickly. It's already the beginning of September. You've got a month and a half before Cédras steps down. You and President Aristide should decide who the new commander is going to be and bring Cédras into it and tell him that you want a transition that works smoothly."

"But how do I go about that?" asked the prime minister.

"I would begin with the president," said Pezzullo. "You've got three men at the top of the command, Generals Charles, Biamby, and Duperval. According to your constitution, if you don't plan to select one of them, you've got to promote some others to the rank of general right away, so that one of them can be selected. That's why you've got to act as quickly as possible in consultation with Cédras so that there are no surprises."[51]

"Yes," said Malval, who was making mental notes.[52]

"This is not a time for delay," said the blunt-speaking Pezzullo. "Do it now."

Malval smiled. "I know there are lots of problems with my country, but I'm optimistic," confided Malval. "You're going to be surprised by what happens here."

Pezzullo was intrigued. "What do you mean?"

"You're going to see Aristide, who is this populist figure on the left of this country become the darling of the right," said Malval. "He's going to rally the right and bring all these private sector people together."[53]

Pezzullo was indeed surprised by what he was hearing. "That would be a miracle," said the diplomat, wondering what Malval was basing his optimism on.

"That's what I think is going to happen," concluded Malval. "You'll see for the first time a leader bringing people on both sides of the political spectrum together."[54] There was a genuine look of hope in the new prime minister's eyes.

"If he does that," said the skeptical Pezzullo, "President Aristide will go down in history as a great hero."[55]

CHAPTER 13

Prime Minister Malval

"In Haiti, you always blame the other person. You never take responsibility. It's a national disease."

—ALICE BLANCHET, aide to Prime Minister Malval

Publisher Robert Malval was one of the first people to call President Aristide after he had been ousted in September 1991 and was living in exile in Venezuela. Malval urged his friend to mobilize the international community to restore him to office. But now as the international effort was bearing fruit in the form of an agreement signed by General Cédras to restore Aristide to office by October 30, 1993, the urbane publisher was growing disillusioned with the man he had agreed to serve.

It didn't help that the day after Malval was formally installed as prime minister—September 3, 1993—President Aristide left for Europe on a fifteen-day book tour. "What a contemptible thing to do," Malval said later. "Also, it was a joke, because he was promoting a book that he hadn't even written."[1]

President Aristide's trip raised more than a few eyebrows at the UN, in Port-au-Prince, and in Washington, because a lot of work had to be done if the deposed president was to return to Haiti on schedule. Amnesty and police laws had to be written and passed, a new commander-in-chief of the FADH had to be selected and other steps completed to fulfill the Governors Island Agreement signed by President Aristide and General Cédras in early July.

Prime Minister Malval, who was committed to making the transition work, found his efforts hampered from two sides. On the military side stood a nervous General Cédras and an antagonistic General Biamby and Colonel Michel François. On the constitutional side were President Aristide and his advisors in Washington, who thought the agreement had been forced on them by the international community and didn't provide for the one thing they felt could ensure their security—the destruction of the Haitian military. They had also saddled Malval with a government that was weak and, for the most part, handpicked by Aristide from his loyalists.

One of the most assertive of the new ministers was the minister of education, Victor Benoit, who had stepped aside in 1990 so that Aristide could run under the banner of the FNCD. Now he and his chief of staff, Micha Gaillard, tried to organize secondary school exams for September so that schools could open without further delays. Before baccalaureate exams could take place, teachers had to be paid and maintenance work had to be performed on school buildings. Through the new minister of finance Marie-Michelle Rey, they wrote to President Aristide in Washington asking him to release state funds that were at his disposal. Under an agreement that had been worked out, Ambassador Casimir had the power to oversee and sign for those resources, but the ministry of finance could annul this right at any moment.[2]

Weeks went by without an answer from Washington. Prime Minister Malval demanded an explanation, but didn't get one. Minister of Finance Madam Rey was reluctant to invoke her power for fear of offending Ambassador Casimir and the president. So Victor Benoit and Malval had to raise the money themselves.

Then there was the question of security for the exams. Benoit arranged a meeting with General Cédras. Cédras, who appreciated the new minister's straightforward approach, agreed to cooperate. The baccalaureate exams were held.

It was a positive step forward in a country where conditions were deplorable and growing worse. International relief organizations estimated that they were feeding as many as one million people a day. Basic services such as water, electricity, roads, and telephones were breaking down daily. "Tragedy does not capture what we see every day," said a resident at University Hospital Center of Port-au-Prince—the country's only major public hospital. "We are down to performing examinations without gloves, because there are none. We operate without soap, because there often is none. Sometimes the wards go for days without a simple washing. Why? Because there isn't any water."[3]

When Mike Kozak from the Haiti Working Group arrived in Port-au-Prince the first week of September, he and U.S. embassy chargé d'affaires Vicki Huddleston drove directly to Prime Minister Malval's house. There they found all of the ministers gathered around the dining room table. Kozak and Huddleston pulled Malval into the living room to talk alone.

Malval said: "You've got to help me. Most of my ministers are afraid to go to their ministries or do anything because they're afraid. They want to know what kind of security you're going to provide."

"None," answered Kozak, who went on to explain that while the UN military and police training missions would soon be arriving along with the security detail that was being trained to protect the president, the security of ministries and ministers remained in the hands of the Haitian military. "You need to engage them and put the onus on them to promise protection or be held responsible for any problem that might occur."[4]

Malval asked Kozak to explain the situation to his ministers "because half of the cabinet refuses to do anything because of security concerns."[5]

Kozak remembers being interrupted by Minister of Finance Marie-Michelle Rey, who complained that her house had been machine-gunned and she needed a bodyguard, otherwise she wouldn't leave her house.

"I hate to say this," said Kozak, "but if you had a bodyguard standing in front of your house and the military wanted to machine gun it, they'd just machine gun the bodyguard. Your only security here is going to depend on what you work out with the military. Otherwise you'll end up dead."[6]

The message wasn't well received. The minister of commerce asked: "What kind of arrangements have you made to bring in oil now that the embargo has been lifted?"

"None," answered Kozak. "That's the responsibility of your government. If you have a problem, we will try to help. But we can't substitute our authority for yours."

"There was no sign of any initiative coming from them," the U.S. diplomat remembered. "Everything was: What are you going to do for us?"[7]

It wasn't as though the ministers' concerns about security were without foundation. On September 6 when Port-au-Prince's pro-Aristide mayor Evans Paul was reinstated in office twenty-three months after the military coup, his supporters, reporters, and bystanders were attacked by a mob of civilian police *attachés*. One man was shot dead in the street and another eleven seriously wounded. Information Minister Hervé Denis was injured by flying glass.

There were similar but less violent demonstrations at the Ministries of Finance, Education, and Health. "Two types of things were happening," explained U.S. special advisor Pezzullo. "One was petitioners or feather-bedded officeholders—mostly girlfriends and cronies of the military—who said they had a right to continuance in their jobs. Then there were these toughs trying to harass people. Once you pushed past them, the police would come in and restore order. It was never clear who had sent them. We never had good information, but we suspected that they were operating with at least the tacit blessing of elements within the military."[8] "Unfortunately," added Kozak, "the new government was too timid to order security in advance, so the military always had a convenient excuse for turning up late."[9]

Then on the morning of September 11, Antoine Izméry, an outspoken supporter of President Aristide, was dragged out of a memorial service at the Church of Sacré Coeur in Port-au-Prince and assassinated. Izméry, who was one of the founders of the Joint Committee for the Emergence of Truth (*komite mete men pou verite blayi*, or KOMEVEB), which opposed amnesty to government agents who had violated human rights, held the mass to commemorate the September 11, 1988, massacre at Saint Jean Bosco Cathedral.

Before the service, two former government officials were seen ferrying police and plainclothes soldiers around the Sacré Coeur church. One of them, a former director of the national retirement insurance service, was seen standing beside a parked white pickup truck from the police antigang unit shouting instructions.

As he entered the church, Izméry was approached by two men who warned him that there would be bloodshed if the service took place. In

May 1992 Izméry's brother, George, had been assassinated, and in May 1993 Izméry had been abducted by armed men and tortured.

During the short sermon, Father Antoine Adrien called for "a suspension of all killing" and for "tranquillity, peace and justice."[10] Seconds after the mass, five men in civilian clothes entered the church.

"We were standing around the altar," remembered Father Hugo Triest, "and a guy with this weapon came up and said, 'He's the one' and pointed to Izméry." Another man put a gun to Izméry's head and marched him outside.

On the street, Izméry was forced down on his knees. A man identified by the OAS/UN International Civilian Mission (ICM) as Gros Fanfan—a former Macoute—shot Izméry twice in the head at point blank range.[11]

An ICM investigation concluded that "the assassination was a carefully planned and orchestrated commando-style operation, involving the Forces Armées d'Haiti and their agents, who carried out the execution with impunity."[12]

Since several police vehicles from the antigang unit were seen taking part in the operation, UN/OAS special envoy Caputo laid the blame on the shoulders of police chief Colonel Michel Francois. Later information indicated that although Francois might have known about the impending attack, the mastermind of the operation was General Phillipe Biamby. Quietly operating behind the scenes, he and fellow Duvalierists including Yannick Cédras had begun to organize a paramilitary unit and quasi-political party that would later be called the Front for Advancement and Progress in Haiti (FRAPH or "hit"). Among its leaders were Emmanuel "Toto" Constant, a CIA informer and son of a Duvalier army commander, and Jodel "Jojo" Chamblain, a former Macoute whose pregnant wife had been murdered in 1991 by a pro-Aristide mob. Constant, who spoke English, said he studied mathematics and physics in Canada and later opened a chair and handicrafts factory in Port-au-Prince.

Joining the ranks of FRAPH were other former Macoutes, police *attachés*, and FADH soldiers. In the manner of the secret voudoun society of Bizango, they waged their campaign of terror primarily at night.

Dante Caputo arrived in Port-au-Prince in early September for a two-day trip to organize the transition and remained for two months. He remembers being awakened many nights in September and October by the sound of automatic weapons fire. The OAS/UN International Civilian Mission reported sixty killings or suspected deaths in Port-au-Prince in the month of September alone. This was four times the number reported for earlier months in the year. Their investigations concluded that the majority of the attacks were "targeted political assassinations carried out by paramilitary groups linked to the Forces Armées d'Haiti."[13]

Interestingly, the killings peaked the weekend of Izméry's assassination and fell sharply in the wake of the strong international condemnation that followed. This led the ICM to make the following conclusion: "The fact that there was such a sudden fall in killings attributed to *zenglendos*, armed criminal groups operating at night, particularly in the slums and working class districts of the city, in which the victims were not political activists, supports the analysis that the operations of *zenglendos* are subject to the control of the FADH and are intended to create a climate of fear and intimidation when the political situation is felt to require it."[14]

U.S. special advisor Lawrence Pezzullo traveled to Port-au-Prince the third week of September to let the military know that the United States would not tolerate state-supported violence. First, he, Mike Kozak, and Dante Caputo met for breakfast with generals Cédras, Biamby, and Duperval at Vicki Huddleston's house. "These human rights violations have got to stop. You've got to get a better grip on the police," began Pezzullo.[15]

Caputo pushed General Cédras hard. "Look, Raoul," he said, "you can't convince me that you have no control over these attacks. No one is going to believe that. You should understand that your image is being badly tarnished."[16] Cédras, according to the diplomats, looked visibly uncomfortable and kept repeating that criminal activity had always been a problem in Port-au-Prince.

Then Pezzullo arranged a meeting with the man who was thought to be behind the recent killings, Police Chief Michel François. François arrived at Vicki Huddleston's house with his brother, Evans, and a Lebanese diplomat by the name of Simonese. The colonel wore his steel police helmet and a blue wool uniform in the steamy weather.

Pezzullo began by saying: "When there are violations in this country and they come from the police, the way I'm going to interpret it is that they're coming from you."[17]

This made the young colonel sit up straight. "You know the military way of doing things," said the diplomat looking him straight in the eyes, "you hold the commander responsible. Secondly, this transition can work if you want to make it work. As long as we see you doing your part to make it work, we'll treat you as a friend."

His brother, Evans, started talking about conditions. Pezzullo cut him off. "There are no conditions. Your brother can stay in the military service under the Governors Island Agreement, but only if he leaves his current position and is reassigned, probably outside the country. He's a young man and he might have a future in the military. But if abuses occur, he has to take responsibility."[18]

Pezzullo directed the remainder of his remarks to the thickly built colonel, who was fluent in English. "Whatever you think about your president, your country elected him. Without a constitutional system, you'll never have political peace. You have to respect the wishes of the people."[19]

Colonel François didn't object. He offered none of the usual polemics about Aristide. To make sure the message got through, Pezzullo arranged for someone from the CIA to travel to Port-au-Prince and talk to the colonel once more. According to Pezzullo, the CIA man's "pitch was very tough." In fact, he was later criticized by his superiors in Washington for having told Evans and Michel that their behavior was likely to be injurious to their health.

Days later in an interview with the Haitian newspaper *Le Nouvelliste*, Colonel François proclaimed his innocence and claimed that he had been threatened by U.S. special advisor Pezzullo. Mike Kozak and Chargé Vicki Huddleston quickly dismissed his statement as "complete hogwash."[20]

Dante Caputo, Mike Kozak, and Vicki Huddleston were meeting with Prime Minister Malval either separately or together almost every day. "I would go over in the morning, sometimes with Vicki, and come back and report to Dante," Kozak said. "Then he would go in the afternoon and sometimes I would go with him. To Malval's great credit he really did try to make it work, but he wasn't getting a lot of help from his cabinet."[21]

The new government was literally operating out of Malval's house, which was guarded by a FADH captain and his unit who were loyal to Malval. "It was a scene that needs to be described in Dostoyesvky's terms," said Caputo. "It was the kind of house that was built for a hot climate; very open, but at the same time no light came inside. And all those guys who made up the Malval government—ministers, functionaries, secretaries, aides were camped out there."[22]

According to Malval's executive assistant, Alice Blanchet, the chaos and pressure would sometimes get too intense for Malval's wife and she would order them all to leave. "From day one I always had boxes ready," explained Blanchet, "because every once and awhile she would say she wanted everyone out of the house. And I would say: 'Start packing!' An hour or so later she would calm down."[23]

"The atmosphere was incredible," said Dante Caputo. "Instead of taking any risks, the ministers had retreated into this heavily guarded house. So they were spending twenty-four hours a day together thinking about how they were going to be attacked. Thinking about all the conspiracy theories you can imagine. A pathological atmosphere developed. Every time I went there I got a very anguished feeling."[24]

Still Kozak, Caputo, and Huddleston tried to get them moving. "We were trying to get them to do things, like move the police law," Kozak explained. "Finally, one day, I said to the minister of justice Guy Malary: 'Guy, Julio Larosiliere introduced a police law that the Justice Department people tell me is pretty good with the exception of five or six god-awful provisions. So instead of trying to come up with a new law that will take months to pass, why not co-opt the rightists on this one and say you support the law with amendments?' And Guy said: 'Bring me the bill and I'll look at it.'"

"But none of them had any sense of politics," Kozak continued, "or how to go about getting a majority in Parliament or, even, how to build up public support. They all sort of sat there and said: It's up to Parliament to pass these laws. We don't have anything to do with that. And I'd say: Well, maybe you should make a speech, call some people, send your lobbyists. And they would say: That's up to Americans and UN guys to figure out. It was like PoliSci 101."[25]

It didn't help that the minister of information, Hervé Denis, left in early September for three months in France, where he was having a play of his produced. He told Kozak that it was up to the international community to run his ministry while he was gone.

It turned out that before he left, Denis fired all the employees of the national television and radio. So they went on a job action and occupied the building. "This time I had sympathy for Cédras," Kozak said, "because he was saying that he didn't want to get the military involved in what was essentially a labor dispute. And the Malval government was saying you have to kick these people out, but the minister responsible for the place and the firings had flown the coop."[26]

Other ministers were equally undistinguished. Minister of Defense Jean Belliote was "manifestly afraid" of Cédras, according to Malval.

Kozak explained: "Cédras would say, I can't go out and clear the national television station without an order from the minister of defense. But Belliote was afraid to talk to him, so he'd write these convoluted letters that said in effect: The duty of the army is what the duty of the army is."

"You had to prod these ministers, push them, almost threaten for even the most elemental task," said Alice Blanchet. "The most incredible amount of energy was wasted on nonsense."[27]

Prime Minister Malval was soon inviting Cédras and the whole general staff to his house for meetings at which they engaged in endless debates. "A lot of time was spent talking about security issues. Cédras would use every excuse under the sun," remembered Kozak. "Usually it was Vicki or me beating Cédras over the head to do something until he finally said: 'I need an order from the minister of interior.'"

Then Kozak would go to the minister of interior, Rene Prosper, who would resist, asking: "Why do we have to give the order? What happens if they don't obey?"

"We would scream: Just do it!" said Kozak. "Try it first and we'll deal with that later . . . It was like pulling teeth."[28]

Kozak and Huddleston were also having dinner with the Cédrases several times a week. "It was interesting," reported Kozak. "Cédras tried to maintain his circular, but reasonable, approach to things. But his wife, Yannick, who is a bitch on wheels, just let it fly."[29]

Yannick would tell them that she thought that Aristide was the devil incarnate, that the Papal Nuncio had told her that it was her religious duty to keep him from coming back to Haiti.

Kozak remembered one night when they were sitting on Vicki's porch and Yannick started getting emotional. "You just can't understand what it's like to have rioters looting and soldiers on the streets," she said.

"Yes, I can," said Kozak.

"How?" asked the general's wife.

"I lived in Berkeley in the sixties," answered Kozak, "when we had martial law most of the time. The cops put gas down practically every day and rioters trashed the grocery store a couple times a week."

Yannick listened and then retorted: "We can't let Aristide back, because if he does that sort of thing will happen."

"Well, tell me something," countered Kozak. "If Aristide has this great hold over people, why aren't they doing anything now when they have real reasons to be pissed?"

"Because the army won't permit them," answered Yannick.

"What makes you think the army will permit it once he comes back?" asked Kozak.

"He's got this mystical power," said Yannick.[30]

One night Kozak pulled General Cédras aside and said, bluntly: "The way I see it you've got four options. One, you can do what you're trying to do—use Aristide's failures to excuse your own failures. But that's not a winning strategy, because you start out being the guy who did the coup and he starts from being a democratically elected president. The other option is for you to play your part perfectly. If Aristide doesn't, you show him up; just like you did at Governors Island. That could result in either of two things: Either you're right that he doesn't want to come back, or he comes back with you having taken the high ground and with democratic restraints on him from being abusive."

You mentioned four, said the general. What's the fourth?

"That's the one where we destroy you," said Kozak.[31]

Cédras and most of top FADH officers were convinced that President Aristide had no intention of returning by October 30. "Later," explained Kozak, "in '94 when I was dealing with Michel François on another issue, he told me that he had penetrated Aristide's inner circle and gave me predictions of what Aristide would do a day or two hence, which proved to be accurate. So I believed him."[32]

The mistrust on all sides continued to grow. Prime Minister Malval, in addition to running the government out of his house, had to pay for most of its expenses out of his own pocket. The Government of Taiwan pitched in some money as did other countries, but nothing was forthcoming from the Government of Haiti funds managed out of Washington.

"It was a disgrace," said Alice Blanchet. "We couldn't get any money! We couldn't get anything!"[33] This was despite the fact that, according to the Aristide government's own fourth quarter 1993 budget, $740,000 per month was set aside for Malval's ministerial cabinet. Malval, a scrupulous man, swore he never received a penny of that money, which left at least $2.2 million in Haitian government assets unaccounted for in 1993. In another anomaly, Prime Minister Malval was not able to authorize government checks while ex-prime minister Réne Préval, who now resided with Aristide in Washington, could.[34]

In telephone conversations, President Aristide told Malval that he did not agree with the strategy of cultivating Cédras. "Then how is this supposed to work?" Malval asked in frustration. In a confidential memo sent to Aristide on September 15, Malval made three points: (1) He wanted Aristide's full support for the strategy of working with Cédras to isolate the elements of the FADH opposed to Aristide's return. (2) He felt failure to pursue this tactic would make it impossible for Aristide to return. (3) He wanted to be consulted every time Aristide made an antimilitary statement that Malval had to live with.[35]

Less than a week later, on September 21, ignoring the entreaties of his prime minister, President Aristide called a news conference at TransAfrica—a Washington-based public policy group specializing in African and Caribbean affairs. "Cédras is a killer," said Aristide, "Michel Francois is a killer and, of course, we ask for their removal."[36] He went on to call for the renewal of sanctions, which had been suspended by the UN Security Council on August 27. "The heads have to be removed and with them the attachés who are the Macoutes," declared Aristide without indicating how this was supposed to be achieved.[37]

The deceptions of Aristide and his advisors played directly into the hands of those in the military who wanted to sabotage the Governors Island Agreement. One morning in mid-September, Dante Caputo arrived at Malval's house to find the prime minister more anxious than usual. "Well, Mr. Caputo, we have to talk. We have to talk," said Malval.

"What's up?" asked the OAS/UN special envoy.

"Well, there's something terrible here because you made an agreement with President Aristide that you were going to get rid of the entire high command of the army and you've been telling me the whole time that this isn't true."

Caputo was stunned. "Of course, it isn't true," he said.

"But you signed a secret side letter and I've just received it," said Malval.

"What are you talking about, Mr. Prime Minister?" Caputo sputtered. "May I see the letter?"[38]

Malval handed him a letter written in English on UN letterhead. Caputo quickly scanned to the end of the letter, where he noticed that there was no signature. Infuriated, he handed it back to Malval. "But listen, Prime Minister," he said. "I didn't sign this!"

Malval was taken aback. "Well, the people in Washington said that was a problem with the fax. The fax machine just cut the bottom of the last page and your signature does not appear," he explained.

Caputo was incensed. "Please," he said. "Let's be serious here. I never signed this. Show me my signature. Besides the United Nations doesn't sign side letters. We are not a government. We are a very sophisticated and complex bureaucracy, but we can't make secret deals. If I sign an agreement I have to give it to the secretary general, who has to get the approval of the Security Council."[39]

At this point, Malval didn't know whom to trust. He had been led to believe that the Governors Island Agreement called for Colonel François's retirement by October 15.

Malval was still operating on the assumption that the version of the agreement given to him by Mike Barnes was real. The very next day he invited Colonel François's brother, Evans, over for lunch. At a certain point, Malval said: "Listen, Evans, you're a smart man. Why don't you convince your brother to leave before it's too late."

Evans said categorically: "My brother will go nowhere."

So Malval took out the agreement he had been given and said: "You must see this. . . . It says your brother is supposed to leave the same day as Cédras."

Evans turned purple and asked: "Can I have a copy of this?"[40]

That evening, Malval and his wife, Linda, were hosting a private dinner with the Cédrases. It had been arranged with some difficulty by Leandro Despouy.

The dinner was going well when Malval brought up the question of Michel François.

General Cédras said: "Michel can leave when the legislation is passed to separate the police from the army."

Malval got upset. "But you promised he would leave by October 15."

"I never promised that," explained Cédras. "The Governors Island Agreement said—"

"This is no way to treat people," fumed Malval. "You're playing with deceptions when François is leaving!"

But Cédras was adamant, vowing that he didn't promise anything with regard to François.

"How can you say that when it's right in the agreement?" asked an irate Malval.[41]

Malval turned to his wife, Linda, and asked her to bring a copy of the agreement. Cédras and his wife, Yannick, were exchanging confused looks when Malval added: "Just today I had lunch with Michel's brother, Evans, and I showed the agreement to him."[42]

The Cédrases quickly excused themselves and left.

UN envoy Leandro Despouy was in his office at the Montana Hotel when the telephone rang. It was an agitated Prime Minister Malval.

"Send me the special agreement! I can't find it," he demanded.

"What special agreement?" asked Despouy.

"Please! The one that was negotiated with Dante Caputo at Governors Island."

"The agreement?"

"No, the special agreement signed by Cédras!"[43]

Despouy wasn't sure what he meant. He knew that Cédras had signed a secret letter of resignation. But he wasn't sure if Malval was supposed to know. So he asked again: "What agreement?"

Malval said: "The special agreement promising Michel François would resign. The agreement that was signed in New York."

"How could that be?" asked Despouy. "I was in New York. I was at Governors Island and I know of no such special agreement being signed."

Despouy spent the next five minutes trying to calm the prime minister down. Finally, Malval screamed: "Fax it to me!" and hung up.[44]

Despouy called Caputo, who recounted the similar scene he had with Malval over the side letter. Despouy had just put down the phone when Yannick Cédras called.

"Leandro, there's going to be a civil war!" she shouted.

Despouy tried to calm her. "What's the matter?" he asked.

"The general wants to talk to you," she said.

"Look, I'll meet him tomorrow. What time?" asked the diplomat.

She started pleading: "You have to come now. Please try. It's about the secret agreement. It's causing all kinds of problems. It's better if you come now."[45]

Leandro Despouy got in his car and drove to their house. When he arrived he found Cédras pacing back and forth wringing his hands and Yannick in a state of panic. According to Despouy, she started screaming: "He's going to kill us! He's going to set the house on fire! I'm talking about the colonel! The colonel is coming!"[46]

Despouy noticed that there were only two or three guards present, instead of the usual dozen. The Argentine asked: "What is going on?" It took fifteen minutes before Yannick calmed down enough to explain their dilemma. She was convinced, she said, that Colonel Michel François would come that night to burn their house down.

Throughout all this, her husband paced back and forth silently. Finally, General Cédras stopped and pointed to Despouy. "You have to stay here all night to stop the colonel," he said, according to Despouy. "You're the cause of this! It's your fault. You and Caputo, because of all your agreements and intrigues!"[47] Cédras added that he had called all the members of the FADH general staff to protect him and only Colonel Dorelien had shown up.

It was like a scene out of some weird Greek drama. But behind the scenes the crisis has been defused. After being shown the altered version of the Governors Island Agreement by Malval, Evans had checked with a source close to Aristide who assured him that the version he had been shown was fake. Evans communicated the deception to his brother, who vowed once again never to let Aristide back in the country.

Although the human rights picture had improved since the first weeks of September, it continued to cause concern. The UN/OAS International Civilian Mission, which had more than 250 monitors deployed throughout the country, was doing a good job of reporting on human rights abuses. Their very presence seemed to give confidence to ordinary Haitians, especially those living in outlying communities, who were coming forward to air their grievances against military and civilian authorities. With few exceptions, the ICM monitors were treated with respect and permitted to conduct their investigations without interference. The experience of the ICM monitors bolstered the belief of Pezzullo, Caputo, Kozak, Despouy, and others that the Haitian military would not pose a problem to the UN police and military monitors once they were deployed.

While the ICM was dutifully reporting human right abuses, Pezzullo and Kozak found out that they were reluctant to do anything else to stop them. The U.S. special advisor remembers meeting with the ICM's executive staff at the group's headquarters in the Montana Hotel in mid-September 1993. During the briefing he suggested that the ICM monitors attempt to identify those individuals who were consistent violators of people's rights so that pressure could be brought to bear to remove or neutralize them. He told the group, which included Ian Martin, who had previously served as secretary general of Amnesty International: "We want to be proactive and remove the bad apples."[48] No one voiced an objection.

But Pezzullo learned later that Martin opposed his suggestion, because he felt that it would jeopardize the safety of the monitors and the effectiveness of their mission.

Pezzullo's deputy, Mike Kozak, had much the same experience. Kozak had been talking to the new minister of justice Guy Malary about what to do with the rural justices, the *chefs de section*. According to Kozak, Malary had told him: "It's easy. Some are corrupt and abusive and others are pretty popular and could get elected. We can't just get rid of them and leave a vacuum. What we have to do is take away their power of arrest, so that they can't intimidate people. Then we can deal with them."[49]

So Kozak decided to discuss the idea with Ian Martin, the acting head of the ICM (in the absence of Colin Granderson, who was out of the country). Kozak said: "I was just talking to Guy Malary and his view is that the way to deal with the *chefs de section* is to take away their powers of arrest. Do you have any ideas?"

Kozak said Martin screamed: "You can't do that! They might attack me! They might attack my people!"

"He went on and on," remembered Kozak. "I wasn't asking him to do it himself, but he was so chickenshit that any kind of action against the people in power might provoke some kind of action against him. It was pathetic. Later I heard he was going around telling his ICM people not to talk to the U.S. embassy because they were all CIA."[50]

Meanwhile, U.S. embassy officer Ellen Cosgrove was quietly trying to approach human rights as a legal issue. She was inspired, she said, by a Haitian human rights attorney named Camille LeBlanc. Cosgrove had learned to act quickly when someone was arrested on what seemed like a trumped-up political charge. She would find an attorney and get the person released before nightfall. "The human rights groups would prefer that the accused individual stay in jail," she said later, "so he or she could be beaten. They wanted a body they could document. It was very sad."[51]

For her efforts, Cosgrove was being accused of being a CIA agent by Aristide attorney Bert Wides. According to Cosgrove, the accusations started shortly after Lavalas senator Firmin Jean-Louis made a slightly veiled sexual advance at a meeting, saying: "It would be in your interest to get to know me better."

To which, Cosgrove retorted: "Absolutely not."

The Haitian senator, who Pezzullo characterized as "totally perverse,"[52] told Cosgrove that she might come to regret her decision.

About a week later a story appeared in the Lavalas paper *Liberté* accusing Cosgrove of not understanding democracy and implying that she might be working for the CIA. Although Firmin Jean-Louis later apologized to Cosgrove, the suspicion among partisans of President Aristide that she was somehow a friend of the military stuck. She heard rumors that she had been seen water-skiing with Yannick Cédras and hanging out with military officers. "It was absurd," said Cosgrove, "and insulting."[53]

As September 1993 drew to a close, Haiti's major political actors seemed more intent on sinking the Governors Island agreement than helping it succeed. "It was bizarre," remembered Prime Minister Robert Malval. "Many nights I woke up asking myself: What is going on here? I'm trying to pull something together when all the parts are determined to pull it apart."[54]

CHAPTER 14

Steps toward Aristide's Return

"When they want to kill a dog, they say it's crazy."

—Haitian proverb

Throughout September 1993 and into the first days of October, U.S. special advisor to Haiti Lawrence Pezzullo spent most of his time shuttling between President Aristide and the Clinton administration, trying to get them both to complete the steps that had been agreed upon at Governors Island. Although this was ostensibly what both of them wanted, he encountered resistance from both sides.

The United Nations, on the other hand, was completely cooperative. On September 23, the Security Council unanimously passed a resolution authorizing the deployment of approximately 567 police trainers/monitors and 700 military trainers and engineers. "These personnel will have the practical effect of training the Haitian military and police," read the White House statement, "and in the process will have an important psychological impact on moderating their attitude toward the Haitian populace."[1]

On October 4 Superintendent Jean-Jacques Lemay of the Canadian Mounted Police was chosen to command the police unit. Colonel J. G. Pulley of the U.S. Army Special Forces was named commander of the military unit, which would be made up primarily of U.S. military personnel with some Canadians.

Dante Caputo called the United Nations Mission in Haiti (UNMIH) a "dissuasive force." But the advance team of twenty-five U.S. military trainers and forty Canadian police that arrived in Port-au-Prince the first week in October hardly projected a "dissuasive" attitude.

By all accounts, Colonel J. G. Pulley—soon known in Port-au-Prince as Colonel *Poulet* (chicken)—was not the right man for the job. "He was unsure of himself in that situation, highly guarded, and he didn't possess the leadership skills that were needed," said Pezzullo. [2]

"Colonel Pulley and his troops were staying at the Rancho Hotel ten minutes from the Montana by car," explained UN official Juliette Remy. "The soldiers were locked in their rooms. They had just landed and within days they were inventing stories. I don't know where they were getting them. All you had to do was walk the streets and you could see that there was no threat to *blancs*." [3]

According to Kozak: "It also didn't help that Pulley and his twenty-five men seemed to be constantly rotating back and forth between Port-au-Prince and Norfolk, Virginia. Caputo kept calling Washington and asking: 'Where in the hell is Pulley? Where is Captain so-and-so? I saw them both the other day and today when I ask for them I'm told they went back to Norfolk. '" [4] In addition, the UN/OAS special envoy, who was supposed to be in charge of the UN peacekeeping operation, never saw the reports Colonel Pulley was dispatching to Norfolk and the Pentagon. According to someone who did see the cables, they dealt generally with the level of danger in Port-au-Prince and were based primarily on how much gunfire was heard each night.

"By early October," said Kozak, "most of the shooting was coming from one asshole who lived down the hill from the Montana. He'd get drunk every night and fire off a few rounds into his backyard. Other people were hearing thieves, or ghosts, or spirits. No question, it was a nervous city." [5] In general, human rights violations had decreased since early September and there was no threat to the UN troops. "There was intimidation, sure," reported Pezzullo, "but no acts of violence against foreigners."[6]

The Canadian Mounties, who arrived wearing blue UN berets, were cheered by Haitians as they marched through downtown Port-au-Prince. Caputo and Kozak used them to mount what they humorously referred to as Operation Aida. "We didn't have many troops, so we tried to use what we had to let the Haitian military know they were there," explained Kozak. "We'd put the Canadians in one car and have them drive past a few police stations, then we'd put them in a different car and have them drive around some more."[7]

It had become clear to members of the State Department Haiti Working Group that the Defense Department, and especially their civilian branch known as the OSD (Office of the Secretary of Defense), headed by a State Department officer named Frank Wisner, had no enthusiasm for the Haitian mission. The OSD subscribed to the CIA assessment of Aristide as dangerously unstable and felt that the administration's attempt to restore him to power was misguided. Despite the uniformed services' concern about the introduction of U.S. forces into Haiti, Pezzullo, Kozak, and others reported that the Joint Chiefs of Staff accepted President Clinton's policy and played a constructive role in formulating plans for the military training mission.

Complicating the situation was the fact that people in the Clinton administration like Frank Wisner were now equating Haiti with Somalia. President George Bush had dispatched U.S. Marines to Somalia in 1991 to protect humanitarian efforts in a country plagued by political anarchy. Now under UN command, U.S. troops had put a price on the head of warlord Mohammed Farrah Aidid, saying he was the cause of the lawlessness and violence in the capital of Mogadishu.

But there were big, important differences between Haiti and Somalia that Special Advisor Pezzullo pointed out in numerous confidential memos to Clinton administration policy makers at State, Defense, CIA, and the White House. Unlike Haiti, Somalia was a country in chaos with no central civilian or military authority. Secondly, the UN trainers/ advisors had been invited into Haiti by both General Cédras and President Aristide. Third, the trainers were not being sent to keep or enforce the peace, only to train and evaluate and to dissuade by their presence.

Convinced by Colonel Pulley's alarmist reports that Haiti was a dangerous environment for U.S. military trainers/advisors, officials at the Department of Defense started raising the issue of how the trainers would defend themselves. Caputo and Pezzullo thought that question had been settled three months earlier in May when the aide mémoire defining the role of UN military advisors/trainers had been cleared by the administration and presented to President Aristide and General Cédras. It stated that the UN military and police personnel would be equipped only with sidearms. That language was also incorporated into the Governors Island Agreement signed in July.

But during a briefing in Norfolk only weeks before the trainers were to be deployed, Admiral Paul Miller told Pezzullo that Seabees would be carrying M-16s. "Wait a minute," Pezzullo interjected.

Admiral Miller explained that the M-16 was the Seabees weapon of issue.[8] Trying to head off a potential problem, Special Advisor Pezzullo traveled with U.S. Marine general Jack Sheehan to Port-au-Prince to brief Malval. They explained that, "the Seabees who are coming are issued M-16s, not pistols. But they're not going to carry them. They'll be in a box with an MP standing guard over the box. You'll never see them."[9]

Malval said he didn't consider that a problem. Next, they discussed the need to send in a landing ship since the Pentagon wanted to land some heavy equipment—steamrollers, road graders, and so on. Pentagon officials had told Pezzullo that they thought it would be easier to send the equipment in one ship that could act as a floating hotel and support base for a couple of months, while a camp was being built. Pezzullo ended by saying: "We don't want to do this without your approval."

Malval asked: "How big a ship?"

"It's big," Pezzullo answered. "But it doesn't look like a warship. It will dock in Port-au-Prince around the second week of October. I've already told Cédras about it and he understands."

Malval nodded. "Fine."[10]

Special Advisor Pezzullo, General Jack Sheehan, and U.S. embassy chargé Vicki Huddleston then caught a U.S. military flight back to Norfolk where they were told by Admiral Miller that they had just changed conditions in Haiti from permissive to semi-permissive.

Pezzullo asked: "Admiral, could you please explain. Up until today, I understood that we agreed that we faced a permissive environment. What brought about the change to semi-permissive?"[11]

Admiral Miller's G-2 (head of intelligence) explained that they had received reports of violence in the country and went on to read from reports filed by Colonel Pulley and members of his advance team.

Pezzullo cut him off. "Let me clear this up," said the special advisor, "because we're getting ourselves all excited about something that has nothing to do with reality." Pezzullo then went on to give an assessment of the various threats in Haiti that he had delivered a week before to a meeting of administration foreign policy makers in the Situation Room in the White House. He separated Haitian-on-Haitian violence, which he related to the political rivalry between people who backed President Aristide and those who opposed his return, to what he considered the threats facing the UN military trainers. He ended up by saying there was almost no evidence that these troops would encounter violence. He pointed out that the civilian UN/OAS ICM monitors had been traveling the country for over six months wearing sweatshirts and baseball caps and reporting on human rights abuses by the military. They had experienced only one or two minor incidents.[12]

Pentagon fears were exacerbated on October 3 when eighteen U.S. elite Army Rangers were killed, seventy-five were wounded, and one helicopter pilot was taken prisoner in an ambush in Mogadishu. They had been on a mission to capture and kill warlord Mohammed Farrah Aidid. That night U.S. television viewers watched gruesome footage of the bodies of dead U.S. soldiers being dragged through the streets and desecrated by cheering Somalis.

A week and a half before the ship containing the bulk of the military and police trainers and their equipment—the USS *Harlan County*—was to be deployed, October 9, 1993, Pezzullo was resting at his home in Baltimore. Earlier that Saturday at a meeting at the White House on Bosnia, Secretary of Defense Les Aspin and acting chairman of the Joint Chiefs of Staff Admiral David E. Jeremiah presented Secretary of State Warren Christopher with a list of conditions drafted by OSD that they said had to be met before they would send troops to Haiti.

Pezzullo's phone rang sometime around 3 P.M. The deputy national security advisor Sandy Berger was on the line. Pezzullo remembers that he said: "Larry, we really have problems with [Secretary of Defense] Aspin. We just had a meeting on Bosnia and he said that there were seven showstoppers on the Haiti military program."

"Showstoppers? What the hell's a showstopper?" Pezzullo asked.

"These are things they say have not been done," Berger said nervously. "If they're not done, they say they cannot go forward."[13]

Pezzullo, who had dispatched his staff to endless interagency meetings where these issues had been discussed, dissected, and supposedly resolved, said: "Sandy, this is something out of Kafka."

"One is the Status of Mission Agreement with the Government of Haiti," Berger continued, according to Pezzullo.

"I saw that a month ago," answered Pezzullo. "I saw that with Pulley and Superintendent Lemay and Dante. They had a couple of minor problems that they were going to work out before they sent it to Malval. My impression, and I'll have to check with Dante on this, is that it was given to Malval."

Berger said the second showstopper was the rules of engagement.

"Sandy, they're giving you a lot of crap," answered Pezzullo. "Because the rules of engagement are our internal rules. We don't share those. I saw something last week that talks about what happens if someone steals a spare tire from a jeep."

Berger wanted to know what Pezzullo was talking about.

"You don't send troops into another country without giving them detailed instructions about how they're supposed to react. But that's our business. What's next?"[14]

The rest were things like a request for the use of the port, which had already been done. Pezzullo told Berger: "We're getting sandbagged here, man."[15]

Berger, who was in a hurry, said, according to Pezzullo: "Larry, I'm going to hand this over to you. You make everything sound so easy. But this could disrupt the whole thing."

"Those guys at OSD are going to try to abort this," Pezzullo warned. "If they do, this administration is going to look terrible. We have real problems here with discipline within the administration and if we don't clear it up, we'll never be able to act."[16]

As soon as he hung up the phone, Pezzullo called his deputy, Mike Kozak, in Port-au-Prince. Kozak remembers that he and Caputo were lying on couches in Caputo's office in the Montana listening to CNN headline news. They had both been sick to their stomachs for days. Caputo heard a CNN correspondent say: "The Pentagon announced today that if American forces are attacked in Haiti in any way, they will leave immediately."[17]

He turned to Kozak and asked: "Mike, did you just hear an announcement from the Pentagon or am I hallucinating?"

Kozak tried to sit up. "No, Dante, I heard it. I think I'd better call Larry."[18]

Minutes later Pezzullo was on the line asking them about showstoppers.

"The rules of engagement are all worked out," Kozak explained. "The Status of Mission Agreement has already been signed by Malval. He sent it to the Pentagon and as far as I know, they haven't signed it yet."[19]

Kozak went down the list. The only so-called showstopper that seemed of any importance was the Status of Mission Agreement.

On Monday, Pezzullo called State Department lawyer Rod Chanderson, who said: "Larry, we work on these things all the time at the UN. We've even got a standard formula. Our Pentagon does this all the time. They give you a song and dance. If you can get me hooked up on a three-way call with their lawyer, we can get this settled in five minutes."[20]

With the Status of Mission Agreement taken care of, Pezzullo drafted a memo to Berger and Under Secretary for Political Affairs Peter Tarnoff stating that "the show goes on." But resistance, particularly from the civilian arm of the Pentagon, was holding strong. It was often expressed to Pezzullo through Tarnoff at State or through Berger or Lake at the NSC. Wisner, Tarnoff, and Lake had all served together in Vietnam and Pezzullo suspected that they had formed a cabal of second-guessers who called each other to anticipate reasons why the mission to Haiti would fail.

One of Pezzullo's deputies, Nancy Jackson, attended a meeting with Admiral Shrieffer of OSD on October 7 to make sure everything was in place for the landing of the *Harlan County*. According to Jackson, Admiral Shrieffer stunned the gathering by announcing: "The decision to deploy the *Harlan County* has not been made. We're still waiting for an execute order."

Sitting next to Jackson was Lieutenant Colonel Chuck Swannack from the Joint Chiefs of Staff. Jackson turned to Swannack and asked: "Is that true? Are we missing a piece and this isn't going to happen?"

Swannack shook his head and said: "I don't know what Admiral Shrieffer is talking about."[21]

"Here were operations guys from DOD saying they're ready to go, and the civilian part, the Office of the Secretary of Defense saying, it's not ready," Jackson explained.

The death of eighteen U.S. Rangers on the streets of Mogadishu one week earlier was clearly on Defense Secretary Les Aspin's mind when he appeared on the Sunday morning news magazine show *This Week with David Brinkley* on October 10. Pressed by ABC News correspondent Sam Donaldson about the means available to U.S. military trainers in Haiti should they be attacked, Aspin said that they would be armed with M-16s. When Aspin's statement was rebroadcast in Haiti via CNN, it evoked an immediate reaction from supporters of both the military and President Aristide.

"The people of Haiti demand an explanation," said a spokesman for the FADH general staff. "This sounds like an occupation," said a pro-Aristide radio commentator.[22]

Ten minutes after Aspin's statement had been rebroadcast, Yannick Cédras called UN envoys Leandro Despouy and Dante Caputo at their office in the Montana.

"Leandro, what's this?" Despouy remembered her asking. "The Americans don't want to come?"

The Argentine tried to calm her: "No, they're coming."

"Then why did Aspin make this statement?"

"It's a question of what the order is," said Despouy. "It's just a technical thing."

"No," said the general's wife, according to Despouy, "This was done because they don't want to come."[23]

As a result of the incident in Somalia, the U.S. public had strong doubts about introducing U.S. troops into another international trouble spot. A *USA Totay*/CNN poll released on Sunday, October 10, found that 59 percent of Americans disapproved of U.S. troops being sent overseas under UN command. A *New York Times* editorial that same day warned that "defenseless U.S. troops should not be sent into this snakepit [Haiti]."[24]

In Georgetown, President Aristide remained uncharacteristically silent. According to one American advisor, "he and his advisors were not sad that Governors Island was going down the drain."[25] From U.S. special advisor Pezzullo's vantage point it certainly seemed as though President Aristide had done everything in his power to frustrate the process and annoy the FADH. Despite repeated entreaties from Pezzullo and Vice President Gore, Aristide still hadn't appointed a successor to General Cédras. According to Jackson, the only aspect of President Aristide's return that seemed to interest him was the training of his sixty-man personal security squad.

Prime Minister Malval, in a meeting with President Aristide and his advisors in Washington on October 1, summed up his view of the situation: "Cédras isn't moving and you guys are frozen. I don't know what you have in mind, but I don't see how you can come back by October 30 unless you have a plan to invade the country and fight."

Malval remembered that Aristide replied: "Bob, the white man will take care of it."

Robert Malval asked: "What do you mean by that?"

"The *blanc* will take care of it," Aristide repeated, according to Malval.[26]

Aristide went on to say that Vice President Gore had promised that Colonel Michel François would be removed from power by October 15.

"I don't know if there are two U.S. governments," Malval replied, "but I just had a conversation with Secretary of State Warren Christopher and that's not what he told me."

Aristide smiled and said: "Bob, you don't know how things work in Washington."[27]

As far as fulfilling his side of the Governors Island Agreement, President Aristide had been dilatory at best. The accord provided for two laws that needed to be written by President Aristide and passed by Parliament. The first, contained in paragraph 6, called for "an amnesty granted by the President of the Republic within article 147 of the National Constitution and implementation of the other instruments which may be adopted by the Parliament on this question." The second was referred to in paragraph 7, which stated: "Adoption of a law establishing the new Police Force."

In late September, after some prodding from Mike Kozak and Vicki Huddleston, the new minister of justice Guy Malary proposed a police law that was taken from a bill previously introduced by Alliance deputy Julio Larosiliere. Despite pressure from the police chief, Colonel François, in the form of bribes and threats, the Chamber of Deputies quickly passed the bill. It then went to the Senate, where Alliance senators held it up, vowing they would pass it when the amnesty law was signed.

The amnesty law was another problem. While President Aristide could—according to the Haitian Constitution—grant amnesty by decree, General Cédras and his supporters insisted on a law passed by the Parliament. They argued that a presidential decree could easily be revoked by Aristide when he returned to Haiti. The amnesty they had in mind cleared any member of the military accused of crimes that had taken place between President Aristide's ouster in September 1991 and the signing of the Governors Island Agreement.

Jocelyn McCalla, executive director of the Committee for Haitian Refugees, and others argued that the military should not be exempted for petty crimes, including corruption and stealing government funds. According to Colonel François, amnesty was not a serious concern. "Look, amnesty is completely irrelevant to the troops," explained François to Mike Kozak. "Because nobody's afraid that Aristide is going to prosecute us under the court system. If he wants to come after us, he is going to send his people to kill us in the night or put burning tires around our necks. The reason he's not going to go through the court system is that he knows we can kill him if he does."[28]

Others in the FADH, including General Cédras, did not share that point of view. They were hoping to find a way to continue to live peacefully in Haiti once they had resigned from the FADH. Cédras also wanted to show that he had the army's interests at heart so that soldiers wouldn't come after him and accuse him of selling them out.

For his part, President Aristide seemed to dodge the issue. At the first meeting between Aristide and Clinton at the White House in early April 1993, the exiled Haitian president had made a reference to amnesty that in Pezzullo's opinion "straddled the question."[29]

Vice President Al Gore challenged the Haitian president by saying: "Mr. President, I'm not satisfied with your answer. Do you want to grant amnesty or not?"[30]

According to Pezzullo, President Aristide told the vice president that he had no interest in vengeance or in persecuting people.

But when President Aristide called Parliament into session in July 1993 following the signing of Governors Island, he deliberately left the amnesty law off the agenda. His foot-dragging provoked a call from Vice President Gore in mid-August. According to Pezzullo, "Aristide basically told Gore that he didn't have any problem submitting a law and asked: What do you want me to say?"[31]

Pezzullo had his office draft a law providing for amnesty for political crimes from the date of the coup to the signing of the Governors Island Agreement. It was sent to Justice Minister Guy Malary, who made some minor changes and faxed it to President Aristide in Georgetown. Aristide's reply, according to Prime Minister Malval, was: "I'll never sign this."[32]

"Then write your own law," Malval countered.[33]

When President Aristide and his advisors finally got around to drafting a law that Prime Minister Malval and the Minister of Justice Malary were supposed to submit to Parliament, it was a law that Malval characterized as "absurd." Mike Kozak, who read the draft, said: "It covered three hours on the night of the coup and excluded 'crimes against humanity' and 'war crimes'—which Aristide consistently interpreted as covering the army's actions."[34] It was so bad that Malval and his entire government threatened to resign if Aristide didn't take it back.[35]

Finally, on Sunday, October 3, President Aristide issued a presidential amnesty for all political crimes committed between the coup of September 1991 and the signing of the Governors Island Agreement.

To the Western observer it might seem strange to issue a presidential decree on Sunday. But to Haitians the meaning was clear. In voudoun, Sunday is a forbidden day.

The decree, according to Justice Minister Malary, was legally binding. But General Cédras had his doubts. At a meeting held at Malval's house in Port-au-Prince on October 4, UN/OAS special envoy Dante Caputo and representatives of the Four Friends of Haiti came together to assure General Cédras and members of his general staff that they would guarantee the amnesty decree.

Mike Kozak said it started with "Cédras moaning and groaning, saying that he had consulted with his lawyers, that it shouldn't have been done on Sunday. He came up with every kind of stupidity."[36] At a certain point, Dante Caputo, who was chairing the meeting, asked Justice Minister Malary to give his interpretation.

According to Kozak, Malary said: "The decree pardons all soldiers for acts they perpetrated from the time of the coup up to Governors Island. It doesn't matter what acts they committed."

Kozak asked Malval: "Is that the position of your government?"

Malval answered: "If the minister of justice says that is the right interpretation, that's the position of the government. We will guarantee it."[37]

Kozak then turned to the Four Friends ambassadors. "Are you as the Four Friends of Haiti willing to act as witnesses and guarantee to the army that this interpretation will be used by this government and every government?" he asked.

The ambassadors all answered in the affirmative.

"Then, what's the problem?" Kozak asked.[38]

Cédras still wasn't satisfied. He knew that by issuing the decree on Sunday, Aristide had sent a message that every Haitian would understand. But instead of explaining this to Kozak and the foreign diplomats, he raised other objections.

A day later, General Cédras met alone with Malary and Malval, both highly cultured, Western-educated men who didn't seem to grasp the significance of the fact that the decree had been signed on Sunday. Toward the end of the meeting with Cédras, Malval remembered that Justice Minister Malary took a very ironic tone and said: "General, if you are feeling guilty about a crime, just tell us what crime it is and we will write it into the document."

Malval said that Cédras gave Malary "such a vicious look that it still haunts me."[39]

Malval said later: "What these guys wanted was an amnesty for all the stealing that they had done. They knew that no one could prove that they had killed x, y, or z, but they were afraid the money they had stolen could be traced."[40]

Dante Caputo had become convinced that both President Aristide and General Cédras wanted a solution imposed on them by the United States. President Aristide wanted a U.S. invasion that would destroy the military and any challenge to his authority, and Cédras wanted the U.S. military to guarantee that his Haitian military wouldn't be destroyed.

During the first week of October, Caputo met with General Cédras in the gardens of the U.S. embassy residence. The two men were sitting alone looking down at the sea below when Cédras turned to Caputo and said: "Mr. Caputo, you always try to implement very complicated solutions. Maybe they're too complicated."

Caputo asked: "What do you mean by this? What's the solution?"

Cédras pointed down to the sea and said: "You know what the solution is: twenty U.S. navy ships right there. That's the solution."[41]

Caputo immediately thought back to the pictures of the American officers in FADH headquarters. "These guys wanted to be raped by the Americans," explained the Argentine. "They wanted to be liked by the Americans. They wanted to go to bed with the Americans for many, many reasons."[42] Caputo felt that the military and their friends in the business community thought of the Americans as friends who would protect them. They regarded the UN and the international community, on the other hand, as supporters of Aristide.

Caputo had personal reasons for believing this; he was receiving threats. "They would call me and say things like: 'You remember the Malvinas war? You remember what the British did to your army? Well, that's what we're going to do to you.'" In the background he could hear bottles breaking, which he said "has something to do with voodoo." As a precaution, he was sleeping in different locations around the city every night.[43]

Mike Kozak, who was also staying in Port-au-Prince, didn't take the threats as seriously. "The Haitian military is counting on our people recoiling," Kozak said at the time. "They are some of the biggest cowards you have ever seen in your life. They couldn't do a Somalia if their lives depended on it."[44]

But the campaign of intimidation continued to raise fears in Washington. On Tuesday, October 4, about thirty armed civilians broke up a meeting of teachers that was being held at the Hotel Christophe with bursts of automatic weapons fire.[45] Three days later on October 7, civilian gunmen seriously wounded two merchants in Port-au-Prince who had defied a call by the Front for Advancement and Progress in Haiti for a general strike to protest the return of President Aristide.

One of the planners of the FRAPH demonstrations, a tall, skinny man with bad teeth named Emmanuel "Toto" Constant, was also a CIA source. According to a CIA official who served in Haiti, Constant had been recruited in the late eighties to help penetrate drug trafficking operations in Haiti. Now, in his reports, Constant was purposely exaggerating the threats to the UN trainers/monitors, predicting widespread violence in the wake of Aristide's return.

The demonstrations and attacks were being carried out by a pool of hired toughs (called attachés), who had once been used by Colonel François. Now they were called FRAPH. "They were mostly skinny guys who hadn't eaten in two days," said U.S. embassy human rights officer Ellen Cosgrove. "Constant, Biamby, and the others would give them a little money and some rum and they'd go wild. Sure, there were some bad guys who went around bragging that they had killed people, but most of them were little guys with pants held up by string because they couldn't afford a belt."[46]

One, a twenty-nine-year-old man named Raymond, said he was unemployed but since joining FRAPH had been paid about forty to fifty dollars a week. He said his job was "to protect the sovereignty of the nation. Aristide is a criminal," he added. "He wanted to burn people alive."[47]

Cosgrove and other embassy officers had seen CIA reports that estimated their strength at twelve thousand. "It was ridiculous," she said.[48] "But once that kind of information gets into the system in Washington," said Pezzullo, "it's hard to kill."[49]

"The CIA station chief had a number of guys like Constant on the payroll," said a State Department official assigned to Port-au-Prince. "They were paid informants, not agents. There's a big difference. And the important thing was always interpreting the information you got from them."[50]

"Part of the problem is people in Washington making judgments about who they're going to believe," said Mike Kozak.[51]

Pezzullo agreed. "You get people who don't have any experience—and you saw this in the Reagan administration, the Carter administration, and with this administration particularly—they come in and even though they've been critical of the CIA, they think: This is the real stuff."[52]

"They end up sharing the Aristide, Bert Wides conspiracy theory," concluded Kozak, "that the CIA runs the world and knows everything that's going on. They don't—not by a long shot."[53]

Events in Port-au-Prince would soon bear that out.

CHAPTER 15

The Harlan County Incident

"What's wrong with the U.S.? Why do the bad guys always win?"

—HAITIAN SUPPORTER of exiled president Aristide

"There are some important things that happened in Haiti that the Agency and the press never picked up," said Mike Kozak. Two weeks before the *Harlan County* was scheduled to arrive in Port-au-Prince, Kozak, Despouy, and Caputo had a meeting with a group of Haitian senators that included Alliance senator Julio Larosiliere. "They told us that Colonel Michel François had proposed to stage a coup against the Malval government and block the whole process," reported Kozak.[1]

General Cédras called the FADH general staff and all the commanders together and Colonel François presented his plan for a coup d'état. Cédras argued against it, saying that a coup would only provoke more embargoes and international pressure. François appealed to the officers' nationalism, vowing that they had to protect Haiti from the *blancs*.

When the issue was put to a vote, François lost. He then pleaded that they do something to save face. Colonel François argued that if the Haitian military allowed foreign troops to land in Haiti without a protest they would look like a bunch of wimps.

A deal was struck. Neither the FADH nor any elements controlled by the FADH would resist the UN trainers. But if other friends of the FADH wanted to organize a nonviolent demonstration at the docks, they could.

"It's interesting," noted Kozak, "because this was the first time Cédras had won a struggle with François."[2]

The next night General Cédras and his wife, Yannick, invited Kozak and U.S. chargé Vicki Huddleston to their house in Petionville for dinner. "It was the only time he exuded any confidence," Kozak recalled. "He was ready to make decisions. He had his notepad out and instead of doodling on it, which is what he usually did, he was going down the list of current issues, saying: 'All right, we'll do that.' He looked like a man in charge."[3]

Kozak left Port-au-Prince on Friday, October 8, to spend the weekend with his wife in Miami and was scheduled to return on Monday to meet the USS *Harlan County*. "Things were so much on track," remembered Kozak, "that I talked to Larry and Vicki on Sunday and we decided that I should go up to Washington to talk about the next steps."[4]

The 560-foot USS *Harlan County* steamed into Port-au-Prince harbor at 2:00 Monday morning, October 11, 1993. On board were 193 U.S. and 25 Canadian military personnel. The captain of the ship, U.S. Navy commander Marvin E. Butcher, whose frame of mind was described as "hysterical" by Vicki Huddleston, found his berth at the dock occupied by a rusting tanker of Cuban registry. He started sending frantic messages to Norfolk and Washington.

Chargé Huddleston had turned over preparations for the docking to a U.S. Coast Guard commander who dealt regularly with Max Paul, a friend of Colonel François and the man who ran a port that in most parts of the world would pass as a junkyard. On Monday morning, Huddleston sent the Coast Guard officer back to talk to Max Paul. Reeking of rum and grumbling, Paul promised that the berth would be cleared by dawn the next day.

By 7 A.M. Monday, a group of about sixty FRAPH members started arriving at the gate to the port. Some carried pistols and sticks, but most were unarmed. It was not the turnout that organizer Emmanuel "Toto" Constant had hoped for. "We were all scared," he said later. "My people kept wanting to run away. But I took the gamble and told them to stay."[5]

Also gathered at the entrance were two dozen reporters from CNN, ABC, the *New York Times*, and other major media outlets. At around 7:30 a convoy of cars and four-wheel-drive vehicles, including one carrying U.S. chargé Vicki Huddleston, approached. The demonstrators started jumping around wildly, waving their arms and screaming "*À bas Caputo! À bas* UN! *À bas* Malval! (Down with Caputo! Down with the UN! Down with Malval!)" Some were heard yelling in English: "Get out!" and, even: "We start another Somalia!"

The demonstrators surged around the cars, kicking their tires, waving a couple of guinea hens, and scattering baking soda in a voudoun ritual. Reporters were pushed and one American television crew was threatened at gunpoint. Commander Butcher, aboard the *Harlan County*, reported back to USACOM in Norfolk that he heard shots coming from the docks and offered to land U.S. Marines.[6] The environment, to his mind, was no longer permissive.

"As wild and scary as it appeared," said one Haitian with close ties to the military, "it was carefully choreographed. The demonstrators had strict orders not to shoot anyone, just to raise the level of fear."[7]

U.S. embassy officials tried to get the gates to the port opened. Unable to do so, they got back into their cars and drove away. The whole incident lasted fifteen minutes. As soon as she got to the U.S. embassy, Chargé Huddleston called Lawrence Pezzullo in Washington to say: "There's nothing to worry about. We'll get the ship docked."[8] UN/OAS special envoy Dante Caputo was on his way to talk to Cédras.

It was about 8:30 in the morning when Pezzullo put down the phone. He had just arrived at his office in the State Department. Now he received a message that Secretary of State Warren Christopher wanted to see him immediately.

Arriving at Secretary Christopher's office, the special advisor found ten people gathered around a television in the corner watching the demonstration replayed on CNN. "I just spoke to Vicki Huddleston," Pezzullo reported, "and she's convinced that we'll get the ship in. Dante is also working on it."[9]

Pezzullo went on to explain that there was no danger to the ship. The secretary listened without offering an opinion, then told Pezzullo: "We're going to the White House. We'll be leaving around ten o'clock."[10]

Back in his office, the special advisor telephoned Huddleston in Port-au-Prince. "Everybody up here is worried," he told her. "I just got back from the secretary's office where they're sitting around watching replays of the demonstration on CNN."

"We'll take care of it," Huddleston said. "I called Malval and he's going to see Cédras. We'll get it done."

"That demonstration at the port didn't help," added Pezzullo.

The chargé had a suggestion: "We could always get the ship landed somewhere else. We could land it at the Mevs' pier."

"Look at the possibilities," instructed Pezzullo, "and get it worked out."[11]

While the special advisor was on the phone with Huddleston, Secretary of State Christopher was meeting with his senior advisors on the seventh floor. Under Secretary Tarnoff was there, as was Thomas Donilan, the secretary's advisor. According to someone who attended the meeting, they all took the same position as Pezzullo and the secretary concurred.[12]

When Christopher and Pezzullo arrived at the Situation Room of the White House at 10 A.M., Lake, Berger, Aspin, Jim Woolsey from CIA, and UN ambassador Madeline Albright were already seated. The atmosphere was tense. Once again, Pezzullo was asked to give his assessment. He characterized the demonstration on the docks as "pure theater that should not be taken seriously." He recounted his conversation that morning with Chargé Huddleston, who had assured him that everything would be worked out. He also reported that Huddleston, Caputo, and Malval were all converging on General Cédras. In the past when thugs had demonstrated at ministries or City Hall, appeals to Cédras had always produced results. "I'm sure we'll see the military restore calm."[13]

CIA director Woolsey disagreed. He said the problem was much wider and was not confined just to the port.

Pezzullo interjected: "This is all trumped up. It's not as if people were waving Uzis. They had bottles of rum, rusted pistols, and guinea hens. It looked worse on TV than it really was."

Tony Lake broke in to tell Pezzullo that the decision to withdraw the *Harlan County* had already been made.

Pezzullo said it felt like he had been hit in the solar plexus. Secretary Christopher didn't say a word. Neither did Les Aspin.

"That's a big mistake, Tony," warned Pezzullo. "Can't we leave it there?"

No, answered the national security advisor.

UN ambassador Madeline Albright said that since it was a UN mission, she had better inform Secretary Boutros-Ghali of the administration's decision.

"No!" Lake said emphatically, according to Pezzullo.

Albright took exception to Lake's tone.

"No!" repeated the national security advisor just as strongly.

Pezzullo remembers that Albright reminded Tony Lake that there were Canadians on the ship and that the Canadian government should be informed.

"No!" Lake said again, according to Pezzullo.

But Albright persisted, arguing that the U.S. government would be embarrassing its international partners.

Pezzullo saw this as an opening. "Look, Tony," he said, "instead of jumping, why don't we give it a little time? Why don't we pull the ship farther out in the harbor? It's a big harbor. We can leave it there for a day or two until everything is worked out."[14]

"No!" said Lake.

That was it. There was no further discussion. The meeting was over.

As Pezzullo left the room, he passed Lake's deputy Sandy Berger. "This is a fucking disaster, Sandy," said Pezzullo. "I hope you understand that."

Berger told Pezzullo to keep in mind that the decision was being taken against the backdrop of Somalia. He said the administration couldn't afford another embarrassment.

Pezzullo left thinking that the decision had been made and that the consequences of withdrawing the *Harlan County* would be disastrous. But later that afternoon, Tony Lake reversed himself and decided to leave the *Harlan County* in the harbor as long as Commander Butcher deemed it safe.

The tense quiet in the Port-au-Prince harbor was broken at dawn the next morning by Commander Butcher playing the U.S. national anthem loudly over the *Harlan County*'s broadcast system. Colonel Pulley, after conferring with General Cédras and U.S. chargé Vicki Huddleston, tried to convince Commander Butcher to land UNMIH forces on a beach north of Port-au-Prince. Butcher answered that a complete shore survey by a U.S. Navy sea-air-land (SEAL) team would have to be completed first. Butcher then offered to transfer the troops ashore by landing craft. Unable to agree on a course of action, the two officers decided to wait.[15]

Shortly before noon, two twenty-five foot Haitian gunboats carrying Haitian police and FADH personnel approached within 2,500 yards of the *Harlan County*. Commander Butcher ordered all the ship's guns manned, and he stationed sniper teams along the deck. Then he called USACOM in Norfolk and, without waiting to speak to the admiral on duty, informed them that he was pulling out.[16]

At around 2 P.M. on Tuesday, Dante Caputo was sitting in his office in the Montana Hotel. He had just spoken to General Cédras, who said that the dock would be secured and a berth cleared for the *Harlan County*. Caputo was relating this information to the French chargé when one of his bodyguards ran in and said: "Mr. Caputo, the *Harlan County* is leaving!"

"What?" asked the startled UN envoy.

"Come . . . you can see it."

"The three of us ran out onto one of the terraces of the hotel and I will never forget that image," Caputo recalled. "There before us was the sea and the *Harlan County* turned around and leaving."[17]

Soon they were joined by Leandro Despouy. "We were like children saying: How can the boat be leaving?" remembered the Argentine. Despouy turned to his stunned colleague and said: "It must be going to hide somewhere nearby."[18]

The two UN diplomats called Vicki Huddleston, who told them that the ship was going to Guantanamo Naval Base in Cuba. UN special envoy Caputo, who was supposed to be in charge of the mission, had not been informed.

That night a haggard-sounding Pezzullo called from Washington to say that he was trying to get people at the White House to change their minds. "It was their decision," he told Caputo, who felt like the ground was being ripped out from under his feet.[19]

At 8 P.M. Juliette Remy picked up the satellite phone in Caputo's office. Vice President Al Gore was on the other end asking to speak to the UN special envoy. Mike Kozak, who had hurried back to Port-au-Prince that afternoon, was also in the room.

According to Caputo, Vice President Gore said: "I want you to know that we had to take this decision. It was difficult for us. We weren't able to inform you. . . . What are your comments?"

"Well, Mr. Vice President," Caputo said, "while we are talking the Haitian army high command is drinking champagne because they think they have defeated the U.S. army. I know they didn't, but it seems that way to them. Mr. Vice President, the consequences of your decision are going to be terrible. This is jeopardizing the lives of the entire cabinet and Mr. Malval. I wouldn't be surprised if some of them get killed. Your action has shown that we're not ready to implement the agreement."[20]

"Dante just laid it out for him," remembered Kozak, who overheard the entire conversation.[21]

After Caputo related the potential consequences, Gore asked Caputo: "What should we do?"

"Sir, order the ship to come back to Haiti immediately and deploy the troops," offered Caputo.[22]

The vice president said that up until that point he didn't understand the consequences of the decision to withdraw the *Harlan County*. He told Caputo that he was going down the hall to talk to President Clinton.[23]

About twenty minutes later, Vice President Gore called Robert Malval at his home. Malval's executive assistant Alice Blanchet was listening on the other line. "I'm calling to tell you that the *Harlan County* is returning," said Vice President Gore, according to both Malval and Blanchet.[24]

Malval immediately called Caputo to relay the good news. "Dante, this is beautiful," said the prime minister. "I received a phone call from Vice President Gore telling me that they have made the decision to bring back the *Harlan County*. They're going to be here tomorrow morning!"[25]

"Great! It worked!" gushed a delighted Caputo.

At one in the morning, Vicki Huddleston called to tell Caputo that she had just heard from an admiral from the Atlantic Command in Norfolk who told her: "Things are moving now. If I receive the order, the ship can return in a few hours. There's no problem."[26]

Despouy remembers that Caputo wanted to call a press conference to announce the *Harlan County's* imminent return.

At three in the morning Caputo got another call from Vicki Huddleston saying that the ship would be leaving Guantanamo at five and arrive in

Port-au-Prince at 11:30 or 12:00. According to a Haitian general, the news spread to FADH headquarters, where officers and soldiers started shedding their uniforms in fear that they would be hunted down and punished by incoming U.S. troops.[27]

By 10:00 Wednesday morning it was clear that the White House had changed its mind again. Now they were pretending that Robert Malval had misunderstood Vice President Gore. "I understand English very well," Malval said later, "and I know what I said and what I heard."[28] His executive assistant, Alice Blanchet, concurred.

"There was some heavy-duty lying going on in the Clinton White House," confided a State Department official.[29] In order to clear up the matter, Pezzullo asked the White House for notes of the vice president's conversation with Malval. "The vice president was very precise and we always had transcripts from his conversations," said Pezzullo, "and that's the one time we never saw anything."[30]

"My own impression is that President Clinton and Vice President Gore committed themselves and then they changed their minds again," said Caputo. "Most likely Gore went to see the president and after explaining the reason, the president realized that the decision he had taken was wrong. Then there was complete confusion."[31] The upshot was that the *Harlan County* had left and was not coming back.

In private meetings with Malval and Dante Caputo, General Cédras expressed shock at the U.S. decision. "I can't believe they turned around the ship," he told Caputo.[32] Ironically, the U.S. retreat had weakened Cédras's position since he had signed the Governors Island Agreement and argued that the military must uphold its end of the bargain.

"What have you done to me?" Mike Kozak remembered that General Cédras asked. "I negotiated with Michel François to make sure there were only a few guys at the docks so that they wouldn't give you any trouble. And you guys run away from that?"[33]

Washington seemed to be putting the onus for what happened at the port on Cédras. In a statement to reporters, President Clinton said the U.S. soldiers would not return to Haiti until the country's military leaders guaranteed the security of the advisors and the safe return of President Aristide. "I have no intention of sending our people there until the agreement is honored," he said. "What I intend to do now is press to reimpose the sanctions."[34]

That same afternoon, the UN Security Council voted unanimously to reimpose oil sanctions against Haiti. When President Aristide spoke to reporters from the steps of his Georgetown house he sounded surprisingly calm. "What we have to do now is push to pressure in order to have some killers saying yes to the world, to democracy, because we have to save lives. We cannot let killers after two years deny what the world said . . . If we don't do that, what will happen to the U.S.?"[35]

On October 13 Prime Minister Malval called President Aristide in Washington and asked: "Now that the *Harlan County* isn't coming back, what are we going to do?"

Malval remembered that Aristide replied: "I've got a new card in my hand. But I cannot deal it yet."

"Don't play games with me," Malval said strongly. "Me and my family have our lives on the line here."[36]

Malval instructed all members of his cabinet to keep a very low profile. Jocelyn McCalla, who along with Justice Minister Guy Malary and others had tried to bring civilian charges against ex-Haitian military strongman Prosper Avril back in 1990, met with the justice minister at his Port-au-Prince office on Wednesday, October 13. Malary had received numerous threats against his life, but didn't appear concerned. "Part of it is that in Haitian society, with the exception of the Duvalier years, violence and repression have been practiced against the lower classes," McCalla explained. "Most middle- and upper-class people thought they might be harassed or arrested, but were almost never killed."[37]

The UN, U.S., and Four Friends diplomats tried to stem the damage. But there was little they could do. Leandro Despouy, Dante Caputo, and Lawrence Pezzullo all seriously considered resigning on October 13. "I told Caputo, nobody's going to believe us at this point," said Despouy. "We had no credibility."[38]

Ten o'clock that night Dante Caputo got a call from Superintendent Lemay saying that the fifty-nine Canadian police trainers/monitors who were already in Haiti would be leaving immediately. Lemay explained that the recall of the trainers was an internal political decision taken in Ottawa and had to do more with upcoming parliamentary elections than the situation in Haiti. Nevertheless, the trainers were gone in less than five hours. They left behind bulletproof jackets for Caputo and Despouy. They were small comfort to Caputo, who was new being pressured by

Ian Martin to withdraw the more than 250 ICM human rights monitors deployed throughout the country.

In an effort to salvage what he could of the Governors Island Agreement, U.S. special advisor Lawrence Pezzullo flew to Port-au-Prince on Thursday morning accompanied by marine general Jack Sheehan and General William Herzog of the Atlantic Command. That same morning President Clinton held a press conference at the White House. "Malval is the key to making this whole thing work," Clinton told reporters. "I want to send a very clear signal today that the United States is very concerned about his ability to function and his personal safety and the safety of his government."[39]

Two hours after President Clinton's statement, Justice Minister Guy Malary, his chauffeur, and one police bodyguard were gunned down in broad daylight as they drove to the Hotel Montana to meet with UN/OAS envoy Leandro Despouy. News of Malary's death set off a panic that caused shopkeepers to quickly close their businesses and hundreds of business executives and merchants to leave town.

U.S. special advisor Pezzullo was greeted with the news of Malary's murder minutes after he landed in Port-au-Prince. He and Generals Sheehan and Herzog drove directly to the U.S. Embassy, where Pezzullo was besieged with calls from Washington. Secretary Warren Christopher told Pezzullo that an emergency meeting of the National Security Council had been called for Friday morning and Secretary Christopher was being asked to recommend steps to save the situation from deteriorating further.

Meanwhile, General Herzog drove to the Rancho Hotel to visit Colonel Pulley and his very nervous contingent of U.S. trainers. "When he came back, he was broken-hearted," Pezzullo recalled.[40]

The previous day, Dante Caputo had directed Colonel Pulley and his soldiers to provide security for UN personnel who were being ordered to evacuate the country. Colonel Pulley refused to do so because of the potential threat to his men. Instead, U.S. Marines assigned to guard the U.S. embassy volunteered to escort the UN personnel to the airport, which proceeded without incident.

In the aftermath of the U.S. withdrawal and the Malary assassination, Dante Caputo agreed under pressure from Ian Martin and UN headquarters to order the 250 ICM human rights monitors evacuated to Santo Domingo. The problem was that they were scattered all over the country and had collected confidential information that could endanger witnesses and sources if it fell into the wrong hands. Now they had ten hours to put their confidential files on computer disks for safekeeping and meet in Port-au-Prince.

Some monitors who had been in the country since March were anxious to leave; others were annoyed. "If the United States and Canada gave up so easily, then we are fair game here," reported one Canadian monitor. "I'm somewhat saddened," said a European member. "We came here to do a job and that job has been interrupted. Hopefully, we can return."[41]

When Pezzullo met with Dante Caputo on Thursday evening, he faced "as shaken a man as I've ever seen."[42]

"Larry, when I saw that ship turn around in the harbor, I couldn't believe my eyes," said the Argentine.[43]

That night Pezzullo sat with Mike Kozak, General Sheehan, General Herzog, and Dante Caputo in Caputo's modest office in the Montana Hotel and commiserated over drinks. Someone recommended stationing U.S. Navy destroyers off the coast as a way to enforce the UN embargo and show the Haitian military a measure of U.S. resolve, now that they were convinced that none existed.

The next morning Pezzullo communicated this idea to Secretary Christopher, who said he would table it at the White House. "It won't compensate for what has happened," cautioned the special advisor, "but at least it will buy us some time."[44]

Mike Kozak and Pezzullo then traveled to Pétionville to meet with Prime Minister Malval, who was deeply disturbed by the death of his friend and colleague Guy Malary. When Pezzullo and Kozak asked him who he thought was responsible, Malval came up with a thesis that surprised both Americans. "Everything points to Colonel Michel François," he said, "which leads me to believe that François is being set up by right-ist forces within the military."[45]

This led to a discussion of the larger issue of the FADH with Malval's minister of interior, René Prosper—a retired colonel who was the brother of Yannick Cédras. Prosper broke down the FADH into three groups.

At the very top was a small group that supported General Cédras because they owed their positions to him. The second larger group was allied to Colonel François. They remained loyal to the police chief because he treated them well and shared the money he made from the ports, state industries, contraband, and drug trade. "They're good soldiers," Prosper said, according to Pezzullo, "but they're a tough, corrupt, self-serving bunch." The third group he identified was much larger than the other two. These were officers and soldiers who were disappointed in Cédras's leadership and resented François because he was corrupt. They were looking for a way to protect their future and save the FADH. "That's the group we should be working with," concluded Prosper.[46]

General Phillip Biamby, who was still operating quietly and effectively behind the scenes, wasn't mentioned.

The centerpiece of Pezzullo's trip to Haiti was a meeting that afternoon with General Cédras. It took place on Vicki Huddleston's terrace and was attended by Generals Sheehan and Herzog and Mike Kozak. General Cédras arrived in uniform with General Duperval. The two Haitians looked grim.

Pezzullo didn't try to hide his anger. "General, do you remember what I said to you when you agreed to sign the Governors Island Agreement?" the U.S. special advisor asked. "I knew you felt badly about the way you had been treated by President Aristide. I told you: I wanted you to know that I thought you had acted with dignity and served the military well. Well, I have to say that my opinion of you has changed. What you've done these last couple of days is a disgrace to your uniform, a disgrace to your military, a personal failure, and a terrible insult to my country."

When Cédras tried to explain, Pezzullo cut him off. "It's the fifteenth of October, General. You're supposed to resign today. Are you ready to?"[47]

General Cédras reached into a manila folder and produced a letter he had just sent to Prime Minister Malval.

"No, no, no," interjected Pezzullo, waving it away. "I've read that letter. It's full of conditions. You know damn well what you agreed to. You said you would retire on the fifteenth of October, period. Now you're trying to impose conditions. It's completely unacceptable, and you know that!"[48]

For once, General Cédras didn't seem to know what to say.

Then General Sheehan spoke. "General, once I knew a soldier whom I respected. Now I find myself talking to a sleazy courthouse lawyer." The special advisor got to his feet and left with the two American generals.[49]

By nightfall the U.S. Navy cruiser *Sterett* was visible off the Haitian coast. The next day two other Aegis class cruisers, the *Vicksburg* and the *Gettysburg*; two frigates, the *Klakring* and *Jack Williams*, and the destroyer *Canon*, were positioned off Haiti. That same day Canadian prime minister Kim Campbell announced that two Canadian destroyers and a supply ship would soon join the U.S. warships in enforcing UN sanctions.

Before he returned to Washington, Pezzullo sat down with the ministers of Malval's government and representatives of the Four Friends of Haiti. "It was like being at a wake," the special advisor recalled. "Dante was trying to put the best face on things, but after the pullout of the *Harlan County* it was clear to everyone that the diplomatic situation was bleak."[50]

Pezzullo said he left depressed. In fact, everyone in the international community was saddened and disheartened, particularly by the death of Justice Minister Guy Malary. "I had worked closely with him and considered him a friend," said UN representative Juliette Remy.[51] U.S. embassy officers Vicki Huddleston and Ellen Cosgrove had eaten breakfast with Malary only days before he was murdered. "He said: 'I've sent my kids out of the country. I'm so, so tired, they can kill me, but I'm not going,'" Cosgrove remembered.[52]

According to Leandro Despouy and others, Malary had raised the ire of extreme rightists in the military because of his efforts to get Supreme Court chief justice Emile Jonassaint to step down. It started back in early September, when President Aristide sent Malary an order to retire the eighty-year-old Jonassaint.

Guy Malary, Robert Malval, and foreign diplomats had not realized the order's significance. Not only was Jonassaint a highly regarded political figure in Haiti—he headed the Constitutional Assembly of 1986—but he was also a major voudoun *houngan* and an ally of General Raoul Cédras, General Phillipe Biamby, and others in the FADH. He was important in the current political situation, because Cédras and the FADH general staff felt that if they ever chose to invoke Article 149 of the Haitian Constitution and declare the presidency "vacant," Jonassaint, as chief justice of the Supreme Court, would make a sympathetic interim president.

After weeks of negotiation with members of Parliament and Haitian jurists, Malary had reached an agreement the evening of October 13 that cleared the way for Chief Justice Jonassaint's retirement. On Thursday morning, October 14, the fifty-year-old Malary went to his private law offices for the first time in several days. When he finished speaking to Leandro Despouy on the telephone, he received another threat on his life.

Minutes later, Guy Malary left his law offices, accompanied by a police bodyguard and driver, to meet with Despouy at the Montana Hotel. His car was cut off by heavily armed gunmen, then it veered out of control and turned on its side. The gunmen peppered it with bullets from their automatic weapons. Then they removed the bodies of Malary, the driver, and the bodyguard and lined them up head to toe.

Had Malary been set up? Some Haitians, including his widow, think he was. Emile Jonassaint was also the judge who had been assigned to adjudicate a dispute over property between Guy Malary and his first wife, who was now married to President Aristide's former prime minister, Réne Préval. Préval, who later succeeded Aristide as president, was one of Aristide's principal advisors in Washington.

The unsigned order to retire Chief Justice Emile Jonassaint had been sent to Malary from Washington. Had Préval sent the order knowing that it would get Malary in trouble with the military?

CHAPTER 16

Dissension in Washington

"I'm standing here in the big road. I ask who else will take
a stand? Everybody runs for cover. . . ."

—*Jou Malè* (Day of Shock), BOUKMAN EKSPERYANS

"There is something peculiarly Roman in the air in Haiti," wrote British novelist Graham Greene in *The Comedians*. "Roman in its cruelty, in its corruption and its heroism." In October 1993, the assassination of Guy Malary, the corruption of the Haitian military, and the heroism of its prime minister Robert Malval all seemed to fit.

The retreat of the *Harlan County* on the afternoon of October 12 had people all over the world scratching their heads. "Americans could have docked that boat if they wanted to," said a thirty-four-year-old electrician named Hervé standing in a shantytown in Port-au-Prince. "There is no stronger country than the United States."[1]

"In their dreams, the Haitian military never thought that anyone would withdraw without a single shot being fired or anyone hurt," reported a source close to the military. "That was the moment the battle, if not the war, was lost."[2]

U.S. and UN diplomats were left with the unfortunate task of trying to fit the pieces of the Governors Island Agreement back together. Dante Caputo, Lawrence Pezzullo, and Leandro Despouy all considered resigning but held out hope that the extraordinary international cooperation they had achieved could somehow find a resolution to the crisis. They also felt a sense of responsibility to Prime Minister Robert Malval.

Faced with daily threats against his life, Malval continued to work out of his handsome two-story stone house in the Delmas suburb, high above Port-au-Prince, guarded by members of the Presidential Guard, who mounted machine guns on the upper floor to fend off attack. "All I can tell them is to come and get me," he told reporters in response to the threats he received from military officers. "If they eliminate me, there will be a very high price to pay, and some of them will definitely be taken out as well."[3]

Malval had an important political ally in Alliance senator Julio Larosiliere, who believed that by simultaneously passing the police and amnesty laws called for in the Governors Island Agreement, Parliament could still pave the way to President Aristide's return by October 30. But Larosiliere was unable to reach a quorum among the remaining seventeen senators and seventy members of the Chamber of Deputies.

Alliance members accused President Aristide's Constitutionalist allies of failing to appear. Constitutionalists like Deputy Patrick Norzeus claimed that the bill was just another Alliance ploy. "The Alliance has always found a way to block any real push to bring Aristide back," he told reporters.[4] A combination of die-hard anti-Aristide and pro-Aristide senators was enough to block a quorum. For his part, President Aristide continued to express his lack of enthusiasm for either piece of legislation despite the commitment he signed at Governors Island.

Those seeking a political solution remained frustrated in the middle. On one side were military leaders like Colonel Michel François, General Philip Biamby and, now, General Raul Cédras. On the other side stood the Aristide loyalists. Ironically, the retreat of the *Harlan County* reduced General Cédras's and Colonel François's control of the army because of the emergence of the Front for Reform and Progress in Haiti (FRAPH). A loose group of Duvalierists organized by FADH chief of staff Phillipe Biamby, FRAPH was now emboldened by its success on the docks.

"That's the day FRAPH was born," declared one of its leaders Emmanuel "Toto" Constant. "Before, everyone said we were crazy, suicidal, that we would all be burned if Aristide returned. But now," he added with a giggle, "we know he is never going to return."[5]

As FRAPH branches opened across the country, local army commanders started to become alarmed. "They were complaining that the FRAPH had better arms and equipment than they had," said one U.S. intelligence official.[6] At a meeting with his zone commanders in November after local commanders catalogued instances in which FRAPH had come into their districts and were pushing their weight around, General Cédras pounded the table and pointing at General Biamby yelled: "You've got to stop this!"[7]

General Phillipe Biamby had used FRAPH behind the scenes to establish his own position. He was now the most powerful, ruthless, and anti-Aristide member of the FADH.

The Aristide camp in Washington seemed equally uninterested in trying to achieve a political compromise. More than a week passed and Prime Minister Robert Malval still hadn't heard a word from President Aristide. As he watched CNN news on Saturday, October 23, Malval learned that Aristide had been a guest at Congressman Joe Kennedy's wedding in Boston.

"What the hell are you doing?" the prime minister asked Aristide over the phone the next morning. "We're in the midst of a political crisis here and you're going to a wedding?" Malval lost his temper. "When are you going to deal that famous card you referred to?"[8]

President Aristide had no answer. "He was happy," Malval reported later. "He was happy that the accord was dead and that he didn't have to return by the end of October."[9]

Convinced that he no longer had a role to play, Prime Minister Malval submitted his letter of resignation to President Aristide on October 28. That same day, President Aristide addressed the United Nations General Assembly in New York. Speaking passionately in French and Creole, Aristide called for a total trade embargo of his country to force its military rulers to resign.[10]

The next day, Friday, October 29, Malval received a phone call from President Clinton asking him to reconsider.

"I told him that under the present conditions, staying on was impossible," Malval remembered.

"We are all working hard to make this work," President Clinton pleaded, according to Malval. "Please stay on and give it another try."[11]

Malval agreed to remain in office for another fifteen days. One of the reasons he changed his mind was the national conference called by UN/OAS special envoy Dante Caputo for the first week of November. "What we were trying to do," explained Mike Kozak, who helped organize the conference, "was to try to shame Cédras and the creeps into compliance with Governors Island, which was a tall order. We had the sanctions back on and we were going to stage a conference and invite all the political players. That's all we had to work with at the time."[12]

The UN embargo, which had been reimposed on October 18, was already having an effect. As long lines grew at the country's few gas stations, economists estimated that Haiti's oil supplies would be depleted in six to ten weeks. Some observers wondered how much lower Haiti's economy could slip without collapsing altogether. During the last two years, according to a report from the World Bank, Haiti's economy had shrunk more that 15 percent.

On October 29, the Clinton administration froze the U.S. bank accounts, real estate, and other assets of forty-one Haitians who worked for the de facto military regime. The list included General Cédras and the police chief, Colonel François. Gradually it was expanded to include over six hundred military officers, officials, and businessmen associated with the de facto government. Treasury Department officials estimated that the freeze would cover tens of millions of dollars in assets.

Dante Caputo and Mike Kozak drove to General Cédras's house on the first of November to try to convince him to attend the national conference. Delegations from the Malval government, Parliament, the private sector, and the diplomatic community had already accepted invitations. But Cédras typically was afraid to commit himself. And once again, President Aristide's actions gave him a convenient out.

"Instead of helping us put pressure on Cédras," said Kozak, "Aristide handed him a gift-wrapped excuse by announcing that he would be represented at the conference by two *blancs*—Mike Barnes and Ira Kurzban."[13]

The naming of two U.S. lawyers was also a slap in the face to Prime Minister Malval. "In effect, Aristide wasn't giving him the authority to represent him at a conference that was taking place in Port-au-Prince," said Malval's executive assistant Alice Blanchet.[14]

Malval claimed he took it all in stride. "Michael Barnes told me he had been sent by Aristide because he knew the background," Malval explained. "I told him: If you've come as a legal representative of the president, no problem. But if you've come to represent the government, there is a problem and a big one."[15]

Both men attended the conference on the morning of November 5— Robert Malval representing the government of Haiti and Michael Barnes sitting as the representative of the head of state.

"I got dressed that morning to ride over to the conference with Dante," Mike Kozak recalled, "and I looked greener than my suit. I said: 'I think I'll go do something useful like throw up.' So Dante went to the conference and I got sick at the hotel. I think what I did was just as useful."[16]

After waiting fifty minutes for General Cédras to appear, Robert Malval stood and walked out, followed by Mike Barnes, diplomats, and other political leaders. Caputo in a brief statement to the press said: "Our engagement here is for the long term," but gave no indication of what the next steps would be.[17]

Back in Washington, U.S. special advisor Pezzullo hoped to get a strong statement out of President Clinton to push General Cédras to the negotiating table. "Instead I got a four-hour meeting in Tony Lake's office with Tony, Sandy Berger, and Peter Tarnoff from State. They gave a lot of unwanted security advice that I was supposed to pass on to Malval."[18]

The situation in Washington was, in Pezzullo's words, "surreal." On October 20 he was asked to appear before the House Intelligence Committee. Before seven members of the House, including the Democratic chairman Daniel Glickman and Republican Robert Dornan of California, the special advisor and an admiral from Defense Intelligence (DIA) gave their assessment of the situation. "We both said that the Haitian military was entrenched, but there were schisms within the military that we thought we could exploit."[19]

The next witness was an analyst from the CIA named Brian Latell, who read from the dated psychological profile of President Aristide written by CIA staff psychiatrist Richard Ammerman. "He concluded by saying that Aristide was a manic depressive with schizophrenic tendencies," Pezzullo recalled.[20]

The special advisor, who had read the profile back in March, tried to discount it. "What you just heard is a report based on drugs allegedly found in Aristide's medicine cabinet," he began, "and by comments from other people who have an interest in showing the man to be unbalanced. I've been dealing with President Aristide on almost a daily basis for seven months. Although I would characterize him as a rigid man who has trouble compromising, these psychological problems are certainly not traits that I've observed."[21]

One congressman asked: "Why is President Clinton using his resources to return a maniac?"[22]

Across the street, at the Senate Intelligence Committee, assistant secretary of state for inter-American affairs Alec Watson was being subjected to the same sort of grilling by Senator Jesse Helms. Watson later said he was "profoundly distressed" by the tone of the CIA evaluation.[23]

Upon returning to the State Department, Pezzullo called the White House to register a strong protest. Then he drafted a pointed memo to Secretary of State Warren Christopher. It said, in effect, that there was no discipline within the administration, that the NSC didn't know what it was doing, that the CIA and OSD had been opposed to the policy of returning President Aristide from the beginning. The memo ended with a call for Secretary Christopher to take command of the policy.

But Christopher never saw the memo. Instead, it was intercepted by Under Secretary of State Peter Tarnoff, who called the special advisor and said: "If the secretary sees this he'll go ballistic."

"Good," countered Pezzullo. "He should come to grips with the truth."[24]

Mike Kozak went to the White House to ask Sandy Berger to order CIA chief James Woolsey to issue a clarification of the Aristide profile. Berger told Kozak that he couldn't interfere with the CIA, but Nancy Soderberg of the NSC staff was writing a rebuttal that the White House would issue to the press. Kozak was surprised that the White House would choose a public debate with the CIA, rather than ordering Woolsey to issue a full and accurate report.[25]

To Kozak and others, it seemed as though Brian Latell's profile was part of a concerted effort by Republicans on Capitol Hill and members of the CIA and the Pentagon to get President Clinton to change his position.

Following the briefings, Senator Helms denounced Aristide as a "psychopath" undeserving of U.S. support.[26] The Senate majority leader, Bob Dole, threatened to introduce legislation to restrict President Clinton from committing forces for use in Haiti, except for reasons of national security. "I don't think he'd win any blue ribbons in most places," Senator Dole said of the ousted Haitian president. "I wouldn't risk any American lives to put Aristide back in power."[27]

Mike Kozak remembers chairing an interagency meeting in late October where Admiral Lou Shrieffer of the Pentagon's OSD said: "I'm just sick and tired of whoever is imposing this stupid pro-Aristide policy," according to Kozak. "It's absolutely mindless. Whoever is doing it must be smoking something we're not allowed to smoke at the Pentagon."

"I'm glad to hear there's great support for the president's policy over at the Pentagon," Kozak replied.[28]

The very departments (CIA and Defense) that were responsible for the withdrawal of the *Harlan County* were now pushing for a complete policy review. At a principals' meeting in the White House Situation Room on October 27, Secretary of Defense Les Aspin suggested that the administration consider withdrawing its support for President Aristide altogether. He cited Aristide's shortcomings and the unlikelihood that Cédras and company would relinquish power without a struggle.

When neither Secretary Christopher nor National Security Advisor Tony Lake spoke up, Pezzullo cut in. "Look, no one in this room has been more frustrated with Aristide's machinations than me," he said. "But he is the elected president of Haiti and it's difficult to see how political peace can be achieved in that country without his return. I believe that we should stay the course with our current strategy of pressure through sanctions on the military and pressure on Aristide to cooperate in reconciling the various political forces so he builds a base for a viable democracy when he returns."

The administration appeared to be in complete disarray. On October 24, Democratic congressman Frank McCloskey of Indiana called for Secretary of State Christopher to resign. "He has severely damaged the national interest through failed leadership in difficult situations," wrote McCloskey in an op-ed piece for the *New York Times*. "Mr. Christopher has defined the return of President Jean-Bertrand Aristide as a strategic interest. But as his elastic views of America's interest show, the use of 'strategic' can really only refer to President Clinton's short-term domestic political interests."[29]

Special Advisor Pezzullo continued to lobby for discipline within the administration and a strong statement from President Clinton to let everyone know definitively "that the policy was not up for grabs." What he got instead were more meetings at State and the White House and memos from the National Security Council raising more fears and options. "It was enough to make you question your sanity," Pezzullo remembered.[30]

Starting at sundown, Friday, October 30, and lasting throughout the night, the streets of Port-au-Prince echoed with gunfire as FRAPH members and soldiers celebrated the passing of the deadline set in Governors Island for President Aristide's return. "This was supposed to be like New Year's Day," said Samuel Delva, an Aristide supporter living in the low-lying slums of the country's capital. "We thought we would be delivered. Now we are shedding tears."[31]

"I cannot blame the average man for losing hope right now," said Prime Minister Robert Malval. "Sometimes I too feel that this is a truly meaningless situation."[32]

"As we got into November those were dark, depressing days in Haiti," remembered UN/OAS envoy Leandro Despouy.[33]

"There was absolutely no political movement," echoed Juliette Remy, who remained with Despouy until November 28. "No work was being done. We were completely demoralized and spent a lot of time trying to protect those parliamentarians who were trying to work the police and amnesty laws."[34]

On November 16, Prime Minister Malval sent the Haitian president another letter of resignation. This time Aristide told Malval that he should seek asylum in a foreign embassy.

"I fought against the Duvalier government," Malval answered defiantly. "They set my printing plant on fire, and you think I'm going to leave now?"[35]

Malval understood that as long as the Haitian military felt that his government provided a veneer of constitutionality, he was safe. He also realized he was practically the only major political figure on the scene who could still talk to General Cédras. So he devoted his last month in office to going around and talking to the different sectors in Haiti. Mainly, he listened. "I told the army I was resigning on December 15 and I would act as a postman," Malval recalled.

After talks with members of the military, private sector, political parties, labor unions, media, and Catholic Church, Malval started to draft an appeal for a new social contract that would begin with a reshaping of his government. His paper began with the observation that Haitian society was dangerously fragmented and could easily descend into chaos. He suggested organizing a national conclave of representatives from all sectors of Haitian society to build a national base of support for political cooperation and reconciliation to rescue the country.

Malval faxed the document to Dante Caputo, Lawrence Pezzullo, and President Aristide in late November. An hour later members of President Aristide's staff issued a response saying: "Any attempt to share power with killers or putschists is something that President Aristide cannot accept."[36] Nothing in Malval's paper suggested sharing power with the military.

Then, Malval got a call from Aristide's U.S. ambassador Jean Casimir, who said, according to Malval: "The president won't even consider it."[37]

With his support among U.S. officials and the international community at an all-time high, Prime Minister Malval decided to travel to Washington to try to convince President Aristide personally of the need for a national dialogue. "Without the support of Aristide," Malval said later, "I knew that my plan would go nowhere."[38] He arrived in Washington on December 1, vowing once again that he would resign by December 15.

Malval and President Aristide met alone in the president's Georgetown office on Thursday morning, December 2. The first thing Aristide told his prime minister is that he didn't want him to resign on the fifteenth. Malval pointed out that General Cédras didn't want him to resign either. "Both of you are comfortable with me," the prime minister said, "but I'm not comfortable with either of you."[39]

The next day, Friday, Malval was invited to the State Department, where he met with Peter Tarnoff, Tony Lake, Sandy Berger, and others from State, Defense, and CIA. "They were all very impressed not only with Malval himself but with his assessment of the situation in Haiti," said Pezzullo.[40]

Even Vice President Al Gore stopped in at one point to express his interest in Malval's plan. As he left the State Department, Malval told the special advisor that he was optimistic about getting President Aristide's approval. Pezzullo said that if President Aristide agreed to hold the national conference, the two Haitian leaders could meet with President Clinton "as a sort of capstone."[41]

When the prime minister met with President Aristide again on Saturday, Malval made it clear that he thought Aristide had no other choice but to try to convene a national conference over which the Haitian president could preside. "I don't know how this will work out," said Malval, "but you have the historic responsibility to take matters into your own hands."[42]

Aristide expressed concern about the outcome. What would happen to the high command?

"After what happened to you in October," answered Malval, "you will be in a position to force Cédras out right away. I think you'll have the support of the whole international community."[43]

From Georgetown, the prime minister called Special Advisor Pezzullo to report: "Aristide said 'yes' but he wants something on paper." Malval then invited Pezzullo, Kozak, Caputo, and U.S. ambassador to Haiti William Swing to his room at the Willard Hotel. For the next four hours, the five men talked and Alice Blanchet took notes and started drafting a proposal. After translating the final proposal into French, Blanchet faxed it to President Aristide in Georgetown.

Sunday morning, Malval received a faxed reply to the international community that had been written by Michael Barnes. It said, in effect, that a national conference could only be convened after President Aristide had physically returned to Haiti.

Malval called President Aristide and said: "Your response to the international community is not what I expected. It's a clear 'no.' If that's your answer, fine, but I'm going to call the State Department and tell them to cancel the meeting at the White House. I don't see the point."[44]

Aristide immediately faxed Malval back, saying that they had to go to the White House.

Malval faxed a reply: "If you don't support the national conference, what's the point?"[45]

Malval decided to announce his resignation at a press conference at 11 A.M. on Monday at the Willard Hotel. At 10:45 A.M. Michael Barnes knocked on his door and asked: "The President wants to know ... If there is a national conference will it remain within the boundaries of Governors Island?"

"Michael, be serious," Malval answered. "The whole reason for a national conference is to give a new dynamic to Governors Island."[46]

Barnes then dialed a private number for President Aristide and told him that he didn't have any choice but to accept the national conference. When the lawyer hung up, Malval interjected: "Of course he has a choice. He can say 'no.' If this conference is going to work, Aristide has to participate."

Barnes said that President Aristide wanted to go forward.[47]

The prime minister and Aristide's lawyer went downstairs to tell the press that President Aristide would convene a national conference that Malval hoped would "find an acceptable way out of the crisis for all the parties involved." He announced that he would continue in the capacity of acting prime minister when his term expired on December 15.

After the press conference, Malval invited Barnes up to his room. "Michael, are you in compliance with what you just heard?" the prime minister asked.

"Yes, absolutely," Malval remembered that Barnes replied.[48]

Malval called Pezzullo. "Larry, under the circumstances I think we can meet with President Clinton. It's going to be just me and President Aristide there."

The meeting at the White House was quickly scheduled for 6:00 that evening. Dante Caputo had arranged a meeting for the following day, Tuesday, December 7, between Malval and UN secretary general Boutros-Ghali in New York. On Wednesday, Malval was leaving for Rome. There wasn't much time.

Shortly after 5 P.M. Monday, Malval climbed into President Aristide's limousine with Ambassador Jean Casimir and Foreign Minister Claudia Werleigh. "We talked about everything except the national conference," remembered Malval. "Everyone was in a jubilant mood."[49]

Waiting to greet them in the Oval Office were President Clinton, Tony Lake, Sandy Berger, and Lawrence Pezzullo. "Malval was very jovial," remembered Pezzullo, "but Aristide walked in looking grim."[50]

As he had been back in April, President Clinton was gracious and warmly greeted both President Aristide and Prime Minister Malval. Then

President Clinton turned to Malval and said something like: I heard that you were in town meeting with your president and I understand you have a new proposal.

On that cue from President Clinton, Malval began to outline his idea and why it was needed.

Clinton then asked Malval when the national conference might take place.

"I still have to put the plans together," answered Malval. "I'm leaving here tomorrow and meeting with Boutros-Ghali. Then I have to return to Haiti and talk to some people. I'm thinking of an open forum in which everyone can lay their cards on the table."[51]

President Clinton asked Malval what chance he thought the conference had of succeeding.

"Maybe fifty-fifty," replied Malval.[52]

Aristide sat like a rock; his face showed no emotion. President Clinton turned to him at one point and said something like: This is hopeful news, Mr. President. If you can put this thing together, it seems to me something that both of you should be proud of. Whether it works or not it deserves a chance.[53]

Aristide starting talking about genocide in Haiti and the need to stop the killers.[54] Next, Casimir spoke at length about human rights abuses, followed by Ms. Werleigh.

"I could see that President Clinton was getting very uneasy," remembered Malval. "We were there to talk about a way to end the crisis in my country and Aristide and his aides were going on about people getting shot in the streets."[55]

Finally, President Clinton turned to President Aristide and, according to both Malval and Pezzullo, asked: "Is it okay with you if I call in the press and tell them I support the Malval plan?"

"Aristide just smiled," Malval recalled. "He didn't say 'yes,' but he didn't say 'no,' either."[56]

After the meeting, Malval returned to President Aristide's apartment with the rest of the Haitian delegation. "Everyone seemed very happy," remembered Malval. "Then my wife and I got in the car and went to the airport for our flight to New York."[57]

CHAPTER 17

The Resignation
of Malval

"You made the psychological error of taking my sense of honor
and loyalty for weakness."

—resignation letter of Prime Minister ROBERT MALVAL to
President Aristide

While Prime Minister Malval was at UN headquarters telling
Secretary-General Boutros-Ghali that "the idea of a national conference has no meaning without President Aristide's support,"[1] President
Aristide and his advisors were huddled in the President's Georgetown
office thinking of ways to trip him up. According to Aristide advisor Bob
White, the Haitian president and the people close to him had two concerns. First, was their perception that Robert Malval was stealing their
thunder. "Watch out for Malval," warned one of Aristide's lobbyists, "he's
becoming more important than you."[2]

Second was their fear that a national conference would only revital-
ize the Governors Island Agreement. They were now convinced, based
on conversations they had with friends in the administration including
Nancy Soderberg of the NSC, that the removal of the entire high command of the FADH should be a precondition for Aristide's return.

"I felt that the key error of Governors Island was to force Malval and his cabinet to deal with General Cédras," explained Aristide advisor Bob White. "That legitimized Cédras and his people to a considerable degree."[3] In confidence, President Aristide had started to say that he didn't believe Haiti needed a military at all.

UN/OAS special envoy Dante Caputo was concerned about the fuzzy nature of Malval's plan and wanted the details fleshed out. UN secretary-general Boutros-Ghali suggested that the Four Friends of Haiti, who were meeting in Paris the next Monday, could be helpful. "Why don't you adjust your schedule so that you can meet with them in Paris?" asked the secretary-general, according to Malval.[4] Aristide's ambassador to the UN, Fritz Longchamps, agreed.

So Dante Caputo drew up specifics to be discussed in Paris, while Malval flew to Rome, where the Vatican secretary of state Cardinal Soldano made no secret of his negative impression of President Aristide. "I saw him at a meeting in Rio and Aristide was very obscene," said the Vatican secretary of state, according to Malval. "He cursed me and said the people of the Vatican are worse than dogs."[5]

Feeling optimistic that they had turned an important corner, Malval and his wife, Linda, spent a relaxing weekend in Rome. Sunday morning his chief of staff, Frantz Voltarie, called from Washington with the news that Mike Barnes and Jean Casimir had issued a statement saying that President Aristide would not support the conference since it would "most certainly require President Aristide to accept some form of power-sharing with forces acceptable to the military."[6] Malval was crushed. In addition to opposing the plan, President Aristide announced that he was withdrawing all authority from Prime Minister Malval to deal with foreign issues.

A defeated-sounding Malval reached Dante Caputo by telephone in New York. "I don't see any reason to continue on to Paris," he told the special envoy.[7] Caputo urged him to go. U.S. special advisor Pezzullo and his deputy Mike Kozak arrived in Paris without hearing the news.

"Mike and I were ushered into the conference and were greeted by a sea of glum faces," Pezzullo recalled.[8]

Malval's executive assistant, Alice Blanchet, reread the statement issued by Mike Barnes and Jean Casimir. Malval stood and said: "There's nothing left for me to do but return to Washington and resign," then left.[9]

On the flight back to Washington, Malval composed his letter of resignation. "I was disgusted and pumped up," he later recalled.[10]

Meanwhile, back in Paris, the Four Friends returned to the conference center, where they drafted a new initiative. It began with a reaffirmation of Governors Island. Disavowing the option of outside military intervention, their *Statement of Conclusions* went on to say that "it is the task of the *Haitian parties* to work out the procedures and political requirements required to bring compliance by both sides."

In effect, they were saying to President Aristide and General Raoul Cédras: You have to solve your own problems. They suggested that "Mr. Malval's ideas of a national conference offer a practical way to address this issue."

Articles Four and Five of their *Conclusions* spoke directly to the Haitian military: "The sanctions adopted by the Security Council are based solely on the failure of the Haitian military authorities thus far to fulfill their commitments. Accordingly, should the Haitian military in good faith take all necessary action within its capacities to bring about fulfillment of the Governors Island Agreement ... the sanctions should be suspended regardless of the actions of the other parties."

But, if the military failed to comply by January 15, the Four Friends recommended: "The Security Council should meet to consider additional measures."

The Four Friends adjourned Tuesday evening with the understanding that they would clear their *Conclusions* with their respective governments and reconvene in Washington.

On Wednesday, December 15, Robert Malval went to President Aristide's Georgetown office to deliver his resignation. According to Malval, it was a frank and brutal session, with Malval telling the Haitian president at one point: "You think you're smart, but you're dumb. You have two choices now, ask for U.S. intervention or just forget the whole thing."[11]

Returning to his home in Port-au-Prince, Malval continued to speak out. "Our country is stuck between a man who refuses to resign and a man who has made a choice to remain abroad as a sort of flag bearer, a mythic symbol," he told reporters. He went on to describe Aristide as "a man with a serious ego problem" who along with his advisors in exile "is playing with our lives, with the future of Haiti."[12]

Former U.S. ambassador Robert White, who was serving as an unpaid political advisor to the Haitian president, defended Aristide's decision. "When you get into a conference like this, you know they are going to squeeze you," said White. "If the president had accepted the conference and then refused to go along with any new constraints on him, he would have looked all the more intransigent. As it is, no serious pressures have ever been brought on the military."[13]

But that wasn't true. The UN Security Council had imposed severe sanctions on the de facto military regime in Haiti. And the United States had frozen the private assets of military officers and civilians.

What was true was that Aristide and his advisors were lobbying for tougher sanctions against the de facto military government. And, once again, the Clinton administration was questioning its policy.

The news out of Haiti was that economic sanctions were making a desperate humanitarian situation worse. A study issued the first week of November by international public health experts at Harvard University made front-page news in the *New York Times*. "Study Says Haiti Sanctions Kill Up to 1,000 Children a Month," screamed the headline. The study, entitled *Sanctions in Haiti: Crisis in Humanitarian Action*, concluded that "the human toll from the silent tragedy of humanitarian neglect has been greater than either the violence or human rights abuses." In addition to its claim of one thousand Haitian children dying a month, it claimed the embargo had contributed to as many as one hundred thousand new cases of malnutrition.[14]

Although the authors of the study later claimed that their findings had been exaggerated and misinterpreted, news that the sanctions were contributing to the suffering in Haiti sent a chill through the Clinton administration. President Clinton had never been able to dispel the racist tenor of his policy of returning fleeing Haitians while readily admitting people escaping from Cuba as political refugees.

Now thousands of desperate Haitians started to besiege the three refugee processing centers inside Haiti. "It started to pick up in the second week of November and I think it will continue to be high," explained one official.[15] "They are going to hit the boats," said one Western diplomat. "It's only a matter of time."

The last thing the Clinton administration needed was another exodus of boat people to Florida's shores. They wanted to avoid headlines like

"Haitian Mother Leaps with Baby into Ocean" found in the December 22, 1993, edition of the *Washington Post*. Therefore, they were hesitant to beef up sanctions against the military government of Haiti as suggested by the Four Friends.

Special Advisor Pezzullo explained the dilemma to policy makers at the White House in the first week of December. "As we found in June, sanctions and embargoes are a short-range tool," he said. "In fact, the psychological threat of sanctions is often more powerful than the sanctions themselves."[16] Furthermore, he argued, pressure on the Haitian military was of no use, unless equal pressure was applied to President Aristide. Pezzullo didn't want the administration to lose sight of the central tenant of U.S. policy: The necessity of getting both sides to negotiate a *Haitian* solution to the crisis.

Aristide wanted the military to capitulate even if it meant bringing his country to its knees. To this end, he lobbied for extending sanctions and the embargo. When Dante Caputo asked him in late December if he wasn't concerned about the suffering of Haitians as a result of the sanctions, Aristide replied, according to Caputo: "Oh, Mr. Caputo, you don't understand. My people love sanctions. I had a letter the other day from a woman who told me she liked the sanctions so much that she named her baby 'Sanctions.'"[17]

Pezzullo urged the Clinton administration to use the leverage of negative publicity generated from Malval's resignation to push Aristide to the negotiating table. But the administration was again in disarray. On December 15, the White House announced that Secretary of Defense Les Aspin was stepping down. People close to Aspin complained that he was being made a scapegoat for the debacles in Somalia and Haiti.

That same day, after a twenty-four-hour visit to Haiti, the assistant secretary of state for human rights and humanitarian affairs, John Shattuck, said he wanted the administration to review its policy of forcibly returning all Haitian boat people. The Coast Guard estimated that it had returned almost forty thousand Haitians since the 1991 coup.

A day later it was reported that National Security Advisor Tony Lake admitted in a meeting with human rights officials that the administration's policy of returning Haitian refugees was "a dark stain" on its record. Lake later denied he had made that statement, saying instead that he told the group: "This was a policy none of us likes, including myself. But it was a policy that was necessary for us to follow because the alternative was worse—risking a humanitarian disaster at sea, possibly risking tens of thousands of lives."[18]

In this atmosphere of confusion and fear, the Four Friends reconvened in Washington during the third week of December. Their deliberations bore two aide mémoires. One, addressed to President Aristide, urged him to name a new prime minister and form a broad-based government of "national concord" as agreed to in the New York Pact. The last paragraph stated that the Four Friends were proposing a government of national reconciliation, not "power sharing" with the military as Aristide lobbyists had alleged.

The second aide mémoire, addressed to the Haitian military, informed them of what unilateral action they could take to get the Four Friends to recommend lifting the sanctions. If these actions were not taken by January 15, 1994, however, the Four Friends would go to the UN Security Council and ask that the sanctions be enlarged and strengthened.

On Monday, December 20, representatives of the Friends delivered their aide mémoire to President Aristide. Pezzullo and Caputo remembered that the Venezuelan representative said: "Mr. President, there is no one in the world community who will understand a president who doesn't act when his country is suffering the way yours is."[19]

The next day President Aristide's public relations firm issued a communiqué which quoted him as saying: "The current conditions of insecurity in Haiti will not allow for a national conference at this time." Instead, he said, the conference should be organized only "after his physical return to Haiti."[20]

Later in the day, President Aristide issued another press release that suggested that U.S. policy toward repatriating Haitian boat people should be reconsidered. "Having given the international community close to one year to resolve the crisis and having faced the weapons in their country for over two years, the voice of the refugees must now be heard," declared Aristide.[21]

It was a total rebuke to the Four Friends and a warning to the Clinton administration. Aristide was saying in effect: If you try to pressure me, I'll abrogate the 1981 agreement that allows the United States to forcibly return Haitian refugees. And then you'll have a political mess on your hands.

President Aristide's rejection of the Four Friends plan was disturbing news even to some of his own supporters. "The only choice left for the international community is disengagement," said one prominent Haitian friend of the exiled president.[22]

"Mr. Aristide's limited view of his own role and responsibility is troubling," read an editorial in the *Washington Post*. "He seems to consider it somebody else's job to restore him to power."[23]

Before he was pressed to defend his position, Aristide was rescued once again by his military opponents in Port-au-Prince. The very same day, General Cédras refused to receive a military delegation sent by the Four Friends to present the aide mémoire.

In an attempt to blunt the criticism he was receiving, President Aristide announced the next day, December 23, that he would be convening a meeting of Haiti's pro-democracy forces and representatives of the United Nations and Haitian refugee groups in Miami on January 15. The agenda of the conference, according to a statement released by the Haitian embassy in Washington, was "to protect Haitian refugees and Haitians threatened by the military."[24]

Special Advisor Pezzullo learned that Aristide advisor Ira Kurzban was at the center of the strategy to press the refugee issue. According to the exchange of diplomatic notes between the government of Jean-Claude Duvalier and the United States that took place in 1981, President Aristide was required to give six months' notice to abrogate that agreement. Kurzban, who had a long record of defending the rights of Haitian refugees, knew that this would be a real shot across the bow to the Clinton administration.

Aristide had at least two things working in his favor. With the political and economic crisis worsening, the possibility of an exodus from Haiti was clearly building. Secondly, the contradiction of imposing economic sanctions on Haiti while forcibly repatriating refugees had come under increasing criticism by human rights groups and the general public.

A three-way contest of wills was developing with the Haitian people caught in the middle. But the most powerful of the three, the international community, had a sizable chink in its armor. By the end of 1993, Aristide's advisors in Washington had identified weakness in the Clinton administration and were ready to mobilize human rights and refugee groups, several Democratic legislators, the Congressional Black Caucus, and the press to exploit it.

During the first week of January, Special Advisor Pezzullo dined at the Cosmos Club in downtown Washington with the Haitian president, Ambassador Casimir, Bob White, Mike Barnes, and Mike Kozak. Pezzullo said: "Mr. President, if you intend to make this conference a forum on the Clinton administration refugee policy, you're declaring war. And where do you go for support if the administration backs away from you?"

The Haitian president answered calmly that he didn't intend to declare war on the Clinton administration, but couldn't ignore the suffering in his country.

"Look, we know about the refugee problem," Pezzullo continued. "There are two ways to resolve it. One, we let all the Haitians into this country, which would be very difficult for this administration to accept politically and would only encourage more Haitians to flee in danger-ous boats. Second, you make Haiti a politically and economically viable country, which is something we want to help do."

As the conversation continued, President Aristide seemed to warm to the idea of turning the planned Miami Conference into a political forum to focus on issues of reconciliation.[25]

"You've got to open your arms to everyone," Pezzullo added. "Even invite the military."[26]

The dinner ended with Aristide lawyer Mike Barnes pledging to work with Pezzullo and Kozak to reprioritize the agenda of the conference. But at a White House meeting on the afternoon of January 13 chaired by Tony Lake, President Clinton's foreign policy advisors seemed to be backing away from President Aristide altogether.

"It was as bizarre as bizarre could be," Pezzullo recalled. "They weren't sure if I should go to the conference at all."[27]

At a luncheon with reporters on January 5, President Clinton had expressed his frustration with the exiled Haitian president: "I think his own prospects are clouded by what happened with Malval. And that's something we're going to have to really sit down and think through and reassess."[28]

The following day, Robert D. Novak in a column entitled "Adieu to Aristide" declared that Malval's resignation "had buttressed the Clinton administration's desire to free itself from the exiled Haitian president."[29] Novak quoted a passage from Malval's letter of resignation where the prime minister said he pleaded with Aristide "to free some state funds at your disposal in Washington" to open Haitian schools. "We never received those funds," Malval wrote, despite the fact that Aristide "receives $1.8 million a month in Haitian government funds blocked by the U.S. Treasury." In the same column Aristide's ambassador Jean Casimir claimed that in the past six months $1.1 million had been spent "to obtain the publication of articles expounding the views of the constitutional [Aristide] government."

"That's the only method I know to make the White House or State Department listen to you," Casimir told Novak. "It is not by mere chance that the largest circulation newspapers have been publishing editorials favorable to the restoration of democracy in Haiti."[30]

After spending a week working to win White House approval Pezzullo, Kozak, and Nancy Jackson traveled to Miami to attend Aristide's conference on January 15. "When we arrived there it was clear it had been geared to assault the administration on refugee and human rights," Pezzullo recalled. Gathered in front of the hotel was a large group of demonstrators. There was a big sign that read: "Pezzullo = Cédras."[31]

The U.S. diplomats made their way into the auditorium that held about two to three hundred people. As the conference was called into order, Pezzullo found his place on the dais between author Taylor Branch and Florida congresswoman Corrine Brown. Reverend Jesse Jackson spoke first, whipping up the crowd. "President Clinton was in Moscow this week," said Jackson, "but he did not have to meet with the fascist leader. He chose to reinforce Yeltsin. We should not be obliged to meet with the fascist forces in Haiti." This brought a huge roar of approval from the partisan crowd.

Next came a whole series of emotional speeches from members of the Congressional Black Caucus. Then Pezzullo spoke extemporaneously. "It's time for building bridges in Haiti," he began. "The country is suffering." He went on to say that he was appalled by some of "the demonization that is going on. You will recall," he said, "that right in the midst of our Civil War, President Lincoln never insulted or demonized anyone.

Nations are forged by people who see beyond the anger and hatred of the day."[32]

These remarks were preceded by those of President Aristide himself, who, in Pezzullo's words, was "remarkably moderate."

After lunch, Pezzullo calmly made his way through the demonstrators gathered outside of the hotel and returned to Washington. Mike Kozak and Nancy Jackson stayed behind to attend the other sessions.

All of them agreed that President Aristide performed well under very difficult conditions. Although nothing concrete came out of the conference, the exiled president did meet with a broad range of delegates, including Senator Julio Larosiliere and KONAKOM leader Victor Benoit. He told both men they were leading candidates to be his next prime minister. Although they came from different sides of the political aisle, Larosiliere and Benoit agreed to work together.

And Workshop A, held on the afternoon of the 15th, did draw up a set of recommendations:

1) That the President of the Republic begin the procedure of naming a new prime minister and establishing a government of national concord.
2) That the President of the Republic obtain from the international community the lifting of the embargo when the following have been accomplished:
   a) the early retirement of General Cédras with the guarantees contained in the amnesty order issued by the president;
   b) the ratification of a new prime minister;
   c) the installation of a new prime minister;
   d) the return to safety and respect for human rights.

Port-au-Prince mayor Evans Paul, who attended the conference, summed up the dynamic like this: "Those of us who are living in Haiti, living the reality there with all its threats and privations, are readier to consider compromises," he said. "The people who live here in exile are more interested in sticking to positions of principle."[33]

"I think the Aristide entourage was pretty surprised," said Juliette Remy, who attended as a UN observer. "The parliamentarians were pushing pretty hard for a commitment from the president about forming a new government and finding a way out of the political impasse."[34] It turned out to be a good conference that raised a lot of hope. But the hope turned out to be misplaced.

CHAPTER 18

The Parliamentarians' Plan

"Although the car slides down the hill easily enough, it takes a lot of gasoline to get back home again."

—MRS. FRANÇOIS BENOIT, wife of Haiti's former minister of foreign affairs

The Four Friends aide mémoire delivered to both President Aristide and General Cédras in mid-December stated categorically that if the military leaders in Haiti did not revive the process set out at Governors Island by January 15, a voluntary OAS economic embargo would be extended and made mandatory under Chapter 7 of the UN charter. But the Clinton administration, sensitive to press reports that children were dying of malnutrition, was getting cold feet. Meanwhile, Father Aristide—champion of the poor and downtrodden in Haiti—campaigned vociferously for a total embargo.

On the humanitarian front, keeping the lines of supply open to CARE and other nongovernmental relief organizations that were feeding as many as one million people a day was of paramount importance. So far the military leaders in Haiti had done nothing to interfere with their operations.

Nor was there a serious risk of a humanitarian disaster as trumpeted by some people in the press. Relief organizations such as CARE, Catholic Relief Services, and others had been operating in Haiti for over fifteen years. Lawrence Pezzullo, who had been the executive director of Catholic Relief Services before taking his post in March 1993, understood that the problems of the relief agencies in Haiti were largely logistical—namely, distributing the food and medicines to hard-to-reach areas of the country. Diesel fuel and gasoline were critical.

But in January 1994, a new problem presented itself. Because of the embargo on oil shipments imposed in October, gasoline and diesel fuel were in increasingly short supply. According to a *New York Times* report filed on January 6: "Local trucking companies that CARE relies on have largely stopped delivering diesel and gasoline, which are available only on the army-controlled black market because the cost of fuel has soared to as much as $12 to $20 a gallon."[1]

Ambassador Richard Brown of the Haiti Working Group, in what Pezzullo called "the cardinal success story of this whole period," organized thirty-some NGOs under the umbrella of the Pan American Health Organization (PAHO) to collate the fuel needs of all international and local relief agencies operating in Haiti and allocate supplies through the Shell Oil Company. PAHO, at Rich Brown's behest, drafted agreements for President Aristide to sign.

But when the draft agreements were presented to President Aristide in late December, Aristide refused to approve them. Special Advisor Pezzullo threatened to tell the press that the Haitian president was blocking a fuel shipment to humanitarian organizations in Haiti and Aristide quickly changed his mind.[2]

Now, Ambassador Brown faced two other challenges. One was getting a waiver to the UN embargo. This hurdle was easily cleared. The second, guaranteeing the security of the fuel, was much more problematic.

The configuration of Port-au-Prince harbor made it impossible to land an oil shipment without attracting serious attention. The Haitian military could block the arrival of the tanker or seize the fuel docking facilities, and a mob action like the one staged for the *Harlan County* could scare off the ship's captain.

To address these fears, Pezzullo wrote a letter to FADH commander General Raoul Cédras, in which he carefully explained the purpose of the shipment, when it would arrive, how it would be monitored, and so on. "We don't need your protection," wrote Pezzullo, "but we want to ensure that the process goes forward without interruption."[3] For good measure, he sent a message to Generals Cédras and Biamby and Colonel François through other channels telling them that they would be held personally responsible for any interference with the oil shipments by the Haitian military.

Before the first tanker could sail, the U.S. government had to insure the ship and post money for the fuel ahead of time, which would later be reimbursed by the NGOs. On the morning of January 10, Pezzullo was summoned to Under Secretary of State Peter Tarnoff's office along with Ambassador Jack Leonard (country director for the Caribbean), Rich Brown, and Mike Kozak. Tarnoff started by raising questions about "the explosive nature" of the shipment.

"Peter, first of all, we have no choice," Pezzullo replied. "If we're going to maintain sanctions to press the Haitian military, we've got to make sure that the humanitarian side is taken care of. If we don't bring in the fuel, we can't maintain the sanctions."

Tarnoff said that there was a great danger of the ship's being seized.

"If they take the ship, we'll kick their butts!" Pezzullo shot back. "That would be an act of war."[4]

Tarnoff wanted the shipment stopped and continued pounding on two points—one, the shipment was too dangerous and, two, it hadn't been cleared. Even though he, the NSC, and others had cleared all the arrangements, Tarnoff said that didn't constitute "approval." He called an interagency meeting for 5:00 that afternoon to decide the ship's fate.

Back in his office, Special Advisor Pezzullo drafted a memo to Tarnoff. "If we turn back the ship," he wrote, "we might as well throw the whole policy away. It would be a monumental act of cowardice."[5]

At 4:00 P.M. the new U.S. ambassador to Haiti, Bill Swing, called from Port-au-Prince to say that he had received a letter from General Cédras. It was a reply to Pezzullo's note explaining the shipment.

"I want to tell you that I read your proposal," wrote Cédras. "I think what you're proposing is a great idea in that it makes available fuel supplies to all relief organizations operating in this country. I agree with the process you have put in effect to monitor deliveries. You have the complete support of the Armed Forces of Haiti."[6]

Pezzullo immediately sent a copy of Cédras's letter up to Tarnoff's office and the interagency meeting was called off. "It was like something out of a magic show," remembered Pezzullo. The tanker docked on January 14, unloaded its 300,000 gallons of fuel, and the NGOs filled up their trucks without incident. The episode cemented in Pezzullo's mind something he had learned about dealing with Haiti: "When you're deliberate and you make clear what you're doing, and you do it thoroughly and in a way that leaves no room for misinterpretation, you can get things done."[7]

Unfortunately, maintaining a clear and consistent policy in the Clinton administration was often frustrating. On January 16, the day after the Miami Conference, Special Advisor Pezzullo and Mike Kozak sat in a secure video conference room at the State Department to confer via video screen with representatives from Defense, the NSC, and the CIA and give a favorable report on the meeting in Miami. Pezzullo concluded by saying: "Now, we've got to move forward with the Four Friends and increase the sanctions. It's the one-two punch."[8]

Sandy Berger from the NSC immediately started raising objections, drawing a distinction between formulating a policy and applying it. The Four Friends' aide mémoire of December had been approved by the White House, Defense, CIA, and State. "Sandy Berger wanted the sanctions, but he didn't want to enforce them," Kozak explained. "It was crazy stuff."[9]

Again, he raised the specter of a humanitarian disaster. Mark Schneider, assistant administrator for Latin America and the Caribbean for the U.S. Agency for International Development (USAID), stated that there was no evidence that Haitians were dying of famine. His agency was spending approximately $60 million a year in Haiti on one of its largest per capita humanitarian efforts in the world and providing an additional $17 million per year in food to be distributed by NGOs. In addition to its feeding programs, USAID was providing access to basic health services to nearly two million Haitians.[10]

"Right now, as best as we can tell, and I don't know anyone who has better information than we do, there is no physical evidence of a significantly worsened humanitarian situation in Haiti," said a USAID official in late December.[11]

Yet Berger and others within the administration were still convinced that a humanitarian catastrophe in Haiti was waiting to happen. At a meeting at the White House in early January, Deputy Secretary of Defense John M. Deutsch (who was later named director of the CIA) argued that if the United States maintained and extended the embargo, it was going to face a crisis like Somalia where we had to send in troops to ensure that foodstuffs got through.[12]

On January 19 representatives of Venezuela, Canada, and France were busily drafting a UN resolution to extend the embargo, while Special Advisor Pezzullo was at the White House trying to get NSC director Tony Lake to clarify the administration's position. "I hope you understand that this is not a question of me intellectually differing with you," Pezzullo said. "If it were only that, fine; but we, as government officials of the United States of America, made a public commitment."

"Let's not get caught up in that," responded Lake, according to Pezzullo. "Let's study the different options and what the effects are going to be."[13]

At another White House meeting on January 25, Special Advisor Pezzullo was presented with a paper drafted by the NSC that proposed two options to end the crisis. The first one was a military invasion of Haiti, which would oust the de facto military leaders and restore President Aristide to power. The second option called for dropping plans to return President Aristide and working out a deal with General Raoul Cédras. The paper suggested that the Parliament declare President Aristide incapacitated under Article 148 of the Constitution and somehow resurrect Prime Minister Malval. Before the international community would lift sanctions, General Cédras would have to retire and Colonel François would have to be reassigned.

Pezzullo characterized the two options as "desperate, duplicitous, and absurd."[14] Soon after the White House meeting, the CIA station chief in Port-au-Prince received a message from Washington instructing him to raise the Article 148 scenario with Robert Malval. Uncomfortable with the sudden change in policy, the CIA station chief showed the message to Ambassador Swing advising him that if he raised the 148 scenario with

Malval, the outgoing prime minister might sign on. Swing suggested that the station chief do nothing until he'd heard from Pezzullo.

"Larry, can you explain what's going on at the NSC?" Mike Kozak asked the special advisor during the last week of January. "You and I are getting publicly criticized by Aristide's advisors for not extending the sanctions, when we're the only ones in the administration who are standing up for them." The administration's retreat from their promise to extend the embargo was being referred to as "Harlan Country II" throughout the State Department.

When President Aristide and Ambassador Jean Casimir got wind of the 148 scenario, it strengthened their conviction that the *blancs* couldn't be trusted and that the United States had a hidden plan for Haiti. This enabled conspiracy-theorist Bert Wides to supplant more reasonable Aristide advisors like Mike Barnes and Bob White.[15] Also, according to White, it made anything short of U.S. military intervention harder to sell to the Aristide camp.[16]

On the military side, the strange signals out of Washington convinced General Cédras and his military supporters that the time had come to legitimize their rule. They even talked about turning FRAPH into a political party, and in late January FRAPH leader Toto Constant said he was considering a run for the presidency. "We will lead a national reconciliation," he told a reporter from the *New York Times*. "Everyone will be included except Aristide, who must understand that his time is over."[17]

On January 28 some three to four hundred Haitian businessmen and bankers staged a strike to protest the international sanctions. That same day hundreds of protesters calling themselves the Grand Coalition of the North were sent by General Phillipe Biamby (with Cédras's support) to pressure the Parliament into passing either Article 148 or Article 149, or disbanding altogether. The passage of either article by Parliament would, in effect, declare the presidency vacant to be filled in the interim either by acting prime minister Malval or Chief Justice Emile Jonassaint. Both houses of Parliament were in session. It was anyone's guess whether or not nervous senators and deputies would bow to threats from the mob.

But, suddenly, the mob was broken up by policemen sent by Colonel François. Why? After talking to both Minister of Education Victor Benoit, leader of KONAKOM, and Alliance senator Julio Larosiliere (the two men who had been approached by President Aristide in Miami to be his next prime minister), Colonel François had become convinced of the need to reach a new political reconciliation and revive the Governors Island Agreement. Also, he knew that the business community was increasingly desperate to get out from under the sanctions and the effects of the political crisis. And they were the ones who were supplying money to pay his troops.[18]

In the midst of this latest crisis, Senate president Firmin Jean-Louis and newly elected Chamber president Bob Mondé traveled to Washington to consult with President Aristide about the appointment of a new prime minister. They were accompanied by Senator Larosiliere and Benoit.

Ambassador Swing and Pezzullo discussed the idea of expanding the group under the auspices of the Center for Democracy to build parliamentary support for the new prime minister and his government. Bob Mondé, who had been elected by a coalition of rightists and socialists and was a close ally of Colonel François, wanted a balanced delegation. He suggested deputies from both the Constitutional FNCD side and the Alliance—FNCD deputy Jean-Jacques Seignon and Alliance deputy Jean Eddy Talandieu Desjardins. Victor Benoit asked to bring his chief of staff Micha Gaillard.

But President Aristide, mistrustful of U.S. motives, was in no mind to accept what he saw as another scheme to legitimize his own successor. He had just returned from a trip to Canada and was angry that the total embargo of Haiti promised by the Four Friends had never been adopted by the UN Security Council.

At a meeting with Canadian foreign minister André Ouellet in Ottawa on January 24, President Aristide had threatened to tell his supporters among the large population of Haitians living in Canada to vote in favor of the referendum separating French-speaking Quebec from Canada. The Canadians quickly changed their approach. According to Kozak, a Canadian assistant secretary of foreign affairs admitted that "Canada's existence as a nation now depended on Aristide's goodwill."[19]

Even without President Aristide's public support, Pezzullo, Caputo, Kozak, Despouy, and other U.S., UN, and Four Friends diplomats still felt that the Haitian legislators had a chance to break the political stalemate. A confluence of factors—the effect of the sanctions on Haitian businesses, the eagerness of the Four Friends to end the political impasse, and divisions within the FADH—all seemed to be working in their favor. Besides, as Pezzullo later acknowledged "it was the only card left."[20]

UN/OAS envoy Leandro Despouy arrived in Washington with the Haitian delegation on February 6. The Haitians installed themselves at the Vista Hotel just up 15th Street from the *Washington Post*. It was a modern hotel with a glass atrium lobby that had been immortalized by Washington, D.C., mayor Marion Barry, who had been videotaped in one of its rooms smoking crack with a female friend.

The conference got off to a slow start on Monday, February 7, as the Haitians met with representatives of the Four Friends, the Haiti Working Group, the OAS, and the UN. "The first couple of days there was more haranguing than anything else," Nancy Jackson recalled.[21] The legislators wanted everyone to understand their version of what was going on in Haiti. Also, individual legislators had different ideas of what the conference was supposed to accomplish.

The heavy-set and volatile Bob Mondé believed that he was in Washington to get the sanctions lifted, and he didn't want to accept that Aristide's return had to be part of the equation. Mondé made no secret of the fact that he was in constant telephone contact with Colonel François. On the other side of the political spectrum, FNCD senator Firmin Jean-Louis had come to Washington because he wanted to be named the next prime minister. His political opportunism had gotten him elected to the presidency of the Senate in early August. Now he was hoping that a similar act of political blackmail could make him the leader of a new government.

The parliamentarians met privately with President Aristide on February 9. "Aristide didn't commit himself to anything; he listened," said one Haitian legislator. "We told him how volatile the situation was in Haiti; how without a government we were all afraid; how sanctions were hurting the people."[22]

When they asked President Aristide what they could do to move the process forward, he said: "Look, I endorse Governors Island and I endorse the Miami Conference resolution," according to the same Haitian legislator. "But all I hear from you senators and deputies are different plans." He implied that if the legislators could come up with a plan that dovetailed with Governors Island and the Miami Conference resolution, he would be willing to endorse it.[23]

The parliamentarians emerged from the meeting with a clear sense of what they had to do. "It wasn't a lovefest," noted Nancy Jackson, who spoke to them soon after, "but they understood the parameters."[24]

Beginning that night and into Thursday, they started to hash out their positions. "It was difficult to get them to concentrate at first," said Juliette Remy, who stayed in the hotel as a UN observer.[25] But Washington's record snowfall and extremely cold temperatures left the legislators with little else to do but sit and talk. "For the first time I think both the left and right realized that they had become captives of their own rhetoric," Jackson concluded.[26]

"It was especially hard for Bob Mondé, because he wanted to control things," added Remy, "and he was constantly going in a direction that would leave the others disappointed and upset." Despouy spent hours listening to Mondé and explaining the positions of the other legislators.[27]

Slowly, Mondé started to accept the idea that Aristide's return to Haiti had to be part of a political solution. On the other side, FNCD legislators began to appreciate the fact that Mondé couldn't return to Haiti with a document that explicitly called for Colonel Michel François's resignation. "Eventually they got around that," Jackson reported, "by referring to the Governors Island Agreement. They said their document does not supersede Governors Island, which said nothing about François [except that a law would be passed to separate the police from the army, which meant that François would have to be reassigned]. That was their concession to Bob."[28]

The legislators also set out to address the timing concerns of President Aristide. Since the events of October, Aristide's advisors had argued that a new government couldn't assume power as long as General Cédras remained as commander-in-chief. According to the parliamentarians' proposal, the approval of the new prime minister by both chambers would be timed to coincide with the passage of the amnesty law and General Cédras's resignation.

"There was definitely a sense of tradeoffs among the group, and recognizing what could and couldn't be sold in Haiti," reported Jackson. "Politically they were being very astute."[29]

The fact that Bob Mondé was in constant telephone contact with Colonel Michel François in Haiti had a sobering effect. "It made us feel that we were dealing indirectly with someone who controlled the guns in Haiti," reported Micha Gaillard. "So what we were doing had a real chance of getting results."[30]

By Friday, February 11, the parliamentarians had a working document that they presented to Lawrence Pezzullo, Dante Caputo, and representatives of the Four Friends. During the meeting at the Vista Hotel, Bob Mondé raised the issue of when the international community would be prepared to lift the sanctions. This elicited a strong response from the French observer to the OAS, who said that the Haitians could not force France into granting further concessions. "France has occupied Haiti before and can do it again!" the French ambassador exclaimed, according to Pezzullo.[31]

This caused several Haitians to jump up from their seats and protest, none more vociferously than Mondé, who yelled: "Remember 1804! We went on a *maroonage* then and we can do it again!"[32]

"He was livid," remembered Pezzullo, who watched Mondé stomp out of the room. A few minutes later the special advisor learned that Mondé had collapsed.

With Mondé in the hospital, momentum to finalize the plan slowed. Micha Gaillard, who was acting as emissary for the group to Aristide and his advisors, was trying to secure a meeting with the Haitian president. "They kept coming up with excuses," Gaillard recalled. At the same time, Aristide aides were already denouncing the parliamentarians' plan in the press as "a power-sharing" gesture. "The only strategy seems to be for Aristide to name people to his cabinet acceptable to the thugs," said one Aristide advisor.[33]

While in the hospital, Mondé asked that Deputy Duly Brutus of the PANPRA democratic socialist bloc and Alliance deputy and former president of the Lower Chamber Antoine Joseph join the delegation. They arrived on Monday.

Senator Firmin Jean-Louis, claiming that the arrival of the two new delegates had shifted the political balance and that he hadn't been consulted, announced he was quitting and returning to Haiti. Later, he admitted to Kozak that he had never "left" but had just gone on an extended weekend with his girlfriend.[34]

In order to restore the ideological balance, the Constitutionalist members invited Port-au-Prince mayor Evans Paul, FNCD senator Yvon Ghislain, and FNCD deputies Edmond Mirold and Rindal Pierre Canal to join the group. Evans Paul was key, because of his close political ties to President Aristide.

President Aristide refused to discuss the contents of their proposal when he finally sat down with the parliamentarians on February 17. Afterward, Aristide said to reporters: "It is unclear that these parliamentarians speak for their institution or command sufficient support to promote any specific proposal."[35] U.S. representative Joseph P. Kennedy II warned in a press release that the parliamentarians' plan, which "does not offer a concrete strategy for Aristide's return," may "enable the Clinton administration to skirt the challenge of restoring Aristide."[36]

The Haitian legislators left the meeting completely disillusioned. "They felt on the one hand that the whole international community was behind them and here was their own president stonewalling the whole thing," concluded Remy.[37] "I don't know him anymore," said Micha Gaillard of KONAKOM and the FNCD, who had been a friend of Aristide's since his days as a parish priest.

While the legislators were meeting with their president, Dante Caputo and Leandro Despouy were in New York City briefing UN secretary-general Boutros-Ghali, who told them that he would endorse the parliamentarians' proposal if it were presented to him in writing. Energized by this news, the parliamentarians worked through the night.

On Saturday morning, Nancy Jackson from the State Department's Haiti Working Group was presented with a document and a letter addressed to the UN secretary-general.

The Parliamentarians' Plan, as it was called, reiterated most of the recommendations made at the Miami Conference. The letter to UN secretary-general Boutros-Ghali laid out a number of key procedural issues, including: "President Aristide obtains the early retirement of General Cédras before the installation of the new government, to keep it from suffering the same fate as the Malval government." It also suggested that certain legislative actions could be taken concurrently, "e.g., (1) confirmation of the prime minister and passage of the amnesty law, and (2) confirmation of the prime minister and of the new commander in chief." The letter ended by stating categorically that "these procedures for implementing our proposal are aimed essentially at breaking the deadlock preventing implementation of the Governors Island Agreement and the New York Covenant, and are based on the resolution, supported by President Aristide, that was developed by Workshop A of the Miami Conference."

On Saturday, Dante Caputo informed the delegation that he had arranged for them to travel to UN headquarters in New York City where they would formally deliver their recommendations to Boutros-Ghali and the Four Friends. In rapid succession the Parliamentarians' Plan was officially endorsed by the OAS, the UN, and President Clinton.

That's when the war of words between the Aristide camp and supporters of the plan began to escalate. The U.S. press seemed to take President Aristide's side, referring to the parliamentarians as "foes of the President," when, in fact, many of them were members of his political coalition. Parroting Aristide's propaganda, articles in the *Washington Post* and in the *New York Times* referred to the proposal as "a power-sharing plan," when, in fact, there was nothing in it that infringed on the Haitian president's authority as delineated in the Haitian Constitution.

On Wednesday, January 23, forty U.S. congressmen—mostly members of the Congressional Black Caucus—signed a letter to President Clinton urging him to move swiftly at the UN to impose "a tough package of sanctions." President Clinton was especially sensitive to the feelings of the Congressional Black Caucus because he needed their support for his own legislative agenda, including his wife's new health care bill.

Representative Joseph P. Kennedy II from Massachusetts, siding with the Black Caucus, argued that sanctions "could invigorate these political and diplomatic efforts while reaffirming the actions that must be taken by the Haitian military."[38]

"Sanctions alone will not bring an end to this crisis if there is not some avenue available for a political settlement," explained State Department spokesman Mike McCurry.[39]

In an address at Dartmouth College on Wednesday night, President Aristide asserted: "The idea that parliamentarians or other democratic forces can act independently in the face of current military intimidation and violence is unrealistic."[40] Congressman Kennedy in an opinion piece published in the *Boston Globe* wrote that "pressure on him

[Aristide] to meet military intransigence by making concessions are read by them as proof that the US is not serious about restoring democracy and allowing the president's return."[41]

The day before the delegation of Haitians returned to Haiti, they presented their plan formally to the Four Friends in New York. "It was enthusiastically received by everyone, particularly the French," reported Juliette Remy. "Some of the Friends couldn't understand why Aristide was refusing to support a plan that he had approved at the Miami Conference."[42] UN secretary-general Boutros Boutros-Ghali had invited President Aristide, who declined because he was leaving soon for Paris and Geneva to address UNESCO and the UN Commission on Human Rights.

At a press conference at Boston's Logan Airport prior to his departure, the exiled Haitian president said: "Everyone has his own responsibility. President Clinton has his responsibility. I have my responsibility. The Haitian people have their responsibility. The international leaders also. The coup leaders also. The Haitian people assumed their responsibility, they are dying, even in the sea fleeing political repression, after losing 5,000 people."[43]

CHAPTER 19

President Clinton
Changes Policy

"I believe the one with the power wins. The weak one loses."

–President JEAN-BERTRAND ARISTIDE

In late December, Ellen Cosgrove of the U.S. embassy in Port-au-Prince noticed that an old man who repaired rubber tires in her neighborhood had disappeared. A few months later, Cosgrove ran into his daughter and asked: "Where have you been? And what happened to your father?"[1]

The girl told a harrowing story of leaving by boat and of her father being thrown overboard by the organizer because he was too old and sick. Denied political asylum in the United States, the daughter wound up in Cuba and, later, chose to be repatriated.

Scenes like these were repeated with increasing frequency through the early weeks of 1994 as life in Haiti grew increasingly more desperate. By some estimates as much as 90 percent of Haiti's manufacturing sector had been destroyed.

Assembly operations that once employed 50,000 Haitians now had jobs for only 6,000. "I'm contemplating moving to Miami or Mexico," said Louis Saint-Lot, a California-educated businessman who once ran one of the country's largest T-shirt factories, supplying Disneyland and

Major League Baseball.[2] The plants, which paid workers about three dollars a day, had been characterized as sweatshops by labor activists. But economists estimated that five to ten family members subsisted on each assembly worker's pay.[3]

As the assembly plants closed, health workers from Johns Hopkins University noticed a sharp increase in HIV among poor women in Port-au-Prince. "This was happening at the same time that Aristide lobbyists like Randall Robinson and Susan Sarandon were trying to get the last assembly plants shut down," reported Cosgrove. "As these factories closed these women were being forced into prostitution. What did people think in their little dream world that these people were going to do to support themselves?"[4]

The tragic irony was that Father Aristide, who many saw as a savior, was willing to see his people suffer in return for political leverage to use against the Clinton administration and the military regime.

In the month of February 1994 alone the U.S. Coast Guard reported that 347 Haitians had been rescued. That number was dramatically higher than the nine who had been picked up in February 1993. Since the UN/OAS sanctions were reinstated in late October 1993, the U.S. Coast Guard had reported a steady increase in Haitians trying to reach the United States by sea.

President Aristide, his advisors, and some human rights activists maintained that the departure of Haitians was directly linked to political events in Haiti. "The death toll rises weekly as those who support democracy in Haiti are murdered, tortured or forced to flee the repression that has gripped our nation," said President Aristide in early February 1994.[5] But U.S. State Department officials of the Bureau of Population, Refugees and Migration claimed this wasn't true. Rather, statistics showed that the departure of Haitians coincided with actions taken in the United States. If Haitians thought they would be permitted to enter the United States, they took to the boats.

Although President Aristide liked to claim that very few Haitians left the country during his eight months in office—"the refugee outmigration essentially stopped," said Mike Barnes before a Senate subcommittee[6]—this was not borne out by the facts. The U.S. Coast Guard reported that it interdicted 1,318 from February through September

1991. This figure is higher than the 1,132 the Coast Guard reported picking up in the eight months (June 1990 through January 1991) preceding Aristide's inauguration. In October 1991, arguably the worst month of military repression in Haiti, only nineteen Haitians were stopped at sea. In November 1991, after news reached Haiti that the United States had decided not to return a boatload of Haitians, the number soared to 6,012.

Then, in December 1991 a federal district court judge in Florida issued a temporary restraining order halting the forced repatriation of Haitian refugees. The number of Haitians seized by the U.S. Coast Guard remained in the thousands, reaching 13,053 in May 1992. After President Bush signed Executive Order 12807 on May 24, 1992, authorizing the interdiction and return of all Haitian refugees with no prior screening for asylum seekers, the number of Haitians seized by the Coast Guard the following month dropped to 473.

Under the new policy every Coast Guard cutter was supplied with preliminary questionnaires and a Creole-speaking interpreter to assist those applying for political asylum. When the cutter reached shore, those who seemed to have legitimate claims were taken to a processing center for further interviews. In addition, the U.S. Immigration and Naturalization Service (INS) ran three in-country processing centers in Haiti. As of February 25, 1994, out of 19,164 Haitians applying at the Cap Haitien office for asylum, 151 had been approved by the INS.[7]

By the end of February 1994 the economic situation in Haiti was growing bleaker by the day. Some wealthy businessmen and military officers were getting rich by smuggling in oil and other badly needed commodities, but most Haitians were getting squeezed.

That is why the Parliamentarians' Plan to break the political impasse was greeted with enthusiasm in Haiti. "You had labor unions, church groups, and business organizations such as the *Centre pour la Libre Entreprise et la Démocratie* all endorsing it," said Nancy Jackson of the Haiti Working Group, who arrived in Port-au-Prince the last week of February.[8] On March 2 the Chamber of Deputies approved the plan by a 35 to 10 vote.

This provoked an angry reply from President Aristide in Geneva, who called the Parliamentarians' Plan "a bad draft."[9] In the Haitian Senate centrists from the FNCD, the Alliance, and the democratic socialist

PANPRA group led by the questor of the Senate, Julio Larosiliere, backed the plan with the support of Police Chief Michel François. Opposed to the proposal were supporters of General Phillipe Biamby and General Raoul Cédras and President Jean-Bertrand Aristide.

While the Parliamentarians' Plan hung in limbo in the Haitian Senate, U.S. columnists used misinformation spread by Aristide's advisors and his public relations firm McKinney & McDowell to rip it apart. "The plan lets coup leader Raoul Cédras approve the prime minister," wrote Derrick Z. Jackson in the *Boston Globe*.[10] This was false.

"Haiti is a wonderfully clear-cut case of good vs. evil," went Mary McGrory's simplistic characterization in the *Washington Post*.[11]

"In their hearts, U.S. officials do not want Mr. Aristide to return," stated an editorial in the *New York Times*.[12]

"Recently, the Clinton administration has pressured Aristide to accept a proposal by Haitian legislators that is a thinly veiled attempt to make him a figurehead and invest real power in a prime minister whose selection would require the tacit approval of Cédras," reasoned columnist DeWayne Wickman in *USA Today*.[13]

A crowning moment for the pro-Aristide lobby came on March 8 when U.S. special advisor Lawrence Pezzullo was called to testify before the Subcommittee on Western Hemisphere and Peace Corps Affairs of the Senate Committee on Foreign Relations, chaired by Democrat Christopher Dodd of Connecticut. Senator Dodd opened the meeting by stating: "General Abraham sat on his hands while opponents of democracy tried unsuccessfully to disrupt the 1990 elections."[14]

"Now we are being told," said Dodd, "that if we can just find the magic formula, if we can just squeeze the right concessions out of President Aristide, the military leaders in Haiti might be convinced to step aside."[15] Before Pezzullo had a chance to explain that the Parliamentarians' Plan was not intended to squeeze concessions out of Aristide, Dodd called a series of witnesses hostile to the plan, including Democratic representative Carrie Meeks of Florida, Democratic senator Tom Harkin of Iowa, and Aristide attorney Mike Barnes, who once again misrepresented the Governors Island Agreement.

"At Governors Island," Barnes said, "President Aristide received a commitment that the entire high command of the Haitian army and the police chief, Michel François, would all either retire from the army or leave the country and take military posts outside of Haiti." He went on to contend that the Parliamentarians' Plan was "a major retreat from Governors Island." In truth, there was no substantive difference between the two accords.[16]

"I think your assessment is absolutely correct," answered Dodd, who from that point on referred to the Parliamentarians' Plan as the "Mondé plan."

"Who is the author of it?" asked Dodd.

"I do not know who the author of it was," answered Barnes. "I assume someone in the State Department."[17]

On March 5, President Aristide had returned from nine days of consultations in Europe and met with Secretary-General Boutros Boutros-Ghali at UN headquarters in New York to formally register his objections to the Parliamentarians' Plan.

"Aristide was very hard to pin down," said Juliette Remy, who attended the meeting along with Dante Caputo. "He was very nice, formal and cordial, but didn't want to discuss anything of substance. Instead, he spoke in generalities about the world and spiritual matters, with lots of metaphors."[18]

"He offered no concrete proposals," remembered Caputo, "but he kept going back to two things: the international community had to impose a full embargo, and until the coup leaders were removed there was nothing to discuss."[19]

Following the meeting with Boutros-Ghali, President Aristide met with the press and called the Parliamentarians' Plan "counterproductive." "The international community has expressed its political will, but it is ambiguous, it is weak," said the ousted Haitian leader. He went on to demand that leaders of the military coup that forced him from power step down before he made any move. "We must have the departure of the military," he proclaimed.[20]

This was the beginning of an all-out press and public relations assault on the Clinton administration. Its objective: to get the Clinton administration to remove the military leaders by force and guarantee his security once he returned to Haiti. On March 18 President Clinton received a letter signed by forty members of the Congressional Black Caucus. "The United States' Haiti policy must be scrapped," it began. "While our nation makes public pronouncements regarding our commitment to restore democracy in Haiti, there is a growing perception throughout the world that the United States is actually doing all in its power to prevent it."

In a speech delivered in Miami on March 18, President Aristide went so far as to suggest that the United States, and especially Ambassador Alvin Adams, had secretly aided the coup to depose him in 1991.[21] When U.S. special advisor Pezzullo sent a note to the Haitian president reminding him that Ambassador Adams had actually helped save his life, President Aristide dismissed his earlier remarks as "a joke."[22]

That same week Pezzullo got a call from Representative Joseph Kennedy, who asked: "Isn't there a way to make this whole thing happen at the same time?"

"Well, if you read the Parliamentarians' Plan, that's exactly what it does," answered Pezzullo.[23]

A few days later, Kennedy called to invite the special advisor to brief him about the current negotiations. Pezzullo brought along Ken Merten of the Haiti Working Group to answer questions about the refugee situation. When the two men arrived at a conference room in the rear of the Capitol, twenty or more people were waiting. Among the faces, they recognized eight members of the Congressional Black Caucus, their staffs, Bob White, and Mike Barnes.

As the special advisor started to describe the Parliamentarians' Plan, Congresswoman Carrie Meeks cut him off, shouting: "That's just plain bullshit!"[24]

Then, Florida congresswoman Corrine Brown stood up and screamed: "I don't understand why you don't support President Aristide!"[25]

"The meeting continued like that with everybody shouting," Pezzullo recalled. One of the representatives accused the special advisor and Ken Merten of being racists.[26]

At the urging of Pezzullo and Dante Caputo, Vice President Gore met with President Aristide at the White House on March 25 to address his concerns about the parliamentarians' proposal. Gore got straight to the point: "The President and I understand and sympathize with your legitimate concern that a process lacking proper safeguards might be manipulated to prevent your return to Haiti. We want to seek to address those concerns without losing the real progress the broad support for the parliamentary plan in Haiti represents. . . . We cannot and will not permit President Clinton to be pressed to make unacceptable choices—whether the use of military force or the de facto abandonment of his strong commitments to restore Haitian democracy."[27] Gore then went on to answer the individual concerns that had been raised by President Aristide and his advisors.

Aristide was unmoved. "At Governors Island I tried to explain my concerns that the strategy being adopted there was a strategy of death. And I was right," he said. "To build reconciliation, we have to see that the problem is the coup leaders. To respect Governors Island we need to remove the coup leaders, then the rest can be accomplished. They do not want democracy."[28]

"Do you think stricter sanctions will force the military leaders to concede?" asked Vice President Gore.

"I think they are crucial," answered Aristide. "At the same time . . . the Parliamentarians' Plan needs improvement."[29]

Three days later, Sandy Berger presented President Aristide with a paper detailing suggested amendments to the Parliamentarians' Plan. On March 30, in a letter to National Security Advisor Anthony Lake, President Aristide rejected the new proposal, stating it was flawed in four fundamental respects. First, he said: "No procedure is provided for the 'appointment' of a new high command . . . a radical shift from the commitment made at Governors Island."[30] This was untrue. Under the Haitian Constitution, the new commander-in-chief appointed by President Aristide had the authority to his select his own general staff and make other assignments within the army.

Secondly, Aristide said: "Under the new proposed strategy the United Nations fuel embargo would be lifted before President Aristide's return to Haiti."[31] The Four Friends had long believed that maintaining sanctions on a new constitutional government, which would have to cope with all the problems inherent in governing Haiti as well as trying to recover from two years of de facto rule, would be counterproductive.

Aristide's third objection was that "there is no date certain for President Aristide's return under the new strategy as there was under the Governors Island Agreement."[32] This was a distortion of the facts. Both Vice President Gore and UN secretary-general Boutros-Ghali had pledged to uphold any date set privately by President Aristide and his new prime minister.

Finally, Aristide claimed: "The enactment of the critical law [separating the police from the military] is not contemplated in either the administration's new strategy or the so-called Parliamentarians' Plan."[33] This was false. The Parliamentarians' Plan stated clearly that it incorporated all the provisions of both the Governors Island Agreement and the New York Pact, which were very specific regarding changes in the FADH, including the passage of a law creating a new police force.

When Lawrence Pezzullo met with Boutros-Ghali on March 29, the UN secretary-general said, according to Pezzullo: "We are dealing with a man who will not compromise but believes his position is unassailable. He repeats over and over that the military must be removed without explaining how that could occur without the use of force."[34]

Having made a decision to press the Clinton administration to remove the coup leaders, Bob White acknowledged that Aristide and his advisors were asking for U.S. military intervention. Sensing that the Clinton administration was weakening under public pressure, President Aristide and his supporters stepped up their media assault. They dropped their big bomb on April 5 when President Aristide released a letter to President Clinton saying that he was giving six months' notice of termination of the bilateral agreement that allowed the United States to automatically repatriate Haitian refugees. "Your government, through its policy, is not only returning Haitians to the same police that terrorizes them," wrote Aristide, "it also returns them without safeguards against their immediate or subsequent imprisonment, disappearance or torture."[35]

In conjunction with this move, the Congressional Black Caucus, Artists for Democracy, the lobby group TransAfrica Forum headed by Randall Robinson, and human rights and refugee groups peppered the media with attacks on the Clinton administration's policy. Clinton's repatriation policy "has contributed to a human rights disaster that has tarnished his presidency," declared Juan Menendez of Human Rights Watch.[36]

"One is left to reasonably conclude that our policy is driven by considerations of race," read a letter published in a full-page ad in the *New York Times* and signed by nearly one hundred people including Julia Roberts, Robin Williams, Robert De Niro, and Paul Newman.

"We are declaring war on a racist policy and an inhumane policy," declared Representative Major Owens of the Congressional Black Caucus.[37]

Another element of the public relations campaign waged by Aristide's camp was designed to dramatize human rights abuses. Beginning in late March and early April there appeared a spate of sensational articles. "Secret Prison. Kidnappings and torture. Bodies left on the streets for pigs to devour. The picture that emerges is more that of a charnel house than a national leadership in quest of security," read one in the *Washington Times*.[38]

Human rights abuses "are worse than under the days of Papa Doc Duvalier," claimed Senator Christopher Dodd.[39]

"Horrific as the everyday tableau of killings and suppression may be, the newest tactics aimed at smothering the faintest desire for democracy have paralyzed ordinary Haitians with fear and taken the rest of us virtually beyond comprehension," said Randall Robinson.[40]

In a country with no effective judiciary system it had always been difficult to determine how many people had been killed, beaten, or imprisoned. A report issued by the UN Inter-American Commission on Human Rights on August 27, 1993, estimated that as many as 1,500 Haitians had been killed in political violence since the coup to overthrow President Aristide. Now, President Aristide and his advisors inflated that number to 5,000.

Since the UN/OAS ICM human rights monitors had departed in October 1993, the reporting out of Haiti had been murky at best. On January 31, 1994, thirty ICM monitors had been admitted back into the country. They reported that 112 political murders had been committed since then. "Human rights abuses have increased recently because the army and its allies believe that they have 'stared down' the U.S. government and can act against their adversaries, and frighten the Haitian people into submission," stated a cable from the U.S. embassy drafted by Ellen Cosgrove on April 12.[41]

But, the U.S. embassy cable continued, it was equally apparent that "the Haitian left, including President Aristide and his supporters in Washington and here, consistently manipulate and, even, fabricate human rights abuses as a propaganda tool."[42]

Leaked to human rights workers in Haiti, Cosgrove's cable created a furor in the press. "Ellen Cosgrove sits with terror all about her and casts upon it an eye notable for serenity, disciplined incuriosity about troublingly dreadful details, and imperviousness to notions of possible moral distinction," columnist Murray Kempton wrote.[43]

The cable "shows that at least in the embassy there is an extreme antipathy for Aristide and a willingness to play down human rights abuses to prevent a political momentum to build for his return," said Kenneth Roth, executive director of Human Rights Watch.[44]

"This hurt so much and it still does," said Cosgrove, who was known to hide political dissidents in her own home and to spend months tracking down people arrested for political crimes and securing their release before they could be beaten and killed.[45]

With the Parliamentarians' Plan hopelessly stalled, political actors in Haiti and Washington started searching for other ways to end the crisis. Retired general Hérard Abraham (the man who had supervised the transition to democracy in 1990) approached U.S. embassy political officer Louis Nigro and suggested exploiting the widening rift between Colonel François and Generals Cédras and Biamby. Abraham said that Colonel François, who directly controlled the commanders of the five military companies in Port-au-Prince and had major influence in the heavy weapons company, was willing to persuade Generals Cédras and Biamby to leave power.

General Abraham arranged a rendezvous with Colonel François that took place one night in late March in the Delmas area of Port-au-Prince. "It was real undercover type of stuff," Kozak recalled. "Lou Nigro and I had to change our license plates so that our vehicle wouldn't stand out. We drove to a blacked-out alley that was filled with plainclothes police."[46] The two State Department officials were escorted up to a room. Seated at a large table were Colonel François, his brother Evans, their foreign affairs advisor Simonese, a legal advisor named Alex Tibul, and General Abraham.

Kozak remembered that Colonel François began by asking two carefully phrased questions. "If we persuade Cédras to leave, will you lift the embargo?"

"If you comply with all aspects of the aide mémoire we gave Cédras in December, yes." Kozak answered.

"If the FADH does everything it's supposed to do under Governors Island and all the other agreements and still Aristide chooses not to return, will you give Parliament the okay to invoke Article 148 of the Constitution?" asked François, according to Kozak.[47]

Kozak said that this was a hypothetical question that he couldn't answer.

François, who claimed he had an informer in Aristide's inner circle in Washington, was convinced that President Aristide would not return without a U.S. invasion. François argued that he should stay on to "stabilize" things after Cédras left. Kozak said that this was impossible. "If you stay, the sanctions will continue," Kozak told François.[48] According to Kozak, Colonel François agreed to be reassigned a few days after Cédras's resignation.

At that meeting and another in early April, the basic steps of the plan were laid out. First, Bob Mondé as president of the Chamber of Deputies would summon General Cédras for questioning before Parliament. Cédras would be shown the confidential letter he had signed at Governors Island saying he would resign by October 15, 1993, and he would be pressured to comply. If that didn't work, he would be confronted with financial data that proved he was stealing from the military payroll by collecting pay for "phantom" officers. If Cédras didn't agree to retire promptly, the Parliament would pass a resolution demanding his immediate compliance. And if Cédras didn't respond to this pressure, François's troops would enforce the order of the Parliament.

Once Cédras stepped down, General Duperval, the deputy commander, would declare that henceforth the army would do its duty to remain an apolitical institution dedicated to protecting public institutions and officials, including President Aristide on his return. Next, Duperval would name a new general staff and transfer François and others to "low-profile" positions. The Parliament would then pass a resolution calling upon President Aristide to return to Haiti and to name a new prime minister and commander-in-chief.

With the basic scenario laid out, Special Advisor Pezzullo presented it to Secretary of State Warren Christopher. He reminded the secretary that it had been administration policy for some time to encourage splits in the Haitian military. Now that one had manifested itself, he wanted approval to continue the confidential talks.

Nobody in the State Department Haiti Working Group was surprised when Secretary Christopher turned the proposal down. After all, Christopher wouldn't even defend the administration's policy in the face of Aristide's public relation assault.

On April 12, after failing to convince actress Susan Sarandon to stage a hunger strike, Randall Robinson began one himself. On April 17 the TransAfrica executive wrote an op-ed in the *New York Times* that said, "The President has abandoned Mr. Aristide and has failed to stand up to Haiti's military rulers" and called for Pezzullo's resignation.[49]

The White House withdrew into a major policy review and the State Department Haiti Working Group was not included. "Suddenly, by the second week of April, I was completely cut out of any policy discussions," Special Advisor Pezzullo recalled. "No messages, no requests for information. I'd call the White House and never get a response. I'd write a memo and hear nothing."[50]

On April 21, while President Clinton was attending a ceremony on the south lawn of the White House to announce an aid package to the new South African government, six congressional critics of the president's Haiti policy staged a sit-in in front of the White House. Among those arrested was Representative Joseph Kennedy II. It was day ten of Randall Robinson's hunger strike, which was getting front-page coverage in the press. After meeting with Robinson, President Aristide held a news conference in which he condemned the Clinton administration's stopping of refugees on the high seas and returning them to Haiti as "a cynical joke." He said: "It's a racist policy. It's really a way to say we don't care."[51]

Two days earlier, at a meeting with newspaper editors, President Clinton had attacked his own policy and praised Randall Robinson's fast. "I understand and respect what he's doing, and we ought to change our policy," said Clinton. "It hasn't worked." It appeared that the president of the United States was backing down in the face of public pressure from the ousted president of Haiti.

On the afternoon of April 21, National Security Advisor Tony Lake and Deputy Secretary of State Strobe Talbott went to see President Aristide at the Haitian embassy in Washington. They came to explain changes they were making in U.S. policy. These included pressing to extend the UN embargo as the administration had promised to do, a pledge to remove the military command of Haiti before President Aristide's return, and a vow to reexamine the U.S. policy of returning all Haitian refugees leaving by sea.

"They basically cut a deal with Aristide at that point saying don't criticize us and we'll do what you want," explained Nancy Jackson.[52]

"It was an incredible act of political cowardice that undercut the whole international effort," said Dante Caputo.[53] Still, Randall Robinson refused to end his hunger strike. He had succeeded in getting President Clinton to change one aspect of his policy, now he was insisting that Clinton end the forced repatriation of Haitian refugees.

After reading about the policy change in the *Washington Post*, Lawrence Pezzullo went to see Peter Tarnoff in his office on the seventh floor. "I see you changed the policy," said Pezzullo. "That's life. But I have two objections. One, you're going off in a direction that's ultimately going to be destructive. The U.S. is going to end up sending troops into Haiti. Secondly, the way the shift was made was personally insulting."[54]

On Saturday, April 23, Lawrence Pezzullo met with Secretary of State Warren Christopher in his office and offered to resign. "I don't like the way this thing has happened," said Pezzullo, "but as long as there's no finger-pointing, let's just end it."[55] He agreed to leave on the twenty-eighth.

On Wednesday, April 27, the State Department officially announced Pezzullo's resignation. "Ambassador Pezzullo was associated with aspects of policy in a high-profile way," said an unnamed official. "He helped shape the policy and was its chief executor. It was a policy that so far was not successful."[56] That was followed the next day by stories in the *Washington Post* and *New York Times* quoting unnamed administration sources who blamed Pezzullo for the failure of the policy toward Haiti and the administration's decision to change course.

As the special advisor packed up his possessions, members of the Haiti Working Group draped the entrance to their office with black crepe paper.

In his letter of resignation, Pezzullo wrote: "As I take my leave, I wanted to express my grave concern that we are heading irrevocably down a path toward unilateral military intervention in Haiti. That would be a terrible mistake." He could have been looking into a crystal ball.

CHAPTER 20

Carter/Powell/Nunn

"Push back the egg inside the chicken!"

—popular Haitian saying in September 1994

On April 27, 1994, President Clinton announced that he would ask the UN Security Council to adopt a tough package of economic sanctions against Haiti's military rulers. In addition to calling for a curb on international travel, he said he would push for a freeze on the military leaders' foreign assets and cancellation of their credit cards. "Tightening the sanctions on suffering Haiti is not likely to rescue the Clinton administration from the unwelcome choices ahead," noted the *Washington Post*.[1]

One of the unwelcome choices was what to do about the Haitian refugees, who were being intercepted at sea in increasing numbers. And Randall Robinson's hunger strike continued to focus media attention on the issue. After meeting with Robinson on May 2, Eleanor Clift of *Newsweek* reported: "He's moving slow, he's talking slow."[2] Among his regular visitors was law school classmate Sandy Berger.

Three days after his meeting with Eleanor Clift, and suffering from an irregular heartbeat, Robinson was checked into a hospital for observation. "They don't want me to die," said Robinson. "They know I'm not a loony."[3] "The President has no moral core," Robinson told the *Washington Post*.[4]

Meanwhile, Aristide supporters continued to snipe at the Clinton administration's refugee policy. "There should be no repatriations to Haiti and no interdictions," declared Steven Forester, a lawyer for the Haitian Refugee Center. "To send terrified people back to Haiti at a time when the streets are littered with bodies is like sending Jews back to Nazi Germany."[5]

At a tense meeting in the Oval Office on Thursday night, April 21, President Clinton, Attorney General Janet Reno, Deputy Secretary of State Strobe Talbott, and Tony Lake debated what to do with a boatload of 414 Haitian refugees that had arrived off of West Palm Beach, Florida. The Coast Guard reported that the badly overcrowded sixty-five-foot vessel had spent fourteen days at sea and most of its passengers were sick.

Friday morning, President Clinton signed the order to let the Haitians come ashore. Supporters of President Aristide immediately dismissed the U.S. move as "a half step."[6] President Clinton also announced that Baptist minister and former congressman William Gray III had been named as the new special advisor on Haiti.

At a CNN-organized global news conference on May 3, President Clinton said Haiti's military rulers "have visited abject misery on their people and are now once again killing and mutilating . . . innocent civilians and it is wrong, and we have got to do what we can to try and stop them." When pressed to specify what exactly he had in mind, the president said: "We have not decided to use force. All I can say is we can't rule it out any longer."[7]

President Clinton's remarks brought an immediate reply from his predecessor, George Bush, who told the *Houston Chronicle* that military intervention in Haiti would be "a tremendous mistake."[8] Bush suggested instead that the administration abandon Aristide, who Bush maintained had been unfairly critical of U.S. efforts to help him. Opposition to President Clinton's remarks was also forthcoming from both sides of the aisle in Congress, including Representative Lee Hamilton, Senate Majority Leader George Mitchell, and Senate Minority Leader Bob Dole.

On May 6 the UN Security Council voted 15–0 to impose a complete embargo and targeted sanctions against the de facto military leaders of Haiti.

Another U.S. policy shift came on May 8, the twenty-seventh day of Randall Robinson's hunger strike, when the Clinton administration announced it would change its procedures for processing Haitian refugees. Under an agreement negotiated between Tony Lake and Randall Robinson, the administration vowed that henceforth no Haitian would be repatriated without being given a chance to make a case for asylum. In return, Randall Robinson agreed to abandon his hunger strike.

"This is foreign policy by hunger strike," remarked former vice president Dan Quayle on the ABC News program *This Week*.[9]

The change in policy produced an immediate flood of refugees. While only 2,300 Haitians were interdicted by the Coast Guard in all of 1993, in May 1994 alone 1,448 were rescued on the high seas. On June 16, the Clinton administration announced that new in-country refugee processing centers had been expanded, hospital ships had been positioned off the coast of Haiti, and discussions had been initiated with other countries in the region about establishing refugee safe havens and camps.

This news produced a huge new exodus. From mid-June to early July a staggering 20,000 Haitian refugees were picked up at sea by the U.S. Coast Guard. In the first week of July alone, two hundred boats carrying 4,700 Haitians were intercepted. They quickly overwhelmed the processing system and available accommodations. On June 28, the refugee center at Guantanamo Bay naval base in Cuba, which had been closed in 1993, was reopened.

On July 5, in a move to discourage Haitians fleeing in boats, the United States announced that it would no longer give those picked up at sea the opportunity for resettlement here, even if they qualified. Instead, efforts would be made to resettle qualified refugees in other countries in the region, including Jamaica and Barbados. That announcement, combined with the advent of the hurricane season, reduced the migrant flow.

On May 11, in an act of defiance directed at the United States, Haiti's military rulers installed Supreme Court president Emile Jonassaint as the provisional president of Haiti. A month earlier, on April 10, a group of thirteen right-wing senators and thirty deputies led by Senator Bernard Sansaricq, at the direction of General Raoul Cédras and General Phillipe Biamby, had voted to invoke Article 149 of the Haitian Constitution and declare the presidency vacant. None of the legislators who had participated in the parliamentary talks in Washington sided with the military. In fact, most of the twenty-seven legally elected senators and seventy-nine deputies were absent. That meant that the vote had been taken without a legislative quorum.

General Cédras and General Biamby were among four generals who attended Jonassaint's swearing in at Parliament. After taking the oath of office, the eighty-one-year-old Jonassaint delivered a rambling acceptance speech in which he claimed: "The sickness was in the hands of the whites, and it has been cured today. . . . Today, Haiti is ours!"[10]

The new provisional president, in addition to being a well-known *houngan*, was a believer in astrology, numerology, and other schools of mysticism. He told friends that he believed Haiti was the last remnant of the lost continent of Atlantis. It was coveted by the United States, he explained, because the Americans wanted to locate and steal the magic Philosopher's Stone.

Jonassaint's installation brought angry denunciations from many inside and outside of Haiti. "It's interesting," Robert Malval said later, "that both Cédras and Aristide had decided by this point that the U.S. had to intervene militarily to end the crisis. There was no more compromising."[11]

On the diplomatic front, efforts to resolve the crisis had ground to an abrupt halt. "I came to New York on the second of May to pack my bags and leave," said UN/OAS envoy Dante Caputo. "But I was under pressure from Secretary-General Boutros-Ghali to stay. I knew it was all over. There was absolutely no dialogue with Aristide. It was just a matter of time before the United States invaded."[12]

In a confidential discussion with the secretary-general, a transcript of which was leaked to the press, Special Envoy Caputo warned of the Rosemary's Baby scenario. Namely, the United States would invade Haiti and quickly pull out, leaving the United Nations to pick up the political and economic costs. "What we do not want to do is inherit a 'baby,'" Caputo told Boutros-Ghali. "For the Americans are fixing to leave quickly."[13]

Back in Port-au-Prince, Leandro Despouy revived the coup talks that had been abandoned by the United States in April. Colonel Michel François was still offering to remove Cédras and Biamby and install General Duperval, who would invite President Aristide to return. One Saturday in late May, Mike Kozak was called to Secretary Christopher's office, where he once again outlined the plan and the risks for the United

States. Under Secretary Strobe Talbott said that President Aristide would not be pleased.

"I'm tired of doing what Aristide likes," complained Christopher, according to Kozak.[14] Secretary of State Christopher then authorized Ambassador Swing to attend the meeting with Despouy and Colonel François, but "just to listen."[15]

This became irrelevant when Colonel François was summoned before General Cédras and the general staff and "basically chickened out," according to Kozak. "Biamby spoke about uncovering the plot and François ended up pledging support to Cédras. After that the word got around that Colonel François was staying out of politics."[16]

The plotting in Port-au-Prince didn't stop. In mid-July, Robert Malval started getting calls from junior officers in the army who said they were planning to oust Generals Biamby and Cédras. One group said they wanted to make Malval the new president. "Make your coup, then call back Aristide," Malval told them. "I'll back you up as the head of govern-ment until he returns. You can go down in history as heroes and the United States will be very grateful to you for saving them a lot of money."[17]

Malval claimed that he met with some of the plotters and even aided them with money. "They told me at the time that Biamby controlled the four most important units of the army and that between them they only had two tanks that were operational. The tank drivers were part of the group that wanted to topple the high command." The problem was that the plotters didn't want President Aristide to return. "I told plotters: 'Trust me, if you ask him to return, he won't. He'll be too afraid.'"[18]

During the second week of July, a group of soldiers were accused by General Biamby of plotting against the FADH high command and killed. That same week provisional president Emile Jonassaint ordered the 104 members of the OAS/UN Civilian Mission to leave the country. Dante Caputo called the move "an insult to the international community."

When Leandro Despouy's name didn't appear on the list of OAS/UN officials who would be departing, Jonassaint ordered the security person-nel of the UN to leave as well.

General Biamby warned Despouy that if he wasn't on the last Air France flight out of Port-au-Prince on July 31, he would never be allowed to leave. Despouy's situation was further complicated by the fact that he had been working for months without a contract from either the OAS or the UN. "At that point Leandro wasn't getting paid," said his UN colleague Juliette Remy. "We didn't know if it was because of pure incompetence and stupidity or because someone high up in the UN was deliberately holding things up. Dante, Max Duboyer, and I had to lend Leandro money so that he could pay his hotel bill."[19]

Back at UN headquarters, Despouy's boss, Dante Caputo, continued his efforts to keep the movement to oust the Haitian military as international as possible. On July 31, 1994, Caputo got what he had been lobbying for. By a vote of 12–0 with China and Brazil abstaining, the UN Security Council passed a resolution authorizing the use of force to remove Haiti's military leaders. Resolution 940 authorized "Member states to form a multinational force under unified command and control and, in this framework, to use all necessary means to facilitate the departure from Haiti of the military leadership consistent with the Governors Island Agreement."

The following day de facto president Emile Jonassaint declared a state of siege. "The battle of Haiti is being prepared," he said in a televised speech. "We shall fight it with all our strength and all the means at our disposal."[20] That same day President Carlos Saúl Menem of Argentina declared that his country was ready to pledge six hundred soldiers to a U.S.-led invasion force. Similar pledges followed from Jamaica, Trinidad-Tobago, and other Caribbean countries.

But the Clinton administration still wasn't of one mind. Political advisors to the president told him that with his important health care reform bill facing critical votes in Congress, he should wait until the summer recess to launch a military action. While Deputy Secretary of State Strobe Talbott pressed the administration to set a deadline for an invasion, Defense Secretary William Perry argued strenuously that the military leaders in Port-au-Prince should be given incentives to quit.[21]

In mid-August Fidel Castro took advantage of the Clinton administration's mounting refugee problem by allowing over 12,000 Cubans to leave for the shores of Florida. On August 29, the State Department announced that it was opening talks with Cuba. Meanwhile, the human rights situation in Haiti continued to decline. On the night of August 29, a Catholic priest and close supporter of President Aristide, the Reverend Jean-Marie, was gunned down in Port-au-Prince just outside the gate of the Fathers of Montfortain house. Bystanders said they saw a group of plainclothesmen in an open jeep.

When the OAS/UN Inter-American Commission on Human Rights had visited Port-au-Prince in late May they found the situation had deteriorated markedly since the previous August. "What we have detected is a systematic use of violence by members of the military and the armed forces, FRAPH and other allied forces as an instrument of terror to intimidate the population who, by and large, are defenseless," said commission member Patrick Robinson.[22]

The question that kept being asked in Port-au-Prince and Washington was, when will the United States act? On Thursday night, September 15, President Clinton addressed the nation. "The message of the United States to the Haitian dictators is clear: Your time is up. Leave now or we will force you from power."[23] As he spoke the lead elements of a 20,000-man invasion force were on warships heading for Haiti. According to a plan developed in the Pentagon several months earlier, the initial attack would be launched by more than fifty helicopters from two aircraft carriers—the *Eisenhower* and the *America*. Administration officials said that President Clinton would be prepared to order an invasion by early the following week.

In Haiti, military leaders remained defiant. Government officials and de facto president Jonassaint said they were convinced they would be protected by divine powers. Referring to a small plane that crashed into the White House earlier in the week, Jonassaint's chief of staff Mireille Durocher Bertin said: "The Haitian people strongly believe that the plane was sent to Clinton by voodoo spirits. Jonassaint is convinced that, mystically speaking, the invasion will not happen."[24]

Maybe Jonassaint's spiritual contacts were looking at the same polls as the White House. Because the *New York Times* and the *Wall Street Journal* reported that about two-thirds of the U.S. electorate opposed any military solution to the crisis in Haiti. A day later, President Clinton reversed himself and decided to dispatch a diplomatic mission to Haiti.

On Friday, September 16, Tony Lake and Larry Rossin of the NSC and Mike Kozak from State were preparing to board an airplane for

Port-au-Prince when they were told to wait. "All of a sudden the White House got spasmodic," said Kozak. "There were all kinds of meetings and phone calls back and forth. The next thing we heard was that the White House had concocted, over State Department objections, the President Jimmy Carter–General Colin Powell–Senator Sam Nunn mission."[25]

Deputy Secretary of State Strobe Talbott was, in the words of one State Department officer, "fit to be tied," because he knew that by send-ing former president Carter the administration was effectively throwing out the terms of reference.[26] "With Carter," explained one official, "he's guaranteed to produce a result that the other side, meaning the Haitian military in this case, can accept. Then you can say you're forced to do this because of Jimmy Carter."[27]

UN/OAS special envoy Dante Caputo was at his home in Buenos Aires when UN undersecretary-general for political affairs Mig Goulding called. "Did you know that President Carter, General Powell, and Senator Sam Nunn have just left for Port-au-Prince to negotiate with the military?" Goulding said.

"How do you know this?" gasped a stunned Caputo.

"By watching CNN," answered Goulding.[28]

Once again, UN secretary-general Boutros Boutros-Ghali had not been informed. "We had been asked by the Clinton administration to cooperate," said Caputo, "and there we were finding out about things on CNN. That's when I wrote my letter of resignation."[29]

Early Saturday morning, Mike Kozak, Larry Rossin, Major General Jared Bates, and General Colin Powell departed from Washington on an Air Force jet, stopping briefly in Atlanta to pick up Senator Nunn, President Carter, and Carter's aide Robert Pastor, before continuing on to Port-au-Prince.

While the diplomatic mission made its way over the Caribbean, the Eighty-second Airborne brigade started moving Chinook and Blackhawk helicopters from Homestead Air Force Base in Miami to Greater Inagua in the Bahamas, less than fifty miles from Haiti.

As soon as they touched down in Haiti, President Carter asked to meet with General Abraham, who had worked closely with him dur-ing the 1990 Haitian presidential elections. Abraham told the three Americans that General Cédras was in a very weakened position and probably willing to resign to save his life and the lives of his family. Abraham suggested that the three men negotiate directly with Cédras and his wife, not with the army or the government of President Jonassaint.

Ignoring General Abraham's advice, Carter, Powell, and Nunn traveled to military headquarters where they met with General Cédras, General Biamby, and the general staff. Ambassador Bill Swing was told to wait outside. "I won't be able to talk freely if there's a State Department person present," complained Carter, according to one diplomat who was present.[30] Swing and Kozak cooled their heels for three hours, while Carter, Powell, and Nunn sat in Cédras's office hearing, in one embassy officer's words, "the same old horseshit that we had heard six million times."[31]

Mike Kozak had returned to the hotel and was listening to the radio when the three men returned at 2:00 A.M. "The three were all pumped up," remembered Kozak. As they talked, it became apparent that all three had decided that General Phillipe Biamby should be the next commander of the FADH. Kozak pointed out that Biamby was a dangerous man who had been behind the creation of FRAPH.[32]

Another extraordinary thing happened that night. Unbeknownst to Carter, Powell, Nunn, or even the U.S. embassy, forty members of the Haitian Presidential Guard rose in a revolt supported by Colonel Michel François. According to Leandro Despouy and General Abraham, the soldiers were on their way to arrest General Cédras and the members of his general staff, when they were stopped by General Biamby.

"Gentlemen, you are rebelling so that there won't be a U.S. invasion," Biamby told them, according to Despouy. "If I were in your shoes I would do the same thing. But President Carter is here and tomorrow we will sign an agreement with him saying that there won't be an invasion."[33] The officers and soldiers of the Presidential Guard didn't know President Carter and didn't feel comfortable approaching him. So they took General Biamby's word and returned to their barracks.

In a particularly Haitian twist of fate, President Carter, General Powell, and Senator Nunn had inadvertently stopped the coup.[34] The next morning, after a few hours' sleep, the three-man U.S. delegation set out for General Cédras's house. Once again they met without the benefit of anyone privy to what had transpired in the past eighteen months. "His wife [Yannick] is one of the strongest and most . . . most powerful women I've ever met," Carter said later. "And attractive. She was slim and very attractive."[35] He later admitted that it was at the breakfast meeting at the Cédras's that the real breakthrough took place.

The former president found himself sitting with the general's ten-year-old son on his knee, Yannick serving cookies, and the general's daughter asking him to autograph a picture of himself. "We convinced her [Yannick] that the highest calling of her husband, General Cédras, was not to give his life, or the lives of his wife and children, but to protect the lives of the Haitians whom he was sworn to protect," reported Carter.[36]

Back at the White House, President Clinton assembled Vice President Gore, Secretary of State Christopher, Secretary of Defense Perry, Tony Lake, Sandy Berger, Joint Chiefs chairman General Shalikashvili, and White House chief of staff Leon Panetta in the Oval Office. At 8:50 Sunday morning they received a call from General Colin Powell, who was still at the Cédras's home.

"Look, I think we may be able to have some room here," said Powell, who kept his remarks brief because he wasn't speaking on a secure phone.[37] President Clinton and his advisors remained skeptical. Orders were given to the Eighty-second Airborne to continue their preparation for an imminent invasion.

At 10:15 A.M., the Carter delegation moved to the Presidential Palace, where they met with de facto president Emile Jonassaint. Around noon, President Carter dispatched a Secret Service agent to the hotel to retrieve a secure satellite phone. By the time the agent returned with the phone, the delegation had moved to FADH headquarters.

Around 1:00 P.M., with the satellite phone set up in an adjoining office, former president Carter read a draft agreement to Tony Lake, President Clinton, and others listening in the Oval Office. "They had fallen for the trap," said someone who saw this draft. "The trap was that the military leaders would leave once the amnesty law was passed by Parliament. Under those circumstance the amnesty law was never going to pass."[38]

Larry Rossin of the NSC, who was with Carter, got on the line and argued against accepting those conditions. Tony Lake agreed with him. Then President Clinton spoke directly to the former president: "I have to tell you, in the strongest terms, that you have to get a date certain" by which the Haitian generals will step down. "You can make it October fifteenth, but I have to have that, and if I don't get that, then I'm going to have to ask you to come back," said Clinton.[39]

President Carter asked for more time. Clinton gave him three more hours. Overhearing the entire conversation was a Haitian military aide, who reported everything back to General Biamby.

Around 4:30 P.M., as the negotiations continued, the U.S. embassy received an execute order to go ahead with the invasion. "This made no sense at all," said a U.S. embassy officer who saw it. "You had a former president of the United States as a prime hostage. You had the CIA people who were supposed to secure the LZs [landing zones] bodyguarding Carter. I couldn't figure out what was going on."[40]

Back at military headquarters, General Biamby rushed into Cédras's office carrying a cell phone. He had just learned that aircraft carrying the Eighty-second Airborne were about to be launched. "They were on the verge of saying, 'We will not negotiate anymore, this may be a trick to keep us occupied,'" said Carter later. "We obviously assured them this was not the case, but the thing was about to break down."[41]

According to Carter, General Cédras still refused to sign. He wanted to talk to de facto president Jonassaint. So the group waded through pro-military demonstrators to the Presidential Palace.

The C-130s carrying the Eighty-second Airborne were already in the air. "My guess is that the White House gave the launch order so that they could look tough," explained someone at the U.S. embassy. "They could always recall the troops. They didn't give the launch order until they had a deal, which they knew they could always accept. By the time they went to the Presidential Palace they were arguing over three words. They were three important words. But my guess is that the White House would have caved and accepted an agreement without a date certain."[42]

It was a few minutes after 6:30 P.M. when the delegation reached the Presidential Palace. After explaining the agreement to Jonassaint, he agreed to sign. The agreement signed by Jimmy Carter and Emile Jonassaint said the following:

1) The purpose of this agreement is to foster peace in Haiti, to avoid violence and bloodshed, to promote freedom and democracy, and to forge

a sustained and mutually beneficial friendship between the governments, people and institutions of Haiti and the United States.

2) To implement this agreement, the Haitian military and police forces will
work in close cooperation with the U.S. military mission. This cooperation, conducted with mutual respect, will last during the transitional
period required for ensuring vital institutions of the country.

3) In order to personally contribute to the success of this agreement, certain military officers of the Haitian armed forces are willing to consent to
an early and honorable retirement in accordance with UN Resolutions
917 and 940 when a general amnesty will be voted into law by the
Haitian Parliament, or October 15, 1994, whichever is earlier. The
parties to this agreement pledge to work with the Haitian Parliament
to expedite this action, and their successors will be named according
to the Haitian constitution and existing military law.

4) The military activities of the U.S. military mission will be coordinated
with the Haitian military high command.

5) The economic embargo and the economic sanctions will be lifted without delay in accordance with relevant UN resolutions and the needs of
the Haitian people will be met as quickly as possible.

6) The forthcoming legislative elections will be held in a free and
democratic manner.

7) It is understood that the above agreement is conditioned on the
approval of the civilian governments of the United States and Haiti.

President Carter was led to a basement office in the Presidential Palace
where he called the White House and read President Clinton the agreement. President Clinton authorized him to sign and the deal was done.

By 8:00 P.M. the Carter delegation was on its way to the airport. From
the command center aboard the USS *Mount Whitney* word went out that
the invasion was off.

Back at the U.S. Embassy, they were hearing from sources that Generals Cédras and Biamby were as happy as clams. "They were spreading the
story that what they had agreed to was that the U.S. would send a negotiator to work out the details of a military deployment for trainers and the
professionalization of the FADH," said an embassy official.[43] According
to the agreement signed by President Carter, the Haitian military had
agreed to a "U.S. military mission" but not an actual deployment.

Bob Pastor, who had accompanied President Carter and stayed behind
in Port-au-Prince, was asked if that was true. "That's right," he answered,

according to Mike Kozak. "That's what they agreed to. The terms of the U.S. mission will have to be worked out later."[44]

Ambassador Bill Swing and Mike Kozak called Deputy Secretary of State Strobe Talbott to tell him what this meant. "If you stop the invasion and send a negotiator you'll be negotiating for the next ten years," explained Kozak.[45] "The whole Carter thing was pretty weird," concluded an embassy officer. "It was not a highly precise diplomatic agreement."[46]

At 9:31 P.M. President Clinton went on national television. "My fellow Americans, I want to announce that the military leaders of Haiti have agreed to step down from power," the president said. "I have directed United States forces to begin deployment into Haiti as part of the UN coalition and General Shelton, our commander, will be there tomorrow. The presence of the 15,000-member multinational force will guarantee that the dictators carry out the terms of the agreement."[47]

Military leaders Cédras and Biamby immediately called the U.S. embassy to complain that this was not what they agreed to. President Aristide, in Washington, was briefed on the content of the agreement and admitted to being "troubled."

The following morning, Mike Kozak, Ambassador Swing, Major General Jared Bates, and Bob Pastor went to see General Cédras and General Biamby at military headquarters. "Cédras was sitting with a big shit-eating grin on his face," reported one State Department officer who was present.[48]

"When is your general going to arrive to negotiate with us about the military mission?" Cédras asked.

"Well, as a matter of fact, he will be here in about forty minutes preceded by a reinforced company of troops who are going to take down the airport," General Bates answered, according to Kozak.[49]

"What?" gasped a surprised Cédras.

At that point, General Phillipe Biamby turned to him and said, according to Kozak: "I think I'd better call the guys at the airport and tell them not to shoot. Right now they have orders to resist."[50]

"Can't you tell your guys not to shoot, too?" Cédras asked General Bates.

"Frankly, at this point, we have no contact with our troops," answered the U.S. general.

"The only way we can do that is to go out there," said Kozak.[51]

So the four Americans jumped into the ambassador's armored limousine and raced out to the airport. When they got to the gate, they were told that the car couldn't enter. "So we had to get out of the car and run to the gate at the far end of the runway," reported Kozak. "That's where the helicopters were landing and the troops were jumping off. We sort of converged at the same time."[52]

The four U.S. officials were yelling: "Don't shoot! Don't shoot!"[53]

By Monday evening 3,000 U.S. combat troops had landed in Haiti, taking control of airports and ports. By the end of the week 15,000 U.S. troops had arrived. Thus began the second U.S. military occupation of Haiti in this century, called Operation Restore Democracy.

Haitian military officers liked to say that it was impossible to reverse the 1991 coup because that would be like trying to put an egg back into a chicken. Now people all over Haiti were painting wall murals of hands shoving eggs back into chickens.

History Repeats Itself

"If this is a triumph, it is difficult to imagine what a failure would look like."

—MARK FALCOFF of the American Institute in his evaluation of Operation Restore Democracy

Approximately three years after he was ousted from power, President Jean Bertrand Aristide returned to Haiti. On October 15, 1994, as thousands of Haitians jammed the streets around the Presidential Palace, President Aristide alighted from a U.S. helicopter, greeted gathered dignitaries including the Reverend Jesse Jackson, Secretary of State Warren Christopher, and acting prime minister Robert Malval, entered a bulletproof enclosure, and addressed his people with: "Today is the day when the sunshine of democracy rises forever!"

A little less than ten years later, on February 29, 2004, he was once again forced into exile. Instead of political reconciliation, the growth of democracy, and economic stability, Aristide and his tight circle of cronies delivered political arrests and assassinations, rigged elections, and corruption. The more than three billion dollars the U.S. Government expended on the military occupation and the hundreds of millions invested by the United States and its international partners to rebuild democratic institutions had largely been spent in vain. Robert Malval, Haitian legislators from both sides of the aisle, and U.S. and UN diplomats who had labored hard throughout 1993 and 1994 all agreed that none of the long-term goals of Haitians, the United States, or the international community had been met.

"We raised so much hope and made so much progress in terms of building political consensus in Haiti and international cooperation," UN diplomat Leandro Despouy said in 2004. "But by returning Aristide to power on his terms only, the whole thing went down the drain."[1]

Lessons Learned

"What Operation Restore Democracy has done to Haiti will never be forgiven."

—an editorial in the Haitian newspaper *Le Nouvelliste*, 1996

"He [President Clinton] is like a kid who jumps from a 7th-story window ledge into a fireman's net," wrote *Washington Post* columnist David S. Broder on September 20, 1994, the first day of the U.S. military intervention in Haiti. "After you know he's not cracked his skull, you have to ask: 'What the hell was he doing on the ledge?' "[1]

Broder went on to say that "the intervention defies almost every rule of political prudence that we thought our government had learned from the painful experience of the post–World War II world."[2]

One lesson supposedly learned from Vietnam was that the United States should not commit troops without strong support from the American public. Polls showed that there was no such support for a U.S. military intervention in Haiti. Nor did the Clinton administration seek the approval of the U.S. Congress, even though it seemed likely that U.S. involvement would be costly and lengthy.

As a corollary to the Vietnam lesson, U.S. troops should not be introduced unless the constitutional leaders of the host country extend an invitation. Although Haitian president Jean-Bertrand Aristide mounted a lengthy and expensive public relations campaign aimed at getting the Clinton administration to commit troops to restore him to power, he was careful never to specifically ask for U.S. military intervention. When Special Advisor William Gray III and Tony Lake tried to elicit an invitation to U.S. troops from the deposed Haitian president in the summer of 1994, Aristide told them that the Haitian Constitution prevented him from making such a request and if he did, he could be impeached.

In the end, what the White House got from President Aristide was a weakly worded letter to UN secretary-general Boutros-Ghali asking for "prompt and decisive action to implement the Governors Island accord."[3] Interestingly, this was the same accord that President Aristide and his advisors claimed he had been forced to sign against his will.

Since his overthrow in September 1991, President Aristide had made it clear that he wanted the United States and the international community to solve the crisis in Haiti for him. Over and over at Governors Island in June 1993, Aristide repeated to UN special envoy Dante Caputo: "You have to get rid of the military."

To which Mr. Caputo answered, correctly: "No, Mr. President, you have to get rid of them."

U.S. special advisor Lawrence Pezzullo came away from his first meeting with President Clinton in March 1993 with the impression that "the president felt this was a crisis in our backyard that we should be able to solve quickly." Why shouldn't the United States be able to patch things up in a small country in our hemisphere? the president wondered. All that was needed for victory, it seemed, was to join forces with like-minded countries and rally behind a negotiation headed by the United Nations.

But policymakers in the White House turned a blind eye to 190 years of Haitian history. They didn't understand the Haitian people or their culture, and they were unprepared for the deep currents of distrust and fear that run through Haitian politics. "Haiti is a universe unto itself," observed one State Department officer who had served in Haiti and in Africa.[4] Even more critical was how little sense the Clinton administration had of how to bring the federal bureaucracy to support a multilateral negotiation.

The tactical mistake made by the Clinton White House from the very beginning was to link two issues that they believed they could solve in one bold stroke—the refugee problem and the political crisis in Haiti. There was no question in their minds that the United States had to do something to stop the thousands of Haitians fleeing in boats to the shores of south Florida, since Florida was a politically important state.

Clinton himself tested the volatility of the Haitian refugee issue during the 1992 presidential campaign when he called the Bush administration's policy of returning Haitian refugees to their country "racist." After his election, as thousands of Haitians prepared to leave their country in boats, Clinton reversed himself and adopted the Bush administration policy of forcibly repatriating Haitian refugees.

But the policy was still "racist." And the Clinton White House never found a plausible explanation for why people fleeing Cuba were welcomed like heroes and given political asylum, while Haitians were shunned.

From the outset, policymakers at the White House explained that they would solve the Haitian refugee issue by returning ousted president Jean-Bertrand Aristide to power. But this was a fallacious argument and one that accepted President Aristide's flawed view of why Haitians were leaving their country in the first place.

All the Clinton advisors had to do was look at the numbers of Haitians seized by the Coast Guard to learn the truth. Although Aristide advisor Michael Barnes told Congress that "the refugee out-migration essentially stopped" during President Aristide's eight months in office, the 1,318 Haitians interdicted by the U.S. Coast Guard in those months actually exceeded the 1,132 who were picked up in the eight months preceding President Aristide's inauguration. And in October 1991, the month after the coup that deposed President Aristide and arguably the worst month of military repression in Haiti, only 19 Haitians were stopped at sea.

The exodus of Haitians always had more to do with policy changes in the United States than with events in Haiti. For example, when news reached Haiti that a boatload of refugees was allowed to remain in Florida in late October 1991, Haitians took to the seas en masse. Over 6,000 were seized by the Coast Guard that November. When President Bush signed an executive order on May 24, 1992, ordering all interdicted Haitians to be forcibly returned, the number of Haitians picked up by the Coast Guard dropped dramatically—473 in June and 160 in July.

By linking the Haitian refugee crisis to the diplomatic effort to restore President Aristide to power, the Clinton administration inadvertently gave the ousted Haitian president and his advisors a powerful trump card to play. Through 1993 and into 1994 whenever President Aristide didn't like the tenor of U.S. policy, he threatened to abrogate the agreement that allowed the United States to return fleeing Haitians to their homeland. In April 1994 when President Aristide actually did play this trump card, the Clinton administration, in effect, threw up its hands and surrendered. From that point on they gave Aristide everything he wanted.

The U.S. and UN diplomats understood that the real issue facing Haiti was political reconciliation. They understood that without a real commitment from President Aristide to abide by the spirit and letter of the 1986 Haitian Constitution, the movement toward participatory democracy in Haiti would never progress. Aristide had failed to govern successfully during his first months in office (January–September 1991), and by not forcing him to recognize the necessity of political reconciliation under the rules of the constitution, he was set up to fail again in 2004.

Despite claims by his supporters, Jean-Bertrand Aristide never accepted the basic tenets of constitutional democracy. According to Robert Malval: "He's a man who likes to seduce people and gets swept up in the passion of the crowd."[5]

In his *Autobiography* published in 1993, Aristide says that he believes in "direct democracy" rather than the representative democracy called for under the Haitian Constitution. "I do not believe," he says, "that liberal and parliamentary democracy is in itself . . . the sole result and unique end of the movement for human rights." Rather, the democracy he imagines "should be in the image of Lavalas: participatory, uncomplicated and in permanent motion."

To a large extent, it was this contradiction that led to President Aristide's ouster in September 1991 and again in February 2004. And it was his insistence that he was the sole interpreter of the peoples' will that made him unwilling to compromise.

By giving the impression that their policy was up for grabs, the Clinton White House gave the protagonists in Haiti—President Aristide and General Raoul Cédras—hope that they could ultimately achieve the outcomes they desired. President Aristide wanted the Haitian Army destroyed, and General Cédras wanted Father Aristide to go away and leave Haiti alone. In early 1993 when the administration position vis-à-vis Haiti appeared to be strong, U.S diplomats working with their counterparts at the UN and the OAS were able to produce positive steps toward ending the crisis.

But the decision to withdraw the USS *Harlan County* on October 12, 1993, completely undercut the diplomatic initiative. It was a decision based on the fear that the American public would equate Haiti with Somalia, where only days earlier eighteen U.S. Rangers had been killed and dragged through the streets. In the end, President Clinton's preoccupation with the day-to-day public consumption of his decisions superseded any concern for political realities in Haiti, statesmanship, or a need to maintain U.S. commitments to its international partners.

The message implicit in the retreat of the *Harlan County* was, in the words of *Newsweek* political commentator Joe Klein, "unambiguous, if unintentional: America can be defied, even in its own backyard."[6] In the minds of President Aristide and his advisors, the administration's backtracking fueled their paranoia that Washington had a secret, nefarious agenda for Haiti.

When the State Department Haiti Working Group, UN special envoy Dante Caputo, and the Four Friends diplomats resurrected a strategy for resolving the political crisis in early 1994, the Clinton White House balked once more. First, they were afraid of creating a humanitarian disaster in Haiti, then they couldn't handle the heat they were getting from President Aristide and his champions in the press.

For the first time in history, a president of the United States was bullied into accepting the agenda of a deposed president of Haiti.

In this, the U.S. media and some members of Congress bear some responsibility. What were Congressmen Rangel, Conyers, and Kennedy doing on President Aristide's official delegation to Governors Island? Didn't they realize that their presence might prove awkward for the United States government, which was trying to mediate between President Aristide and General Cédras? On the other side of the issue, General Cédras claims that during the summer of 1994 he was receiving telephone calls from Senate Minority Leader Bob Dole and other Republicans and their staffs saying that they would never support a U.S. military intervention.

How can the United States hope to negotiate a diplomatic resolution to a crisis when members of its own government actively interfere? Lobbying within the U.S. government is one thing. But U.S. elected officials should not be permitted to serve as active advisors to a foreign leader who is involved in negotiations with the United States.

The role of the press was even more insidious. From the beginning of the crisis in 1991, most U.S. reporters chose to cast the political struggle in Haiti as a simple morality play. President Aristide was the populist, democratically elected president who was trying to reform the system, and General Cédras was the brutal bully who sided with rich businessmen to thwart President Aristide's remarkable scheme. Anyone with experience in Haiti knew that the truth was much more shaded with gray.

A reading of U.S. newspaper articles from March 1993 through December 1994 reveals a tale of distortion that was supplied by one side in the Haiti conflict. "It's not by mere chance that the largest circulation newspapers have been publishing editorials favorable to the restoration of democracy in Haiti," boasted Haiti's ambassador to the United States, Jean Casimir, in January 1994. He was referring to $500,000 to $1,000,000 a month President Aristide was spending on public relations. "That's the only method I know to make the White House or State Department listen to you," admitted Casmir.[7] Shamefully, major media outlets like the *New York Times* and the *Washington Post* willingly printed what they were fed.

The Haiti crisis reveals several key U.S. vulnerabilities when it comes to conducting foreign affairs. The role of responsible foreign policy makers should be to stake out clear, realistic goals for our country—goals consistent with our national interests—which can be communicated to the American people, Congress, and our international partners. The objectives of any policy must be rooted in a sustainable political consensus.

For any administration, the absence of a clearly enunciated policy is the political equivalent of a vacuum. If a president fails to set a clear agenda of his own, he risks becoming prisoner of somebody else's. Randall Robinson's hunger strike is a case in point.

At a time when the world community has the chance to build international relations on rationality and principles, Haiti is a case study in multilateralism. The cooperation of the UN and the Four Friends that produced the Governors Island Agreement and the parliamentary initiative of early 1994 can be pointed to as a model for the future. But as the Haiti crisis also shows, multilateralism will not work without the commitment of the United States. And the United States must understand that the price for scuttling international agreements for the sake of political expediency will be suspicion and resentment on the part of our international partners the next time we call on them to help.

Repeated failures in foreign policy are something that the United States and the world cannot afford. And U.S. isolationism is no longer a viable option. Therefore, it is imperative that we learn from our mistakes. To that end, here are some lessons that can be derived from the Haiti experience:

1. There are no easy foreign policy victories. Foreign crises are by their nature complex and difficult. Anyone who tells you they can be solved quickly and easily should be treated with great skepticism.

2. Multilateral negotiations can work if you and your partners agree on goals and methods, and you constantly build trust. They fail when a partner breaks ranks because of domestic political considerations.

3. Know the history, study the culture. Every country on the planet has its own proud and unique culture. National character and national historical trends are not an accident. As much as they defined the past of a particular country, they inform the present and will determine the shape of the future.

4. Be just. Don't appear to side with one protagonist or the other when negotiating the end to a crisis in another country.

5. Don't try to solve one problem by putting it aside and addressing another. For example, restoring a deposed president to power will not solve your refugee problem.

6. Be judicious about committing the prestige of the president. Presidential promises can back a government into a corner.

7. Don't let a foreign leader who comes to you for help pressure your government through lobbying or a public relations campaign. Tell him (or her) that if you want U.S. help, you can't pressure us behind our back.

8. You can't effectively negotiate with foreign leaders if your administration is in disarray and your policy is in flux. Stop negotiating and work toward putting your house in order first.

9. Turf battles within an administration are best dealt with head-on and in private.

NOTES

CHAPTER ONE. **Clinton's Pledge**

1. Interview with Lawrence Pezzullo, December 26, 1994, Baltimore, MD.
2. Ibid.
3. Ibid.
4. Interview with Bernard Aronson, April 17, 1995, Washington, DC.
5. Ibid.
6. Ibid.
7. Anastasio Somoza, *Nicaragua Betrayed* (Boston: Western Islands, 1980), 337.
8. Interview with Lawrence Pezzullo, February 22, 1995, Baltimore, MD.
9. Pezzullo and Pezzullo, *At the Fall of Somoza* (University of Pittsburgh Press, 1993), 218.
10. Notes of Lawrence Pezzullo.
11. Interview with Lawrence Pezzullo, February 25, 1995, Baltimore, MD.
12. Ibid.
13. Ibid.
14. Ibid.
15. Ibid.
16. Ibid.
17. Interview with Lawrence Pezzullo, February 26, 1995, Baltimore, MD.
18. Ibid.
19. Interview with Bernard Aronson, April 17, 1995, Washington, DC.
20. Ibid.
21. *Washington Post*, January 15, 1993, 3.
22. Earl Caldwell, "The Prez Begins to Do Right by Haiti," *New York Daily News*, March 19, 1993.
23. Ibid.
24. Interview with Robert Malval, Miami, Florida, April 8, 1996.
25. Robert Lawless, *Haiti's Bad Press* (Rochester, VT: Schenkman Books, 1992), iv.
26. Christopher Caldwell, "Haiti Mongers," *American Spectator*, July 1994, 32.
27. Interview with Lawrence Pezzullo, March 30, 1994, Baltimore, MD.
28. Gwen Ifill, "Haitian Is Offered Clinton's Support," *New York Times*, March 17, 1993, 1.

29. Interview with Lawrence Pezzullo, March 30, 1994, Baltimore, MD.
30. *New York Times*, March 17, 1993, 13.
31. Ibid.
32. Ibid.
33. Interview with Lawrence Pezzullo, March 30, 1994, Baltimore, MD.

CHAPTER TWO. **Welcome to Haiti**

1. Dwight Worker, "Haiti on the Brink of Ecocide," *E: The Environmental Magazine*, July 1994, 38.
2. Ibid., 40.
3. William Booth, "Bad Voodoo," *GQ*, October 1993.
4. Interview with Dante Caputo, September 30, 1994, New York City.
5. Interview with Lawrence Pezzullo, March 30, 1995, Baltimore, MD.
6. Notes of Lawrence Pezzullo.
7. Interview with Pezzullo.
8. Jorgen Leth and Amanda Mitchison, "The Wrecking Crew," *Independent Magazine*, April 23, 1994, 32.
9. Interview with General Hérard Abraham, January 19, 1995, Queens, NY.
10. Interview with Dante Caputo, September 30, 1994, New York City.
11. Notes of Ambassador Lawrence Pezzullo.
12. Ibid.
13. Ibid.
14. Peter Katel, "Looking Out for Their Own Skin," *Newsweek*, August 30, 1993, 43.
15. Notes of Ambassador Lawrence Pezzullo.
16. Herbert Gold, *The Best Nightmare on Earth: A Life In Haiti* (New York: Prentice Hall, 1991), 258.
17. Bernard Diederich and Al Burt, *Papa Doc: Haiti and Its Dictator* (Maplewood, NJ: Waterfront Press, 1991), 215.
18. Notes of Ambassador Lawrence Pezzullo.
19. Ibid.
20. Ibid.

CHAPTER THREE. **From Slavery to Independence**

1. Robert Louis Stern, *The French Slave Trade in the Eighteenth Century* (Madison: University of Wisconsin Press, 1979), 85.
2. Edward Reynolds, *Stand the Storm: A History of the Atlantic Slave Trade* (London: Allison & Busby, 1985), 33.
3. Ibid., 51–52.

4. Carolyn Fisk, *The Making of Haiti* (Knoxville: University of Tennessee Press, 1990), 26.
5. Ibid.
6. Wade Davis, *The Serpent and the Rainbow* (New York: Warner Books, 1985), 235.
7. Elizabeth Bishop, *Haiti: The Duvaliers and Their Legacy* (New York: McGraw-Hill, 1988), 13.
8. Fisk, *The Making of Haiti*, 19.
9. Cited in Robert Heinl and Nancy Heinl, *Written in Blood* (Boston: Houghon Mifflin, 1978), 37.
10. Thomas Ott, *The Haitian Revolution* (Knoxville: University of Tennessee Press, 1973), 37.
11. Martin Ros, *Night of Fire: Black Napoleon and the Battle for Haiti* (New York: Saredon, 1991), 168.
12. Ibid., 170.
13. Cited in Ian Thomson, *Bonjour Blanc* (London: Huchinson, 1992), 52.
14. Ros, *Night of Fire*, 166.
15. Thomson, *Bonjour Blanc*, 52.

CHAPTER FOUR. **Working with the UN**

1. Jorgen Leth and Amanda Mitchison, "Wrecking Crew," *Independent Magazine*, April 24, 1993.
2. Notes of Lawrence Pezzullo.
3. Interview with Lawrence Pezzullo, March 30, 1995, Baltimore, MD.
4. Ibid.
5. Maya Deren, *Divine Horsemen: The Living Gods of Haiti* (New York: McPherson & Co., 1953), 41.
6. Interview with Dante Caputo, September 30, 1994, New York City.
7. Ibid.
8. Ibid.
9. Ibid.
10. Ibid.
11. Interview with Leandro Despouy, April 25, 1995, New York City.
12. Carole Cleaver, "Carnival Rum, Uneasy Calm: The Other Side of Haiti," *The New Leader*, March 8, 1993, 11.
13. Interview with Despouy.
14. Ibid.
15. Howard French, "U.S. Prepares to Get Tough with Haiti's Generals," *New York Times*, April 21, 1993.
16. Howard French, "Haiti Army Spurns Offer of Amnesty," *New York Times*, April 17, 1993.

17. Interview with Caputo.
18. Interview with Pezzullo.
19. Howard French, "Haiti Pays Dearly for Military Coup," *New York Times,* December 25, 1991, 1.
20. Notes of Lawrence Pezzullo.
21. Interview with Bob White, December 1, 1994, Washington, DC.
22. Notes of Lawrence Pezzullo.
23. Interviews with Pezzullo and Caputo.
24. Ibid.
25. Ibid.
26. Interview with Pezzullo.

CHAPTER FIVE. **Early U.S.-Haitian Relations**

1. Ludwell Lee Montague, *Haiti and the United States* (New York: Russell & Russell, 1966), 34.
2. Winthrop Jordan, *The White Man's Burden: Historical Origins of Racism in the United States* (London: Oxford Press, 1974), 147.
3. Elizabeth Abbott, *Haiti: The Duvaliers and Their Legacy* (New York: McGraw-Hill, 1988), 17.
4. Ibid., 20.
5. James Franklin, *The Present State of Hayti* (London: John Murray, 1928), 25.
6. Abbott, *Haiti,* 20.
7. Michel-Rolph Trouillot, *Haiti: State against Nation* (New York: Monthly Review Press, 1990), 49.
8. Paul Farmer, *The Uses of Haiti* (Monroe, ME: Common Courage Press, 1994), 75.
9. Montague, *Haiti and the United States,* 74.
10. For an account of the early U.S. dilemma regarding Haiti, see Gordon S. Brown, *Toussaint's Clause: The Founding Fathers and the Haitian Revolution* (Jackson: University Press of Mississippi, 2005).
11. Montague, *Haiti and the United States,* 77.
13. Ibid., 94.
13. Abbott, *Haiti,* 33.
14. Franklin, *The Present State of Hayti,* 211.

CHAPTER SIX. **UN Sanctions**

1. Notes of Lawrence Pezzullo.
2. Don Bohning, "U.S. Backs UN Police for Haiti," *Miami Herald,* May 9, 1991.
3. Howard French, "500 Foreign Police Readied for Haiti," *New York Times,* May 19, 1993, 3.

4. Ibid.

5. Ibid.

6. Interview with Michael Kozak and Lawrence Pezzullo, March 17, 1995, Washington, DC.

7. Ibid.

8. Ibid.

9. Ibid.

10. Ibid.

11. Interview with Dante Caputo, September 30, 1994, New York City.

12. Ibid.

13. Interview with Leandro Despouy, May 18, 1995, New York City.

14. Interview with Pezzullo and Kozak.

15. Herbert Gold, *The Best Nightmare on Earth* (New York: Prentice Hall, 1991), 62.

16. Interview with Louise Benechek, January 7, 1997, New York City.

17. Interview with Michael Kozak and Nancy Jackson, December 1, 1994, Fairfax, VA.

18. Interview with Pezzullo and Kozak.

19. Interviews with Pezzullo, Caputo, and Despouy.

20. Interview with Despouy.

21. Fax from Leandro Despouy, October 9, 1995, 9.

22. "Haiti's Premier Quits," *New York Times*, June 9, 1993, 13.

23. *L'actualité en question, Haiti 1993* (Le Nouvelliste: Port-au-Prince, 1994), 135.

24. Interview with Caputo.

25. Interview with Pezzullo.

26. Interview with Despouy.

27. Ibid.

28. Interview with Alice Blanchet, November 14, 1994, New York City.

29. Jorgen Leth and Amanda Mitchison, "The Wrecking Crew," *Independent Magazine*, April 23, 1994, 28.

30. Ibid.

31. Interview with Leandro Despouy, September 6, 1995, New York City.

32. Interview with Pezzullo.

33. Ibid.

34. Interview with unidentified State Department officer, December 22, 1994, Washington, DC.

35. Interview with Despouy.

36. Ibid.

37. Ibid.

CHAPTER SEVEN. **The First U.S. Occupation**

1. Frances Maclean, "They Didn't Speak Our Language, We Didn't Speak Theirs," *Smithsonian*, January 1993, 45.

2. Michael Rolph-Trouillot, *Haiti: State against Nation, Origins and Legacy of Duvalierism* (New York: Monthly Review Press, 1990), 27.

3. Francis Maclean, *Smithsonian*, January 1993, 47.

4. Ibid., 48.

5. Herbert Gold, *The Best Nightmare on Earth* (New York: Prentice Hall, 1991), 17.

6. Paul Farmer, *The Uses of Haiti* (Monroe, ME: Common Courage Press, 1994), 99.

7. Ibid.

8. Hans Schmidt, *The U.S. Occupation of Haiti* (New Brunswick, NJ: Rutgers University Press, 1971), 150.

9. Carolyn Fowler, *A Knot in the Thread* (Washington, DC: Howard University Press, 1980), 15.

10. J. P. Sartre, "Orpheé Noir," *Anthologie de la Nouvelle Poésie Négre* (Paris: PUF, 1948), xiii.

11. Maclean, *Smithsonian*, 56.

12. Ibid.

13. Michael Rolph-Trouillot, *Haiti: State Against Nation, Origins and Legacy of Duvalierism* (New York: Monthly Review Press, 1990), 103.

14. Maclean, *Smithsonian*, 57.

15. Mark Danner, "A Reporter at Large: Haiti," *New Yorker*, December 4, 1989, 114.

16. Ibid., 96.

17. Elizabeth Abbott, *The Duvaliers and Their Legacy* (New York: McGraw-Hill, 1988), 66.

18. Ibid., 54.

19. Abbott, *The Duvaliers and Their Legacy*, 96.

20. Gold, *The Best Nightmare on Earth*, 17.

21. Anthony P. Maingot, "Haiti: The Political Rot Within," *Current History*, February 1995, 60.

22. Ibid., 61.

23. Abbott, *The Duvaliers and Their Legacy*, 157.

CHAPTER EIGHT. **Governors Island**

1. Interview with Mike Kozak, March 2, 1995, Washington, DC.

2. Ibid.

3. Interview with Lawrence Pezzullo, December 1, 1994, Baltimore, MD.

4. Notes of Lawrence Pezzullo.

5. Interview with Dante Caputo, September 30, 1994, New York City.

6. Interview with Leandro Despouy, December 8, 1994, New York City.

7. Ibid.

8. Interviews with Caputo and Despouy.

9. Interview with Leandro Despouy, December 8, 1994, New York City.

10. Ibid.
11. Ibid.
12. Ibid.
13. Interview with Caputo.
14. Interview with Leandro Despouy, December 8, 1994, New York City.
15. Ibid.
16. Ibid.
17. Ibid.
18. Ibid.
19. Interview with Caputo.
20. Interviews with Caputo and Despouy.
21. Interviews with Pezzullo and Caputo.
22. Interview with Leandro Despouy, October 27, 1996, New York City.
23. Interview with Pezzullo.
24. Interview with Bob White, December 12, 1994, Washington, DC, and interview with Lawrence Pezzullo.
25. Interviews with Caputo and Pezzullo.
26. Howard French, "Haiti's Military Leaders Reported Unyielding at Talks," *New York Times*, June 29, 1993, 3.
27. Interview with Robert Malval, April 8, 1996, Miami, FL.
28. Notes of Lawrence Pezzullo.
29. Interview with Malval and notes of Pezzullo.
30. Interview with Pezzullo.
31. Interviews with Caputo and Pezzullo.
32. Notes of Lawrence Pezzullo.
33. Interviews with Caputo and Pezzullo.
34. Howard French, "Haiti's Military Leaders Reported Unyielding at Talks," *New York Times*, June 29, 1993, 3.
35. *L'Atualité en Question: Haiti 1993* (Le Nouvelliste, 1994), 151.
36. Interview with Caputo.
37. Interview with Leandro Despouy, October 27, 1996, New York City.
38. Interview with Caputo.
39. Interview with Pezzullo.
40. Ibid.
41. James Morrell, "The Governors Island Accord on Haiti," *International Policy Report*, September 1993.
42. Interview with Pezzullo.
43. Interview with Robert Malval.
44. Ibid.
45. Ibid.
46. Interview with Leandro Despouy, October 27, 1996, New York City.
47. Ibid.

48. Ibid.
49. Interview with Malval.
50. Interview with a member of Aristide's Presidential Commission, December 1994, Baltimore, MD.
51. Interview with Pezzullo.
52. Ibid.
53. Ibid.
54. Ibid.
55. Interview with Caputo.
56. Interview with Malval.
57. Ibid.
58. Interviews with Pezzullo and Caputo.
59. Interview with Caputo.
60. Interview with Bob White, December 1, 1994, Washington, DC.
61. Interview with Caputo.
62. Ibid.
63. Ibid.
64. Ibid.
65. Ibid.
66. Interview with Pezzullo.

CHAPTER NINE. **The Fall of Baby Doc**

1. Interview with Alice Blanchet, November 14, 1994, New York City.
2. Jean-Bertrand Aristide, *Aristide: An Autobiography* (New York City: Orbis, 1993), 31.
3. Mark Danner, "The Prophet Aristide," *New York Review of Books*, November 11, 1993, 30.
4. Elizabeth Abbott, *The Duvaliers and Their Legacy* (New York: McGraw-Hill, 1988), 252.
5. Aristide, *Aristide: An Autobiography*, 43.
6. Interview with Robert Malval, April 8, 1996, Miami, FL.
7. Aristide, *Aristide: An Autobiography*, 62.
8. Ibid., 63.
9. Danner, "Haiti: Beyond the Mountains, Part 1," *New Yorker*, November 27, 1989, 60.
10. Ibid., 60.
11. Amy Wilentz, *The Rainy Season* (New York City: Simon & Schuster, 1989), 132.
12. Ibid., 84.
13. Danner, "Haiti: Beyond the Mountains, Part 1," 94.
14. Ibid.
15. Danner, "Haiti: Beyond the Mountains, Part 3," *New Yorker*, December 11, 1989, 120.
16. Wilentz, *The Rainy Season*, 391.

17. Interview with Hérard Abraham, January 19, 1995, Queens, NY.
18. Paul Farmer, *The Uses of Haiti* (Monroe, ME: Common Courage Press, 1994), 150.
19. Herbert Gold, *The Best Nightmare on Earth* (New York: Prentice Hall, 1991), 17.

CHAPTER TEN. **The New York Pact**

1. Howard French, "Haitian Military and Aristide Sign Pact to End Crisis," *New York Times*, July 4, 1993, 1.
2. Interview with Bob White, December 12, 1994, Washington, DC.
3. Interview with General Abraham, January 19, 1995, Queens, NY.
4. Notes of Special Advisor Lawrence Pezzullo.
5. Interview with Lawrence Pezzullo, December 1, 1994, Baltimore, MD.
6. Interviews with Lawrence Pezzullo and Mike Kozak; Kozak interview, March 2, 1995, Washington, DC.
7. Interview with Kozak.
8. Interview with Robert Malval, April 4, 1996, Miami, FL.
9. Larry Hohter, "Haitian General Begins a Selling Job," *New York Times*, July 5, 1998, 4.
10. Interview with Leandro Despouy, October 27, 1996, New York City.
11. Interview with Juliette Remy, January 24, 1995, New York City.
12. Ibid.
13. *L'actualité en question* (Port-au-Prince, Haiti: Le Nouvelliste, 1994), 160.
14. Interview with Remy.
15. Ibid.
16. Interview with Despouy.
17. Interview with Remy.
18. Ibid.
19. Interview with Pezzullo.
20. Interview with Dante Caputo, September 30, 1994, New York City.
21. Interview with Pezzullo.
22. Interview with Caputo.
23. Ibid.
24. Interview with Pezzullo.
25. Interview with Caputo.
26. Ibid.
27. Interview with Remy.
28. Interviews with Caputo and Pezzullo.
29. Interview with Remy.
30. Ibid.
31. Interview with Pezzullo.
32. Ibid.
33. Interview with Kozak.

34. Ibid.

35. *L'actualité en Question* (Port-au-Prince, Haiti: Le Nouvelliste, 1994), 166.

36. Interview with FNCD member, August 5, 1995, Washington, DC.

37. Interview with Pezzullo.

38. Interview with Kozak and Pezzullo, December 28, 1994.

39. Interview with Caputo.

40. Ibid.

41. *L'actualité en Question*, 169.

42. Interview with FNCD member.

43. Ibid.

44. Interview with Pezzullo.

45. Interview with Kozak.

46. Richard Bernstein, "Haitians Approve Political Truce," *New York Times*, July 18, 1993, 7.

47. Ibid.

48. Interview with Pezzullo.

49. Interview with Caputo.

CHAPTER ELEVEN. **The Rise and Fall of Aristide**

1. Mark Danner, "The Fall of the Prophet," *New York Review of Books*, December 2, 1993, 47.

2. Ibid.

3. Ibid.

4. Jean-Bertrand Aristide, *Aristide: An Autobiography* (Mary Knoll, NY: Orbis Books, 1992), 115.

5. "Haiti: A Whiff of the Bad Old Days," *Economist* 316, no. 7664 (July 21, 1990): 44.

6. Danner, "The Fall of the Prophet," 47.

7. Ibid., 121.

8. Ibid., 126.

9. Council of Freely Elected Heads of Government, *The 1990 General Elections in Haiti*, 1991, 47.

10. Don Bohning, *Miami Herald*, November 26, 1990.

11. Ibid.

12. Howard French, "Front-Running Priest a Shock to Haiti," *New York Times*, December 13, 1990.

13. Henry F. Carey, "Electoral Observation and Democratization in Haiti," *Electoral Observation and Democratization in Latin America*, ed. Kevin Middlebrook (San Diego, CA: Center for U.S. Mexican Studies, 1998), 147.

14. Danner, "The Fall of the Prophet," 48.

15. Interview with General Hérard Abraham, January 19, 1995, Queens, NY.

16. Radio Métropole broadcast, January 8, 1991.

17. *The 1990 General Elections in Haiti*, 1991, 88.

18. Ibid., 119.

19. Interview with Michael Kozak, March 2, 1995, Washington, DC.

20. Raymond Alcide Joseph, "Father Aristide and Other Haitian Myths," *Forbes Media Critic* 1, no. 3 (1994): 30.

21. Aristide, *Aristide: An Autobiography*, 126.

22. Interview with Haitian FNCD politician, January 2, 1995, Washington, DC.

23. Howard French, "Ex-backers of Ousted Haitian Say He Alienated His Allies," *New York Times*, October 22, 1991, 10.

24. Ibid.

25. Ibid.

26. Interview with Abraham.

27. Interview with unnamed U.S. intelligence officer, August 23, 1995, Washington, DC.

28. Interview with Mike Kozak and another State Department officer, May 22, 1995, Washington, DC.

29. Radio Métropolitan, August 5, 1991.

30. Bella Stumbo, "A Place Called Fear," *Vanity Fair*, February 1994, 117.

31. David Adams, "Haiti's Rich Families Financed Coup That Toppled Aristide," *San Francisco Chronicle*, October 22, 1991.

32. Radio National, September 27, 1991.

33. Ibid.

34. Amy Wilentz, "The Oppositionist," *New Republic*, October 28, 1991.

35. Aristide, *Aristide: An Autobiography*, 156.

36. This is according to the soldier who carried out the order, who passed a lie detector test and is now under the U.S. Witness Protection Program.

37. "Haiti: Why the Coup Matters," *Newsweek*, October 14, 1991, 34.

38. Bella Stumbo, "A Place Called Fear," *Vanity Fair*, February 1994, 75.

39. Ambrose Evans-Pritchard, "Getting to Know the General," *National Review*, November 29, 1995, 25.

40. Ibid.

41. *Vanity Fair*, February 1994, 75.

42. Aristide, *Aristide: An Autobiography*, 158.

43. "Haiti's Military Assumes Power after Troops Arrest the President," *New York Times*, October 1, 1991, 1.

44. *Report to Congress on the Participation or Involvement of Members of the Haitian Government in Human Rights Violations between December 15, 1990, and December 15, 1994*, 9.

45. Ibid.

46. Interview with Abraham.

47. Quoted to Leandro Despouy, interview with Despouy.

48. Interview with FNCD member.

CHAPTER TWELVE. **Reconciliation**

1. Notes of Lawrence Pezzullo.
2. Interview with General Hérard Abraham, January 19, 1995, Queens, NY.
3. Interview with Robert Malval, April 8, 1996, Miami, FL.
4. Interview with Leandro Despouy, March 21, 1995, New York City.
5. Interview with Malval.
6. Interview with Juliette Remy, March 25, 1995, New York City.
7. Interview with Michael Kozak, December 28, 1994, Fairfax, VA.
8. Interview with Malval.
9. *L'actualité en question* (Port-au-Prince, Haiti: Le Nouvelliste, 1994), 175.
10. Interview with Remy.
11. Ibid.
12. Telephone interview with Lawrence Pezzullo, January 17, 1996.
13. Ibid.
14. Ibid.
15. Interview with Ellen Cosgrove, March 22, 1995, Washington, DC.
16. David Binder, "Clinton Urges Haitian Leader to Appoint a New Premier," *New York Times*, July 23, 1993, 8.
17. Howard French, "Reluctant Politician Dives into Haiti's Hot Water," *New York Times*, August 4, 1993, 4.
18. Interview with Louise Benichek, April 4, 1997, New York City.
19. Interview with Remy.
20. Ibid.
21. Fax from Despouy, August 23, 1995.
22. Interview with Remy.
23. Ibid.
24. Ibid.
25. Ibid.
26. Ibid.
27. Interview with Despouy.
28. Ibid.
29. Interview with Remy.
30. Interviews with Remy and Despouy.
31. Ibid.
32. Interview with Despouy.
33. Interview with Remy.
34. Interview with Despouy.
35. Interview with Remy.
36. Ibid.
37. Interview with Malval.
38. Ibid.

39. French, "Reluctant Politician Dives into Haiti's Hot Water," 4.
40. Interview with Despouy.
41. Interview with Malval.
42. Interview with Lawrence Pezzullo, December 26, 1994, Baltimore, MD.
43. Interview with Kozak.
44. David Binder, "Haiti's Premier Is Installed," *New York Times*, August 30, 1993, 3.
45. Fax from Despouy, August 23, 1995.
46. Interview with Pezzullo.
47. Interview with U.S. embassy officer, September 12, 1995, Port-au-Prince, Haiti.
48. Interview with Kozak.
49. Interview with Alice Blanchet, November 15, 1994, New York City.
50. Interviews with Caputo and Pezzullo.
51. Interviews with Malval and Pezzullo.
52. Interview with Malval.
53. Interviews with Malval and Pezzullo.
54. Interview with Pezzullo.
55. Ibid.

CHAPTER THIRTEEN. **Prime Minister Malval**

1. Interview with Robert Malval, April 8, 1996, Miami, FL.
2. Interview with Micha Gaillard, December 28, 1994, Baltimore, MD.
3. Howard French, "Hospital Mirrors Country," *New York Times*, May 2, 1993, 19.
4. Interview with Kozak, May 22, 1995, Washington, DC.
5. Interview with Malval.
6. Interviews with Kozak and Malval.
7. Ibid.
8. Interview with Lawrence Pezzullo, October 5, 1994, New York City.
9. Interview with Kozak.
10. "Prominent Backer of Aristide Slain after Mass," *New York Times*, September 12, 1993, 8,
11. United Nations General Assembly, 48th Session, "The Situation on Democracy and Human Rights in Haiti," November 18, 1993, A/48/532/Add.1, 12–13.
12. State Department, "Report to Congress on the Participation or Involvement of Members of the Haitian Government in Human Rights Violations between 12/15/90 and 12/15/94," 10.
13. UN General Assembly, "The Situation on Democracy," 2.
14. Ibid.
15. Interview with Lawrence Pezzullo.
16. Interviews with Pezzullo, Kozak, and Caputo.
17. Interview with Pezzullo.
18. Ibid.

19. Ibid.
20. Interview with Kozak.
21. Ibid.
22. Interview with Dante Caputo, September 30, 1994, New York City.
23. Interview with Alice Blanchet, November 15, 1994, New York City.
24. Interview with Caputo.
25. Interview with Kozak.
26. Ibid.
27. Interview with Blanchet.
28. Interview with Kozak.
29. Ibid.
30. Ibid.
31. Ibid.
32. Ibid.
33. Interview with Blanchet.
34. Christopher Caldwell, "Haiti-Mongers," *American Spectator*, July 1994, 5.
35. Confidential memo from Robert Malval to President Aristide, September 15, 1993.
36. Steven A. Holmes, "Aristide Asks for Removal of Army and Police Chiefs," *New York Times*, September 22, 1993, 3.
37. Ibid.
38. Interviews with Caputo and Malval.
39. Ibid.
40. Interview with Malval, April 4, 1996, Miami, FL.
41. Ibid.
42. Ibid.
43. Interview with Despouy and Malval.
44. Ibid.
45. Interview with Despouy.
46. Ibid.
47. Ibid.
48. Interview with Pezzullo.
49. Interview with Kozak, December 28, 1994, Fairfax, VA.
50. Ibid.
51. Interview with Ellen Cosgrove, March 22, 1995, Washington, DC.
52. Interview with Pezzullo.
53. Interview with Cosgrove.
54. Interview with Malval.

CHAPTER FOURTEEN. **Steps toward Aristide's Return**

1. White House Press Release, "UN Passes SC Resolution Authorizing Deployment," September 24, 1993.

2. Interview with Pezzullo, February 22, 1995, Baltimore, MD.
3. Interview with Juliette Remy, January 27, 1995, New York City.
4. Interview with Mike Kozak, December 28, 1994, Fairfax, VA.
5. Ibid.
6. Interview with Pezzullo.
7. Interview with Kozak.
8. Interview with Pezzullo.
9. Ibid.
10. Interview with Pezzullo; interview with Robert Malval, April 8, 1995, Miami, FL.
11. Interview with Pezzullo.
12. Ibid.
13. Ibid.
14. Ibid.
15. Ibid.
16. Ibid.
17. Interview with Kozak.
18. Interviews with Pezzullo and Kozak.
19. Ibid.
20. Interview with Pezzullo.
21. Interview with Nancy Jackson, December 28, 1994, Arlington, VA.
22. "L'actualité en question," *Le Nouvelliste*, 234.
23. Interview with Leandro Despouy, March 21, 1995, New York City.
24. "Haiti: Mission Impossible," *New York Times*, October 10, 1993, 14.
25. Interview with Bob White, December 1, 1994, Washington, DC.
26. Interview with Robert Malval, April 8, 1995, Miami, FL.
27. Ibid.
28. Interview with Kozak.
29. Telephone interview with Lawrence Pezzullo, October 30, 1996.
30. Ibid.
31. Interview with Pezzullo.
32. Interview with Malval.
33. Ibid.
34. Interview with Kozak.
35. Interview with Malval.
36. Interview with Kozak.
37. Interviews with Kozak and Malval.
38. Interview with Kozak.
39. Interview with Malval; corroborated by Alice Blanchet.
40. Interview with Malval.
41. Interview with Caputo.
42. Ibid.
43. Ibid.

44. Howard French, "First Foreign Troops Arrive under Peace Plan for Haiti," *New York Times*, October 7, 1993, 12.

45. Howard French, "Unrest Continues in Haiti's Capital," *New York Times*, October 6, 1993, 5.

46. Interview with Ellen Cosgrove, March 22, 1995, Washington, DC.

47. Gary Pierre-Pierre, "Standoff in Haiti: Terror of Duvalier Years Is Haunting Haiti Again," *New York Times*, October 18, 1993, 6.

48. Interview with Cosgrove.

49. Interview with Pezzullo.

50. Interview with U.S. embassy officer, January 7, 1995, Port-au-Prince.

51. Interview with Pezzullo and Kozak, December 28, 1994, Fairfax, VA.

52. Ibid.

53. Ibid.

CHAPTER FIFTEEN. The Harlan County Incident

1. Interview with Mike Kozak, December 28, 1994, Fairfax, VA.

2. Interview with Kozak.

3. Ibid.

4. Ibid.

5. Bella Stumbo, "A Place Called Fear," *Vanity Fair*, February 1994, 120.

6. Walter E. Kretchik, "Planning for Intervention: The Strategic and Operational Setting for Upholding Democracy," U.S. Army Command General Staff College, Fort Leavenworth, Kansas, 41.

7. George J. Church, "In and Out with the Tide," *Time*, October 25, 1993, 27.

8. Interview with Pezzullo, February 25, 1995, Baltimore, MD.

9. Ibid.

10. Ibid.

11. Telephone interviews with Vicki Huddleston and Lawrence Pezzullo, October 14, 1995.

12. Interview with State Department officer, May 26, 1995, Washington, DC.

13. Interview with Pezzullo.

14. Ibid.

15. Kretchik, "Planning for Intervention," 43.

16. Ibid.

17. Interview with Dante Caputo, September 30, 1994, New York City.

18. Interview with Despouy, March 21, 1995, New York City.

19. Interviews with Pezzullo and Caputo.

20. Interview with Caputo.

21. Interview with Kozak.

22. Interview with Caputo.

23. Interviews with Caputo and Kozak.
24. Interview with Alice Blanchet, November 14, 1994, New York City; confirmed by R. Malval.
25. Interview with Malval.
26. Interview with Caputo.
27. Interview with Kozak.
28. Interview with Malval.
29. Interview with State Department officer, May 2, 1995, Washington, DC.
30. Interview with Pezzullo.
31. Interview with Caputo.
32. Ibid.
33. Interview with Kozak.
34. Steven Homes, "Bid to Restore Haiti's Leader Is Derailed," *New York Times*, October 13, 1993, 1.
35. *MacNeil-Lehrer NewsHour*, October 12, 1993.
36. Interview with Malval.
37. Interview with Jocelyn McCalla, May 4, 1996, New York City.
38. Interview with Despouy.
39. Gwen Ifill, "U.S. Presses New Haitian Plan," *New York Times*, October 15, 1993, 1.
40. Interview with Pezzullo.
41. Gary Pierre-Pierre, "Rights Monitors Are Pulled Out of Haiti," *New York Times*, October 16, 1993, 4.
42. Interview with Pezzullo.
43. Interview with Caputo.
44. Interview with Pezzullo.
45. Interview with Malval.
46. Interview with Pezzullo.
47. Ibid.
48. Ibid.
49. Ibid.
50. Interview with Pezzullo.
51. Interview with Remy, January 27, 1995, New York City.
52. Interview with Cosgrove, March 22, 1995, Washington, DC.

CHAPTER SIXTEEN. **Dissension in Washington**

1. Gary Pierre-Pierre, "Standoff in Haiti: Port-au-Prince, City of Many Divides," *New York Times*, October 17, 1993, 14.
2. Ibid.
3. Howard French, "Standoff in Haiti: Haiti General Refuses to Budge," *New York Times*, October 18, 1993, 6.

4. Gary Pierre-Pierre, "Amid Strife, Haiti Parliament Struggles with Itself," *New York Times*, October 31, 1993, 12.

5. Bella Stumbo, "Haiti: A Place Called Fear," *Vanity Fair*, February 1994, 120.

6. Interview with U.S. Embassy officer, April 2, 1995, Washington, DC.

7. Ibid.

8. Interview with Malval, April 8, 1996, Miami, FL.

9. Ibid.

10. Paul Lewis, "Aristide Asks UN to Place Total Embargo on Haiti," *New York Times*, October 29, 1993, 6.

11. Interview with Malval.

12. Interview with Kozak, December 28, 1994, Fairfax, VA.

13. Ibid.

14. Interview with Alice Blanchet, November 14, 1994, New York City.

15. Interview with Malval.

16. Interview with Kozak.

17. Douglas Farah, "Haitian Military Senses Victory over Sanctions," *Washington Post*, November 11, 1993.

18. Interview with Pezzullo, February 25, 1995, Baltimore, MD.

19. Ibid.

20. Ibid.

21. Ibid.

22. Ibid.

23. Steven Holmes, "Admistration Is Fighting Itself on Haiti Policy," *New York Times*, October 23, 1993, 1

24. Interview with Pezzullo.

25. Note from Mike Kozak, June 4, 1998.

26. R. Jeffrey Smith and John M. Goshko, "CIA's Aristide Profile Spurs Hill Concern," *Washington Post*, October 22, 1993.

27. Thomas Friedman, "Standoff in Haiti: Dole to Offer Bill to Limit President on GI Role in Haiti," *New York Times*, October 18, 1993, 1.

28. Interview with Kozak.

29. Frank McCloskey, "Christopher, Resign," *New York Times*, October 24, 1993, 15.

30. Interview with Pezzullo.

31. Howard French, "As Aristide Fails to Return, His Foes Celebrate in Haiti," *New York Times*, October 31, 1993, 12.

32. Ibid.

33. Interview with Despouy, March 21, 1995, New York City.

34. Interview with Remy, January 27, 1995, New York City.

35. Interview with Malval.

36. Notes of Lawrence Pezzullo.

37. Interview with Malval.

38. Ibid.

39. Ibid.
40. Interview with Pezzullo.
41. Interview with Malval.
42. Ibid.
43. Ibid.
44. Ibid.
45. Ibid.
46. Ibid.
47. Ibid.
48. Ibid.
49. Ibid.
50. Interview with Pezzullo.
51. Interviews with Pezzullo and Malval; and notes of Pezzullo.
52. Interview with Malval.
53. Notes of Lawrence Pezzullo.
54. Ibid.
55. Interview with Malval.
56. Ibid.
57. Ibid.

CHAPTER SEVENTEEN. **The Resignation of Malval**

1. Interview with Robert Malval, April 8, 1996, Miami, FL.
2. Ibid.
3. Interview with Bob White, December 1, 1994, Washington, DC.
4. Interview with Malval.
5. Ibid.
6. John M. Goshko, "Haitian Premier Cancels Plans for Reconciliation Conference," *Washington Post*, December 16, 1993, A37.
7. Interview with Dante Caputo, September 30, 1994, New York City.
8. Interview with Pezzullo, February 25, 1995, Baltimore, MD
9. Interview with Malval.
10. Ibid.
11. Ibid.
12. Howard French, "Premier of Haiti Criticizes Aristide," *New York Times*, December 20, 1993, 1.
13. Ibid.
14. Howard French, "Study Shows Haiti Sanctions Kill Up to 1,000 Children a Month," *New York Times*, November 11, 1993, 1.
15. "Thousands of Haitians Ask Asylum in the U.S.," *New York Times*, December 9, 1993, 7.
16. Interview with Pezzullo.

17. Interview with Caputo.
18. Steven Holmes, "Pressure Builds over Return of Boat People to Haiti," *New York Times*, December 17, 1993, 17.
19. Notes of Pezzullo and interview with Caputo.
20. Daniel Williams, "Aristide Rejects New U.S. Effort to Jump-Start Talks," *Washington Post*, December 22, 1993, 2.
21. Steven Holmes, "Exiled Haitian Rebuffs Diplomats," *New York Times*, December 22, 1993, 3.
22. Kenneth Fried, "U.S. Said to Drop Bid to Reinstate Haiti President," *Los Angeles Times*, December 21, 1993, 1.
23. "The Haitian Deadlock," *Washington Post*, December 22, 1993.
24. Steven Greenhouse, "Aristide Organizes Haiti Conference," *New York Times*, December 24, 1993, 3.
25. Interview with Pezzullo.
26. Ibid.
27. Ibid.
28. Mary McGrory, "The Trouble with Haiti," *Washington Post*, January 6, 1994, A2.
29. Robert D. Novak, "Adieu to Aristide," *Washington Post*, January 6, 1994, A27.
30. Howard French, "Aristide Seeks to Rally Support," *New York Times*, January 18, 1994, 10.
31. Ibid.
32. Notes of Lawrence Pezzullo.
33. French, "Aristide Seeks to Rally Support," 10.
34. Interview with Juliette Remy, February 26, 1985, New York City.

CHAPTER EIGHTEEN. **The Parliamentarians' Plan**

1. Howard French, "UN Sanctions against Haiti Are Hampering Relief Efforts," *New York Times*, January 11, 1994, 1.
2. Interview with Pezzullo, December 1, 1994, Baltimore, MD.
3. Notes of Lawrence Pezzullo.
4. Ibid.
5. Ibid.
6. Ibid.
7. Interview with Pezzullo.
8. Ibid.
9. Interview with Mike Kozak, March 2, 1995, Washington, DC.
10. Testimony by Mark Schneider before the Subcommittee on Western Hemisphere and Peace Corps Affairs of the Committee on Foreign Relations, United States Senate, March 8, 1994.
11. Steven Holmes, "Spread of Hunger Denied," *New York Times*, December 2, 1993, 2.
12. Interview with Pezzullo.

13. Ibid.

14. Ibid.

15. Interview with Bob White, December 12, 1994, Washington, DC.

16. Ibid.

17. Howard French, "Gonvaives Journal: The Bogeyman's Back," *New York Times*, January 21, 1994, 4.

18. Notes from Mike Kozak, July 6, 1998.

19. Notes of Kozak.

20. Interview with Pezzullo.

21. Interview with Nancy Jackson, December 28, 1994, Fairfax, VA.

22. Interview with FNCD legislator, January 5, 1995, Washington, DC.

23. Ibid.

24. Interview with Jackson.

25. Interview with Juliette Remy, January 24, 1995, New York City.

26. Interview with Jackson.

27. Interview with Remy.

28. Interview with Jackson.

29. Ibid.

30. Interview with Micha Gaillard, December 28, 1994, Baltimore, MD.

31. Interview with Pezzullo.

32. Interviews with Jackson, Kozak, and Pezzullo.

33. "U.S., Aristide Fight Bitter War of Words," *Baltimore Sun*, February 11, 1994.

34. Notes of Kozak.

35. Norman Kemster, "America Urges Aristide to Agree to Plan for Coalition Government," *Los Angeles Times*, February 18, 1994, 1.

36. Ibid.

37. Interview with Remy.

38. Christopher Marquis, "White House Defends Haiti Policy," *Miami Herald*, February 24, 1994, 20.

39. "Aristide Faulted by US," *Boston Globe*, February 19, 1994, 4.

40. John Milne, "Aristide Renews Call to Tighten Embargo," *Boston Globe*, February 25, 1994, 2.

41. Joseph Kennedy II, "What Should Be Done about Haiti?" *Boston Sunday Globe*, February 27, 1994.

42. Interview with Remy.

43. Derrick Z. Jackson, "Clinton's Inaction Hurting Haiti," *Boston Globe*, March 1, 1994.

CHAPTER NINETEEN. **President Clinton Changes Policy**

1. Interview with Ellen Cosgrove, March 22, 1995, Washington, DC.

2. Susan Benesch, "Firms Run Out of Hope, Cash," *Miami Herald*, February 24, 1994, 20.

3. Ibid.

4. Interview with Cosgrove.

5. Christopher Marquis, "Aristide Rips Repatriation," *Miami Herald*, February 9, 1994, 1.

6. Testimony of Michael Barnes before the Senate Subcommittee on Western Hemisphere Affairs, March 8, 1994.

7. Testimony of Father Richard Ryscavage, Executive Director of the U.S. Catholic Conference Office of Migration and Refugee Services before the Senate Subcommittee on Western Hemisphere Affairs, March 8, 1994.

8. Interview with Nancy Jackson, December 28, 1994, Fairfax, VA.

9. Stephanis Nebehay, "Aristide Calls for Democracy, Rejects New U.S. Plan," *Reuters News Service*, March 2, 1994.

10. Derrick Z. Jackson, "Clinton's Inaction Hurting Haiti," *Boston Globe*, March 1, 1994.

11. Mary McCrory, "Buoying Haiti in Whitewater," *Washington Post*, March 15, 1994, 2A.

12. "Haiti: The Plan No One Wants," *New York Times*, March 15, 1994.

13. DeWayne Wickham, "Regaining Power a Lost Cause for Aristide," *USA Today*, March 14, 1994.

14. Opening remarks of Senator Christopher Dodd before the Senate Subcommittee on Western Hemisphere Affairs, March 8, 1994.

15. Ibid.

16. Testimony before the Senate Subcommittee, March 8, 1994.

17. Ibid.

18. Interview with Juliette Remy, January 24, 1995, New York City.

19. Interview with Dante Caputo, September 30, 1994, New York City.

20. "Aristide Unbending in Talks with UN Chief," *New York Times*, March 6, 1994, 6.

21. Ron Howell, "U.S. Outraged at Aristide's Slap," *New York Newsday*, April 4, 1994, 3.

22. Notes of Lawrence Pezzullo.

23. Ibid.

24. Ibid.

25. Ibid.

26. Ibid.

27. Transcript of Vice President Gore's meeting with President Aristide, March 25, 1994.

28. Ibid.

29. Ibid.

30. Letter from President Aristide to Anthony Lake, March 30, 1994.

31. Ibid.

32. Ibid.

33. Ibid.

34. Interview with Lawrence Pezzullo, December 1, 1994, Baltimore, MD.

35. Christopher Marquis, "Aristide Says He'll End U.S. Immigration Pact," *Miami Herald*, April 6, 1994, 18.

36. Ibid.

37. Michael Norton, "Aristide's Supporters' Fate Worsens," *Washington Times,* April 8, 1994.

38. Ibid.

39. Richard Cohen, "Haiti: Time for Muscle," *Washington Post,* April 7, 1994, 27.

40. William Raspbery, "Equality for Haitians," *Washington Post,* April 8, 1994, 21.

41. Notes of Ellen Cosgrove.

42. Ibid.

43. Murray Kempton, "Blindness in Haiti," *New York Newsday,* May 6, 1994.

44. Elaine Sciolino, "Embassy in Haiti Doubts Aristide's Rights Reports," *New York Times,* May 9, 1994, 3.

45. Interview with Cosgrove.

46. Interview with Michael Kozak, March 2, 1995, Washington, DC.

47. Ibid.

48. Ibid.

49. Randall Robinson, "Haiti's Agony, Clinton's Shame," *New York Times,* April 17, 1994.

50. Interviews with Kozak and Pezzullo.

51. Steven Greenhouse, "Aristide Condemns Clinton's Haiti Policy," *New York Times,* April 22, 1994.

52. Interview with Jackson.

53. Interview with Caputo.

54. Interview with Pezzullo.

55. Ibid.

56. Daniel Williams, "U.S. Advisor on Haiti Is Ousted," *Washington Post,* April 27, 1994.

CHAPTER TWENTY. **Carter/Powell/Nunn**

1. "Choices in Haiti," *Washington Post,* April 25, 1994.

2. Laura Blumenfeld, "Haiti's Fast Friend," *Washington Post,* May 4, 1994, C1.

3. Paul Anderson and Christopher Marquis, "Activist's Fast Galvanizes Opposition to Haiti Policy," *Miami Herald,* May 5, 1994, 6A.

4. Blumenfeld, "Haiti's Fast Friends," C1.

5. Larry Rohter, "US Lets 400 Haitians in Florida," *New York Times,* April 23, 1994.

6. Ibid.

7. Ron Howell, "Force in Haiti?" *Newsday,* May 4, 1994, A21.

8. Ibid.

9. Ibid.

10. Andrew Downie, "Aristide Foe Installed as Haiti's President," *Washington Post,* May 12, 1994, 13A.

11. Interview with Robert Malval, April 8, 1996, Miami, FL.

12. Interview with Dante Caputo, September 30, 1994, New York City.

13. Reprinted in the *Congressional Record,* September 29, 1994, H10357.

14. Interview with Michael Kozak, March 2, 1995, Washington, DC.

15. Notes of Kozak.

16. Interview with Kozak.

17. Interview with Malval.

18. Ibid.

19. Interview with Juliette Remy, January 24, 1995, New York City.

20. Larry Rohter, "Haitian Military Greets Invasion Vote with Defiance," *New York Times*, August 2, 1994, A3.

21. Elaine Sciolino, "Top U.S. Officials Divided in Debate on Invading Haiti," *New York Times*, August 4, 1994, 1.

22. Bill Lambrecht, "Politics of Terror Claiming Victims," *St. Louis Post-Dispatch*, May 23, 1994, 4A.

23. Douglas Jehl, "Your Time Is Up," *New York Times*, September 16, 1994, 1.

24. Larry Rohter, "In Port-au-Prince, Signs of Invasion Are in the Air," *New York Times*, September 15, 1994, A8.

25. Interview with Kozak.

26. Interview with State Department officer, May 1, 1994, Washington, DC.

27. Ibid.

28. Interview with Caputo.

29. Ibid.

30. Interview with U.S. embassy officer, July 22, 1995, Port-au-Prince, Haiti.

31. Ibid.

32. Interview with Kozak.

33. Interview with Leandro Despouy, March 21, 1995, New York City.

34. Interview with Haitian political leader, August 17, 1995, New York City.

35. Rick Bragg, "Varying Views on Role of Haiti General's Wife," *New York Times*, September 26, 1994.

36. *New York Times*, September 26, 1994.

37. ABC News *Nightline*, "From Invasion to Intervention," September 22, 1994.

38. Unnamed U.S. embassy officer, Port-au-Prince.

39. ABC News *Nightline*, September 22, 1994.

40. Unnamed U.S. embassy officer, Port-au-Prince.

41. ABC News *Nightline*.

42. Unnamed U.S. embassy officer, Port-au-Prince.

43. Ibid.

44. Interview with Kozak.

45. Ibid.

46. Unnamed U.S. embassy officer, Port-au-Prince.

47. "Clinton Tells Nation a Three-Year Objective Has Been Attained," *New York Times*, September 19, 1994, A8.

48. Interview with U.S. embassy officer, July 22, 1995, Port-au-Prince.

49. Interview with Kozak.

50. Ibid.
51. Ibid.
52. Ibid.
53. Ibid.

Epilogue

1. Telephone interview with Leandro Despouy, March 24, 2004, Buenos Aires, Argentina.

Conclusions

1. David S. Broder, "Hostage to Haiti," *Washington Post*, September 20, 1994, A21.
2. Ibid.
3. George A. Fauriol, editor, *Haitian Frustrations: Dilemmas for U.S. Policy* (Washington, DC: Center for Strategic and International Studies, 1995), 113.
4. Interview with Louise Bedichek, April 4, 1997, New York City.
5. Interview with Robert Malval, April 8, 1995, Miami, FL.
6. Joe Klein, "The Politics of Promiscuity," *Newsweek*, May 9, 1994, 19.
7. Robert D. Novak, "Adieu to Aristide," *Washington Post*, January 6, 1994, A27.

INDEX